The role of entrepreneurship in the world economy is perhaps more important now than at any time in the twentieth century. This book analyzes the relative importance of small firms in industrial economies. It brings together a series of studies spanning a spectrum of selected countries in developed Western nations and Eastern Europe to identify the exact role of small firms, and how this role has evolved over the last fifteen years. A striking result which emerges is that a distinct and consistent shift away from large firms and towards small enterprises has occurred within the manufacturing sector of all Western countries. At the same time the role of small firms in Eastern European nations has been remarkably restricted and, indeed, all these countries have experienced a shift away from small firms. It is clear from this analysis that a major challenge for political and economic reform in Central and Eastern Europe is to create the strong entrepreneurial sector which exists in the West.

Small firms and entrepreneurship: an East–West perspective

Small firms and entrepreneurship: an East–West perspective

edited by

Zoltan J. Acs
University of Baltimore, USA

and

David B. Audretsch
*Wissenschaftszentrum
Berlin für
Sozialforschung,
Germany*

CAMBRIDGE
UNIVERSITY PRESS

CAMBRIDGE UNIVERSITY PRESS
Cambridge, New York, Melbourne, Madrid, Cape Town, Singapore, São Paulo

Cambridge University Press
The Edinburgh Building, Cambridge CB2 8RU, UK

Published in the United States of America by Cambridge University Press, New York

www.cambridge.org
Information on this title: www.cambridge.org/9780521431156

First published 1993
This digitally printed version 2008

A catalogue record for this publication is available from the British Library

Library of Congress Cataloguing in Publication data

Small firms and entrepreneurship: an East–West perspective / edited by Zoltan J. Acs and
David B. Audretsch.
    p.   cm.
Papers presented at a conference held July 6–7, 1990 in Berlin.
ISBN 0 521 43115 8 (hardback)
1. Small business – Europe – Congresses. 2. Small business – Europe. Eastern – Congresses. 3. Small business – United States – Congresses. 4. Entrepreneurship – Congresses. I. Ács, Zoltan J. II. Audretsch, David B.
HD2341.S623 1992
338.6'42'094 – dc20   92–5263 CIP

ISBN 978-0-521-43115-6 hardback
ISBN 978-0-521-06204-6 paperback

Contents

Figures

Tables

Contributors

Zoltan J. Acs, *University of Baltimore, USA*

David B. Audretsch, *Wissenschaftszentrum Berlin für Sozialforschung, Germany*

Hans-Gerd Bannasch, *Hochschule für Ökonomie, Berlin, Germany*

Hans-Peter Brunner, *Wissenschaftszentrum Berlin für Sozialforschung, Germany*

Michael Fritsch, *Technische Universität Berlin, Germany*

Alan Hughes, *Cambridge University, UK*

B. Invernizzi, *University of Torino, Italy*

Simon Johnson, *Duke University, Durham, NC, USA*

Gary Loveman, *Harvard University, Boston, MA, USA*

José Mata, *Universidade do Minho, Braga, Portugal*

Gerald A. McDermott, *MIT, Cambridge, MA, USA*

Michal Mejstrik, *Charles University, Prague, CSFR*

Riccardo Revelli, *University of Torino, Italy*

Roy Thurik, *Erasmus University, Rotterdam, Netherlands*

Acknowledgments

We would like to thank the Wissenschaftszentrum Berlin für Sozialforschung for financially supporting the conference on "Small Firms and Entrepreneurship: an East–West Perspective," which took place in Berlin on July 6–7, 1990, and from which the contributions included in this volume were selected. Special thanks go to Manfred Fleischer and Christiane Loycke de Roux for their capable assistance not only in organizing the Conference but also in compiling this volume. We are particularly grateful to the helpful suggestions and comments of two anonymous referees who played an important role in shaping this book, and finally to Patrick McCartan of Cambridge University Press, who enabled us to move from the conference to publication of this volume with a minimum of impediments.

1 Introduction

Zoltan J. Acs and *David B. Audretsch*

1. Two views of (small) firms

A heated debate has recently emerged, or been revived, concerning the relative roles and importance of large and small firms. On the one hand is the view, which has prevailed for the better part of this century, that small firms do not perform an important role in the economy and that they will play an increasingly diminished role in the future (Kaplan, 1954; Galbraith, 1957; and Berger and Piore, 1980). This was especially the case in the manufacturing sector where large, and even giant, firms have dominated Western economies throughout the century. In country after country official policies favored large units of production and mechanisms of ownership. These goals were pursued in both free market and planned economies alike. As Galbraith (1957) pointed out, there were strong reasons to believe that large firms exploiting economies of scale were superior to small firms in virtually every aspect of economic performance – productivity, technological progress, and job security and compensation.

Until the mid-1970s the evidence indicated that small firms were indeed becoming less important over time (Brock and Evans, 1986). The view that the cornerstone of the modern economy is the large firm dates back to at least Karl Marx (1912, p. 836), who prophesied the corporate form of organization leading to a "constantly diminishing number of the magnates of capital, who usurp and monopolize all advantages of transformation." The limit was a state in which "the entire social capital would be united, either in the hands of one single capitalist, or in those of one single corporation" (Marx, 1912, p. 836).

An alternative view has recently emerged in the economics literature arguing that small firms and entrepreneurship are playing a much more important role in the economy than had been previously acknowledged. According to this view, small firms make at least four important

1

contributions to industrial markets. First, they play an important role in the process of technological change. Building upon the Schumpeterian (1934) tradition, Nelson (1984), Winter (1984), and Nelson and Winter (1974, 1982) argue that small firms make a significant entrepreneurial contribution, in the sense that they are the source of considerable innovative activity. Second, small firms generate much of the market turbulence that not only creates an additional dimension of competition not captured in the traditional static measures of market structure, such as concentration, but also provides a mechanism for regeneration (Marshall, 1920; Beesley and Hamilton, 1984). In this sense, small entrepreneurial firms serve as agents of change in a market. A third contribution, which is related to the first two, is promotion of international competitiveness through newly created niches (Brock and Evans, 1989). The final contribution emanating from small firms in recent years has been their preponderant share of newly generated jobs (Storey and Johnson, 1987).

This debate regarding firm size is important because the prolonged economic stagnation and widespread unemployment in the 1980s triggered an unexpected reappraisal of the role and importance of small manufacturing firms. By the early 1970s "cracks" had begun to appear in the structure of the manufacturing sector in most developed countries, including in some of the largest firms and industries. At the same time, casual evidence began to suggest that small firms in at least several countries were outperforming their larger counterparts (Böbel, 1984; Jacquemin and de Jong, 1977; Kaufer, 1980; Irsch, 1986; Acs, 1984). Perhaps the best example of this was in the steel industry where new firms entered in the form of "mini-mills" and small-firm employment expanded, while the incumbent large companies shut down plants and reduced employment in a number of countries. Although no systematic evidence exists unequivocally to identify whether small units (firms and plants) of production are equally as efficient as large firms, or are, in fact, actually more efficient than their larger counterparts, Aiginger and Tichy (1991) conclude that the accumulated evidence to date indicates that small firms and plants are at least not burdened with an inherent size disadvantage.

Given the surge in interest in this debate, surprisingly little has been established in the empirical literature to identify what exactly is the economic role of small firms, and to what extent this has shifted over time. While there is no shortage of theoretical arguments about the relative roles of large and small firms, empirical knowledge is generally based upon a collection of anecdotal evidence and case studies. Such anecdotal evidence has not proved adequate to be able to resolve the five major issues typically raised in the debate:

(1) What is the role of small firms, or the extent to which they account for economic activity, and how does this vary across nations?
(2) How does the role of small firms vary across sectors and industries?
(3) Has the firm-size distribution shifted towards or away from small enterprises?
(4) What are the explanations for any shifts that have occurred?
(5) Are these shifts good or bad – what are the welfare implications?

The purpose of this volume is to bring together a series of studies across a wide spectrum of selected countries carefully to identify in a systematic manner the exact role of small firms, and how this role has evolved during the last fifteen years. In particular, the goal of this volume is to provide systematic evidence on the first three issues above so that future debate and research will have a solid set of stylized facts regarding the relative roles of large and small firms upon which to build. In addition, possible explanations and hypotheses to be tested in future research will be offered in the individual country studies in the chapters in this volume. These explanations are generally preliminary and tentative in nature; it is hoped that they will provoke the requisite systematic hypothesis testing in subsequent research. The final issue – the welfare implications – remains beyond the scope of this volume. While there already exists a growing literature arguing that the recent shift towards small enterprises is either positive (Sengenberger, Loveman and Piore, 1990), or negative (Ferguson, 1988; Brown, Hamilton and Medoff, 1990), the purpose of this volume is to get the facts straight first, in order to set the stage for the presumably more complicated and perhaps more heated debate on the welfare implications.

2. Measurement issues

The lack of systematic analysis identifying the role of small firms and how it has shifted over time is attributable chiefly to the unavailability of appropriate data bases. No country has had a monopoly on this problem. Only in recent years have a series of new data sources enabled researches carefully to identify economic activity across a broad spectrum of firm sizes in a meaningful manner that affords comparisons with other countries. For example, in one of the first studies to receive international attention, David Birch (1979) turned to a private source of data, Dunn and Bradstreet, to compare the number of new jobs generated between large and small US firms. Birch was severely limited by data constraints, for which he was subjected to considerable criticism (Armington and Odle, 1982). His initial findings, indicating that 80 percent of new jobs were generated by small firms, were based on the performance of establishments, many of which are owned by larger firms. Much of the job generation Birch attributed to small firms in fact thus occurred in small plants owned by large firms (Armington and Odle, 1982). Similarly, Brown, Hamilton and Medoff (1990, p. 1) conclude, "The prevailing wisdom about large and small firms should be reexamined because in at least two instances, job creation and political power, it is wrong. Perhaps the most widespread misconception about small businesses in the United States is that they generate the vast majority of jobs and are therefore the key to economic growth." In any case, because the concept of job generation does not reflect the extent to which the jobs are in any sense permanent or long term, the measure provides precariously little information about the extent to which the firm-size distribution is shifting.

In this book we are not interested in job generation *per se*, but rather in directly measuring the extent to which small firms account for economic activity, and if this has been evolving in any systematic manner in recent years. That is, we will focus on the firm-size distribution, and how that size distribution has shifted over time.

There are a number of measurement issues which need to be identified, analyzed, and qualified, particularly in light of the lack of precedents and in view of the international comparisons which we wish to make. In particular there are five measurement issues which must be addressed in order to carry out a systematic analysis that both yields meaningful results and facilitates international comparison: (1) the measurement variable, (2) the definition of a small firm, (3) the unit of observation, (4) the appropriate sector of the economy on which to focus, and (5) the relevant time period.

A wide range of variables could be used to measure the extent to which small and large firms account for economic activity – the numbers of firms and establishments, the number of self-employed workers, employment, output, sales, value added, and assets are the most obvious measures. The country studies included in this book focus on the employment measure, not only because this variable most easily facilitates international comparisons by avoiding exchange rate problems, but also because it minimizes the problems associated with monetizing the other measures. Sales or value-of-shipments might be a suspect measure for comparing the relative economic activity within an industry accounted for by large and small firms, since firms of various sizes may represent different locations along the vertical production stream.

The number of firms and establishments as a measure of economic activity has the disadvantage of not being weighted by the amount of economic activity undertaken by each unit. While over 90 percent of firms have fewer than ten employees in most developed countries, employment, sales, and assets tend to be concentrated among the few largest corporations. The number of self-employed workers has recently been used to examine shifts in entrepreneurial activity (Blau, 1987; Evans and Leighton, 1988; Devine, 1990; Meyer, 1990), as well as to analyze particular problems confronting entrepreneurs (Evans and Jovanovic, 1989; Blanchflower and Oswald, 1990). However, there are three major drawbacks to using self-employment data to measure shifts in the size distribution of firms. First, as with the measure of the number of firms, the number of self-employed is not weighted by the extent of economic activity. Second, in the manufacturing sector there are relatively few self-employed workers, so that this measure does not reveal much about what has been happening to the size distribution of firms. Third, government data bases in most countries do not include information on self-employment as an economic category but only as a legal definition.[1] Thus, throughout this volume, we will focus on the employment measures, which in any case are the most widely standardized and the most reliable across a wide array of nations.

The unit of analysis could conceivably be undertaken either at the enterprise (firm) level, or at the establishment level. Establishments in manufacturing are generally referred to as plants. The attractiveness of the establishment measure is that it tends to be the greatest source of scale economies. Shifts in the size distribution of establishments are most likely to reflect changes in the underlying production technology (Carlsson, 1989).

However, the advantage of using the enterprise as the relevant unit of observation was emphasized by Armington and Odle (1982, p. 14): "It is the parent firm that makes the business policy decisions that determine much of the behavior of the neighborhood branch of the department store, the business office of the telephone company, or the local cannery of a large food-processing company. Similarly, most government policies affecting business are directed at the legal and financial entity, the parent firm." Although to some extent the static and dynamic performance of establishments will be identified throughout this book, the main unit of observation common among all of the specific country studies is the enterprise.

How to distinguish small firms from large ones is not obvious from any theoretical literature (Brock and Evans, 1989). While it could be argued that the notion of what constitutes a small firm conceivably varies across industries and even across countries, we adopt here the standard most commonly found in the literature – a "small firm" is broadly defined as an enterprise with fewer than 500 employees (Brock and Evans, 1989; White, 1982; Schwalbach, 1989; Acs and Audretsch, 1990). However, as is the case in most of these studies, results in the specific country chapters are typically compared across a wide spectrum of definitions of what constitutes a small firm. It should be emphasized that this standard is oriented towards distinguishing the economic performance of the largest firms from that of smaller firms, and not vice versa. That is, the common denominator between an enterprise with six employees and 490 employees is that neither can be considered to be among the largest firms. The standard measure used for gauging the extent of small firms in this book is thus the share of employment accounted for by firms with fewer than 500 (or alternatively 100, etc.) employees.

On which sectors of the economy should this measure focus – the aggregate economy, manufacturing, services, or finance? While the role of small firms in the overall economy and the shift in the small-firm share of total employment over time is identified for each country, this book will focus particularly on the manufacturing sector. Dertouzos, Lester and Solow (1989), Wright (1990) and Baumol, Blackman and Wolff (1989) argue that, despite the obvious transformation of economic activity out of manufacturing and into services, manufacturing remains the cornerstone of a modern industrial economy. They emphasize that while the share of employment accounted for by the manufacturing sector has declined in virtually every developed country, the share of manufacturing output has remained about the same.

The time period selected for analyzing shifts in the firm-size distribution is roughly between the mid-1970s and the end of the 1980s, for two reasons. First, although it would be interesting and insightful to be able to trace out the manner in which the size distribution of firms has evolved over a long historical period, the new sources of data enabling such analysis typically do not contain such rich historical data. Second, the preliminary and anecdotal evidence suggests that it is only since around 1975 that the firm-size distribution may have begun noticeably to shift towards small firms. And it is only within the last decade that the debate over the relative merits of small and large firms has really heated up.

In order to provide analyses that can be compared within an international context, a variety of data bases, some of them relatively new, are used throughout the individual country studies contained in this book. For example, in Chapter 2 Alan Hughes employs the data from VAT registration and the Census of Production for the United Kingdom. For the study on West Germany in Chapter 3, Michael Fritsch combines data from the Census of Business and social insurance data. The data on Dutch industries used by Roy Thurik in Chapter 5 are derived from two files of the Netherlands Central Bureau of Statistics: (1) Statistics on Enterprises, and (2) Statistics on Man-Years and Gross Wages. Both files are maintained by the Research Institute for Small and Medium-Sized Business. José Mata in Chapter 6 uses Portuguese data from the Statistics Department of the Ministry of Employment. B. Invernizzi and Riccardo Revelli in Chapter 7 employ data from the social security files for Italy. Acs and Audretsch in Chapter 4 rely on the US Small Business Administration's Small Business Data Base as well as the Bureau of Census data (both the Annual Survey and the Census of Manufactures). The data sources used for the country studies for Eastern Europe can be found in the individual chapters.

3. Justification for international comparison

Why compare the role of small firms across different countries? There are at least three reasons.[2] First, identifying the same empirical patterns in different countries provides at least some evidence that the underlying explanations have broad empirical support. Second, and more specifically, if entrepreneurial activity leads to either an improvement or a deterioration in economic activity, this may help to explain differences in national economic performance. Third, cross-national comparisons can contribute towards identifying those government policies and programs that foster entrepreneurial activity (Reynolds, 1992).

3.1 Research strategies for cross-national comparisons

There are perhaps four different approaches for cross-national comparisons: direct cross-national comparisons; cross-national historical studies; cross-national, cross-market comparisons; and cross-national, cross-regional analysis. Recently Reynolds (1992) has suggested that the character of the business organizations that comprise a regional economy and the national economy may require different approaches. According to Reynolds, each regional economy could be considered to be an independent entity for analysis. This approach would be most fruitful if regional geographic boundaries can be considered to delineate a complete socio-economic system and if there are uniform data available.

The cross-national, cross-market comparison approach has been applied by Geroski and Schwalbach (1991) in compiling a series of country studies examining the role of entrants across manufacturing industries. While this approach proved fruitful in identifying the manner in which similarly defined explanatory variables relate to similarly defined dependent variables, this conceptual scheme does not lend itself to systematic analysis of shifts in the size distribution of firms.

Direct cross-national comparisons are very appealing. They require, at a minimum, the use of the same theoretical conception of the key variables – employment, establishments, enterprises, etc. Carefully implemented direct cross-national comparisons can yield meaningful comparisons of socioeconomic activities across a broad range of nations. Their major limitation is the different methods of data collection among countries, rendering direct comparisons of limited meaning.

In this book we rely upon a direct cross-national comparison, for a uniform time period, and with an emphasis on a single sector of the economy – manufacturing. The main unit of observation has been standardized to be the firm, and each individual country study measures both the share of employment accounted for by small firms, using the common definition of what constitutes a small enterprise, and the extent to which the small-firm employment share has shifted over time.

However, due to the peculiarities of each specific data base used to study each different country, deviations from implementing a rigid standardized methodology are appropriate in order to maximize what can be learned from each data base and about each country. The trick is to employ a common methodology in undertaking the specific country studies in order to facilitate meaningful direct cross-national comparisons, while at the same time allowing sufficient flexibility in each country study as to exploit the information particular to both the individual data base and to the special situation of the country. For example, in Chapter 7 results are reported for the North and South of Italy, rather than for the entire country. Not only do the authors argue for this distinction on economic grounds, but are forced to do so in order to exploit a rich data base.

3.2   Previous research

While the pathbreaking study by Birch (1979) was not international in nature, it nevertheless proved to be a catalyst for the resulting wave of job-generation studies carried out in a host of countries throughout Western Europe. These subsequent studies were important because they brought together an army of researchers to bear on the fundamental questions involving job generation and firm size (Storey and Johnson, 1987; Hull, 1986; FitzRoy, 1989, 1990; Johnson, 1989; Gallagher and Stewart, 1986; Gallagher, Daly and Thomason, 1991).

The first cross-national comparison on the role of small firms was undertaken by the OECD (1985). This study examined the employment share of small firms in seven countries for the early 1980s. Considerable variation in the size distribution of firms across countries was found. The three countries where large firms provided more than 60 percent of the employment were the United States, United Kingdom and West Germany. No attempt was made to examine shifts in the firm-size distribution over time.

Storey and Johnson (1987) undertook the first major cross-national study of the role of small firms in the job-generation process. This was one of the first attempts carefully to examine Birch's findings within an international context. Their tentative findings suggested that the relative success of small firms in generating jobs across a broad spectrum of countries is attributable to the lack of international competitiveness of large enterprises and the subsequent job-shedding and organizational changes.

Sengenberger, Loveman and Piore (1990) carried out the first systematic international study examining the re-emergence of small units of production in advanced industrialized countries.[3] Their main focus was on small establishments and how they have evolved over time. Two major findings emerged from their study. First, the size distribution of establishments at any particular point in time depends on the particular institutional or historical context. As Loveman and Sengenberger (1991, p. 35) argue, "[M]ajor criteria for structuring SME (small and medium-sized enterprise) sectors are the legal status (such as France), the ownership status (as in Hungary), the distinction between 'craft' and 'industrial firms' (as in the Federal Republic of Germany), independent and subordinate firms (as in Japan), or small firms in small-firm industries vs. small firms in industries where large enterprises dominate or where there is a mixed size composition." That is, there does not appear to be a predetermined optimal size distribution of firms. Their second major finding was that neither the size distribution of firms nor that of establishments crucially determines business performance, either in economic or in social terms. Rather, business performance depends decisively upon organizational structure, and on public and private policies.

3.3 The countries chosen for this study

In selecting countries to implement the type of direct cross-national comparisons described above, several criteria were considered. First, it is important to include a diversity of social and economic systems for different countries with a similar level of development. This helps to shed at least some light on the issue of the extent to which the role of small firms is independent of the social and political context. Second, it is important to include a diversity of stages of economic development for countries with at least a fundamentally similar economic and political system, such as Western capitalism. This enables inferences to be drawn on the extent to which the stage of economic development influences the role of small firms. Finally, it is important to include several countries with very different economic and political systems – such as nations in Eastern Europe.

The first three chapters in this book (Chapters 2–4) thus include country studies of three large, dominant economies – two Anglo–Saxon countries, the United Kingdom and the United States, and the most powerful country in continental Europe, the Federal Republic of Germany. These countries were among the earliest to be industrialized. The particular experiences in financial deregulation and similar banking systems in the two Anglo–Saxon countries serve as a contrast to the still heavily regulated and concentrated financial system of the Federal Republic of Germany. Differences in financial systems alone could explain variations in the role of small firms and entrepreneurship between the Federal Republic of Germany on the one hand and the United Kingdom and United States on the other. In addition, there is a strong tradition of "craft" firms, which consist of highly skilled and trained workers in small enterprises in West Germany. Such a tradition is absent in both the United Kingdom and in the United States. The US experience is particularly important because it provides a contrast to the Western European nations, such as the United Kingdom, which have been under the influence of the integration of the internal market within the European Economic Community.

Three small "open" economies from the European continent – the Netherlands, Portugal, and Italy – are included in Chapters 5–7. These countries, especially Portugal, represent somewhat different stages of economic development than those nations included in Chapters 2–4. Italy is included because it was the earliest focus of the re-emergence of small firms (Brusco, 1982) and served as the basis for Piore and Sabel's 1984 study which helped to popularize the debate throughout the West. Holland ranks among the most developed countries in continental Europe and, for a small country is populated by some of the largest companies in the world.

Eastern Europe countries – Czechoslovakia, East Germany, and Poland – are included in Chapters 8–10. While Western countries have faced a difficult task of restructuring during the last fifteen years, the problems confronting these Eastern European countries are even greater. Eastern European nations systematically eliminated most of their small firms, and with them their entrepreneurs. As Simon Johnson and Gary Loveman point out in Chapter 10, small firms and entrepreneurship were simply not compatible with state ownership and control; large units of production were much more conducive to centralized planning. The virtual obliteration of small firms and entrepreneurship deprived Eastern Europe of a key element facilitating industrial restructuring and technological progress (Román, 1989; Puchev, 1990). However, the Eastern European countries do provide a lesson for the West about the consequences of the systematic elimination of small firms and entrepreneurship. The three country studies included in Chapters 8–10 do touch upon the role of entrepreneurship in the transformation process currently under way in Eastern Europe.

Chapter 11 consists of an attempt by Hans-Peter Brunner to draw upon the experience of government policies in developing countries oriented towards promoting economic development and to provide lessons for Eastern Europe. Unlike the preceding chapters, Brunner does not provide a country study, but rather identifies those development issues confronting the "South" and how they are applicable to Eastern European countries currently confronting an unprecedented transformation process. In particular, Brunner provides four lessons from the experience in developing countries which should be applied to generate an entrepreneurial sector in Eastern Europe.

Notes

1 For example, the US Small Business Data Base does not identify the contribution from the self-employed.
2 This section draws on Reynolds (1991).
3 The compilation of studies contained in their edited volume includes Japan, the United States, the United Kingdom, France, the Federal Republic of Germany, and Italy.

References

Acs, Zoltan J. (1984) *The Changing Structure of the U.S. Economy: Lessons from the Steel Industry*, New York: Praeger.

Acs, Zoltan J. and David B. Audretsch (1990) *Innovation and Small Firms*, Cambridge, MA: MIT Press.

Aiginger, K. and G. Tichy (1991) "Small Firms and the Money Mania," *Small Business Economics*, **3**(2), 83–101.

Armington, Catherine and Marjorie Odle (1982) "Small Business – How Many Jobs?" *The Brookings Review*, **1** (Winter) 14–17.

Baumol, William, J., Sue Anne Batey Blackman and Edward N. Wolff (1989) *Productivity and Amerian Leadership*, Cambridge, MA: MIT Press.

Beesley, M. E. and R. T. Hamilton (1984) "Small Firms' Seedbed Role and the Concept of Turbulence," *Journal of Industrial Economics*, **33**, 217–232.

Berger, Suzanne and Michael J. Piore (1980) *Dualism and Discontinuity in Industrial Societies*, Cambridge: Cambridge University Press.

Birch, David L. (1979) "The Job Generation Process," Cambridge, MA: MIT Program on Neighborhood and Regional Change.

(1981) "Who Creates Jobs?," *The Public Interest*, 65, 3–14.

Blanchflower, David G. and Andrew Oswald (1990) "What Makes an Entrepreneur?" Cambridge, MA: National Bureau of Economic Research, 3252.

Blau, David B. (1987) "A Time Series Analysis of Self-Employment in the United States," *Journal of Political Economy*, 95(3), 445–467.

Böbel, Ingo (1984) *Wettbewerb und Industriestruktur*, Berlin: Springer-Verlag.

Brock, William A. and David S. Evans (1986) *The Economics of Small Business*, New York: Holmes & Meier.

(1989) "Small Business Economics," *Small Business Economics*, 1(1), 7–20.

Brown, Charles, James Hamilton and James Medoff (1990) *Employers Large and Small*, Cambridge, MA: Harvard University Press.

Brusco, Sebastiano (1982) "The Emilian Model: Productive Decentralization and Social Integration," *Cambridge Journal of Economics*, 6(2), 124–146.

Carlsson, Bo (1987) "The Evolution of Manufacturing Technology and its Impact on Industrial Structure: An International Study," *Small Business Economics*, 1(1), 21–38.

Dertouzos, Michael L., Richard K. Lester, Robert M. Solow and the MIT Commission on Industrial Productivity (1989) *Made in America: Regaining the Productive Edge*, Cambridge, MA: MIT Press.

Devine, Theresa (1990) "The Dynamics of Female Self Employment," Pennsylvania State University, mimeo.

Evans, David S. and B. Jovanovic (1989) "Estimates of a Model of Entrepreneurial Choice Under Liquidity Constraints," *Journal of Political Economy*, 97(4), 808–827.

Evans, David S. and Linda S. Leighton (1988) "Some Empirical Aspects of Entrepreneurship," *American Economic Review*, 78(3), 519–535.

(1989) "The Determinants of Changes in U.S. Self-Employment, 1968–1987," *Small Business Economics*, 1(2), 111–120.

Ferguson, Charles H. (1988) "From the People Who Brought You Voodoo Economics," *Harvard Business Review*, 87, 55–62.

FitzRoy, Felix R. (1989) "Firm Size, Efficiency and Employment: A Review Article," *Small Business Economics*, 1(1), 75–80.

(1990) "Employment, Entrepreneurship and 1992: Macroeconomic Policy and European Problems," *Small Business Economics*, 2(1), 11–24.

Galbraith, John K. (1957) *The New Industrial State*, Boston: Houghton Mifflin.

Gallagher, C. C. and H. Stewart (1986) "Jobs and the Business Life Cycle in the U.K.," *Applied Economics*, 18(8), 875–900.

Gallagher, C. C., M. J. Daly and J. C. Thomason (1991) "The Growth of U.K. Companies, 1985–1987, and their Contribution to Job Generation," *Small Business Economics*, 3(4), 269–286.

Geroski, Paul and Joachim Schwalbach (eds.) (1991) *Entry and Market Contestability: An International Comparison*, Oxford: Basil Blackwell.

Hull, Christopher, J. (1986) "Job Generation in the Federal Republic of Germany – A Review," Wissenschaftszentrum Berlin, II/LMP, 86–112.

Irsch, N. (1986) *Kleine und mittlere Unternehmen im Strukturwandel*, Frankfurt: Kreditanstalt für Wiederaufbau.

Jacquemin, A. P. and H. W. de Jong (1977) *European Industrial Organization*, London: Macmillan.

Johnson, Peter (1989) "Employment Change in the Small Business Sector: Evidence From Five Manufacturing Industries," *Small Business Economics*, 1(4), 315–324.

Kaplan, A. D. H. (1954) *Big Enterprise in a Competitive System*, Washington, DC: The Brookings Institution.

Kaufer, E. (1980) *Industrieökonomik*, München: Vahlen.

Loveman, Gary and Werner Sengenberger (1991) "The Re-emergence of Small Scale Production: An International Perspective," *Small Business Economics*, 3(1), 1–38.

Marshall, Alfred (1920) *Principles of Economics*, London, Macmillan, 8th edn.

Marx, Karl (1912) *Capital*, trans by Ernest Untermann, vol. 1, Chicago: Kerr.

Meyer, Bruce (1990) "Why are there so Few Black Entrepreneurs,?" Northwestern University, mimeo.

Nelson, Richard R. (1984) "Incentives for Entrepreneurship and Supporting Institutions", *Weltwirtschaftliches Archiv*, 120(4), 646–661.

Nelson, Richard R. and Sidney G. Winter (1974) "Neoclassical vs. Evolutionary Theories of Economic Growth: Critique and Prospectus," *Economic Journal*, 84, 886–905.

(1982) *An Evolutionary Theory of Economic Change*, Cambridge, MA: Harvard University Press.

Nguyen, Sang V. and Arnold P. Reznek (1991) "Returns to Scale in Small and Large U.S. Manufacturing Establishments," *Small Business Economics*, 3(3), 197–214.

OECD (1985) "Employment in Small and Large Firms: Where Have the Jobs Come from?" *Employment Outlook*, Paris: OECD.

Piore, Michael J. and Charles F. Sabel (1984) *The Second Industrial Divide*, New York: Basic Books.

Puchev, Plamen (1990) "A Note on Government Policy and the New 'Entrepreneurship' in Bulgaria," *Small Business Economics*, 2(1), 73–76.

Reynolds, Paul D. (1991) "Strategies for Cross-National Comparisons: Matching Research Issues and Analysis Strategies," *Small Business Economics*, 3(4), 245–260.

Román, Zoltán (1989) "The Size of the Small-Firm Sector in Hungary," *Small Business Economics*, 1(4), 303–308.

Schwalbach, Joachim (1989) "Small Business in German Manufacturing," *Small Business Economics*, 1(2), 129–136.

Schumpeter, Joseph A. (1934) *The Theory of Economic Development*, Cambridge, MA: Harvard University Press.

Sengenberger, Werner, Gary Loveman and Michael Piore (1990) *The Re-Emergence of Small Enterprises: Industrial Restructuring in Industrialized Countries*, Geneva: International Labor Organization.

Shepherd, William G. (1982) "Causes of Increased Competition in the U.S. Economy, 1939–1980," *Review of Economics and Statistics*, **64**(4), 613–626.

Storey, David J. and Steven Johnson (1987) *Job Generation and Labor Market Changes*, London: Macmillan.

White, Lawrence J. (1982) "The Determinants of the Relative Importance of Small Business," *Review of Economics and Statistics*, **64**(1), 42–49.

Winter, Sidney G. (1984) "Schumpeterian Competition in Alternative Technological Regimes," *Journal of Economic Behaviour and Organization*, **5**, 287–320.

Wright, Gavin (1990) "The Origins of American Industrial Success, 1879–1940," *American Economic Review*, **80**, 651–668.

2 Industrial concentration and small firms in the United Kingdom: the 1980s in historical perspective

Alan Hughes

There is a great deal of evidence to show that the jobs and products of tomorrow are highly likely to come from the activities of the small business sector . . . in my judgement the future belongs to them.
John Major (then Chief Secretary to the UK Treasury) May 1989.

1. Introduction

Since the election of the first Thatcher administration in 1979 a great deal of emphasis has been placed by government spokespersons on the virtues of an expanding small-firm sector. A number of policy measures were accordingly designed to further its development in the 1980s. Small-firm corporation tax was reduced from 42 percent to 25 percent (in line with the basic rate of income tax), the Business Expansion scheme was introduced to encourage private equity investment in unquoted companies, the Enterprise Allowance scheme was promoted to subsidize the unemployed in setting up their own businesses, and the Enterprise Initiative was launched to improve management efficiency in selected areas of small business activities. The result it is claimed has been "a remarkable transformation" of the small business sector, with a substantial growth in numbers of businesses of all kinds, and in manufacturing an increase of almost 50 percent in the number of businesses employing under 200 people from 87,000 in 1980 to 128,000 in 1986 (HM Treasury, 1989).

The object of this chapter is to examine the evidence bearing on this "remarkable transformation", and to place it in long-run historical perspective. It looks in turn at changes in the share of large and small firms in the economy as a whole and especially in manufacturing, first in the 1980s and then in the period since 1909. My conclusion will be that this "transformation" is the result of a continuation of longer-run trends which predate the 1980s and that a major part of the changes in the numbers of small business reported in the official statistics for UK manufacturing industry in the 1980s are the result of changes in the way the data are collected. I also argue that changes in the shares of small businesses in employment and net output mask an underlying stability in small-firm employment combined with major rationalization by the largest firms as manufacturing employment contracted in the 1980s. There has been nevertheless an increase in small-business formation, especially at the very smallest level of business organizations employing less than ten people. It is shown that there has been stability in concentration especially in terms of net output since the early 1970s and that the larger plant rationalization of the early 1980s was associated with a widening productivity gap between large and small firms. The problem for policy is now not so much one of small-business creation but of overcoming barriers to growth in the existing small-business population.

2.   The changing stock of businesses in the UK economy as a whole[1]

Changes in the size distribution of firms over time arise from differences in the growth rates of surviving companies, and the numbers and sizes of births and deaths occurring. The only economy-wide data source with a consistent time series of births and deaths arises from the VAT Register. This source shows that there was a clear increase in the number of businesses in the 1980s from 1.3 million in 1979 to 1.7 million in 1989. The annual percentage of registrations over this period remained fairly steady between 12 and 15 percent. At the same time the share of deregistrations also remained fairly constant but between 1 and 2 percent lower. The result was a steady growth in businesses. It is clear, however, that this steady growth was the result of high rates of registration and deregistration, so that there was massive turbulence in the population. Thus between 1979 and 1989 there were 1.7 million registrations and 1.4 million deregistrations (Dunne and Hughes, 1990b). Whilst registration and deregistration do not necessarily reflect economic birth and death, it is clear from other sources that these trends based on VAT statistics are not particularly misleading guides in this respect.

Only the retail sector saw a reduction in the number of businesses in 1979–1988. The most significant increases were, however, confined to services. The numbers of service businesses registered for VAT rose by over 60 percent in this period compared to only 4 percent in the production industries. The dynamism of services was the result not so much of a high rate of registration as a relatively low rate of deregistration compared to other sectors. The relative dynamism of services is not surprising. It reflects the substantial structural shifts occurring in the distribution of economic activity in the United Kingdom in the 1970s and 1980s.

Whilst total industrial and service sector employment (including the self-employed) stood at around 24 million in both 1977 and 1987, service sector employment rose by 2.4 million, so that its share in the economy rose from 58 percent to 67 percent. Over 1 million of the increase in employment was located in banking, finance, insurance and business services. In the latter category, which includes market research, management consultancy, personnel, and public relations there was an increase of nearly 500,000 employees between 1982 and 1987 alone (Graham, Beatson and Wells, 1989; Keeble, 1989). In the long run the overall relative service sector employment trends reflected a growth in demand for services of all kinds as income rises combined with a relatively low rate of productivity growth in the service sector (Rowthorn and Wells, 1987). As far as business service growth is concerned a number of specific factors may also be at work. In the recessionary and unstable years of the early 1980s risk-spreading vertical disintegration by large industrial companies undoubtedly had a role to play (Morris, 1988; Howells, 1989; Shutt and Whittington, 1987). Moreover the increasingly specialized nature of demands for business services and consumer services associated with changing production and information technology, and rising incomes, has probably favoured the creation and survival of smaller firms in this sector (Keeble and Wever, 1986; Keeble, 1989; Wood, 1990).[2]

The impact of the economy-wide pattern of registration and deregistration and business growth on the size distribution of UK businesses as a whole by turnover is given in Table 2.1 This shows that there has been an increase of five percentage points in the share of businesses in the smallest size band, and that it has been at the expense of businesses with a turnover of above £100,000 in 1985 prices. However it is apparent that only the very smallest size classes have benefitted from the overall upward trend in registrations. Moreover, a spatial analysis of these changes shows their very uneven spread, with the South East and East Anglia experiencing disproportionate growth especially in the service sector (Keeble, 1989).

Overall it is clear that there has been an increase in the stock of business registered for VAT in the United Kingdom over the last ten years, and that this has been the result of an increase in registrations since the 1980–1981 recession, rather than a decline in the share of deregistrations. There is a variation across sectors and geographical regions but the evidence suggests that much of the movement has been in the very smallest size bands, with these businesses representing an increasing share of the total. This trend is confirmed by economy-wide data on the employment share of small businesses drawn from the UK New Earnings Survey. Between 1979 and 1986 the share of business organizations in the

Table 2.1. *The percentage distribution of business units in the United Kingdom by turnover size band, 1978–1987*

Turnover size band, £000 (1985 prices)	Number of business units		% change in share 1978/1979–1987
	1978/1979	1987[a]	
0 < 20	10	15	+5[b]
20 < 100	50	52	+2
100 < 1000	34	29	−5
1000 < 2000	3	2	−1
> 2000	3	3	–
	100	100	0

Notes:
[a] The number of units shown for 1987 is the number on the register in 1987, although the turnover values are for 1985/6 the latest year for which information is available. Turnover size bands in 1978/9 were doubled to adjust roughly for the effects of inflation. (The Retail Price Index (1980 = 100) stood at 84.8 in 1979 and 146.5 in 1986.) The 1987 data were adjusted to add back the 238,511 units with turnover below £19,500 which were voluntarily registered.
[b] The sum of the percentage shares and changes in shares do not necessarily sum to 100 because of rounding errors.
Source: Hughes (1989).

survey employing less than 200 people rose from 24.9 percent to 29.0 percent with 3.4 percent of this overall change accounted for by those employing less than 50.

3.   The changing size distribution in manufacturing

We have seen that these economy-wide changes were most dramatically reflected in the service sector with the production industries experiencing much less rapid growth. This seems at odds with the official claims of a substantial increase in small business numbers in manufacturing between 1980 and 1986 referred to in the Introduction. It is therefore worth looking at manufacturing in some detail. In what follows we look both at small-firm shares and then at the position of the very largest firms. We consider data both for business enterprises and the establishments (or operating plants) they own (for a full discussion of the definition of "enterprise," "establishment" and other units which report data for the Official Statistics on UK businesses, see Dunne and Hughes (1990a)).

Table 2.2 divides the enterprises in UK manufacturing into four size classes according to levels of employment.[3] The most obvious point to

Table 2.2. *Establishments enterprises and the shares of output and employment by employment size class, UK manufacturing, 1979–1986*

Size Class 1–99			% share of		
	No. ent.	*No. est.*	*No. ent.*	*Emp.*	*Output*
1979	84229	88226	93.9	17.2	14.6
1983	81474	85753	94.8	22.0	18.0
1984	114186	118352	95.8	23.4	18.8
1986	125503	129656	96.4	24.0	19.3
Size Class 100–499					
1979	4152	6804	4.6	12.9	11.6
1986	3688	6778	2.8	15.9	14.5
Size Class 500–999					
1979	609	2170	0.7	6.6	6.8
1986	508	1787	0.4	7.4	7.2
Size Class 1000+					
1979	751	9876	0.8	63.0	67.0
1986	544	7631	0.4	52.8	59.1

Note: There are substantial changes in the Census coverage between 1983 and 1984 which boosts the recorded number of small enterprises (see text, p. 22). In 1980 a revised definition of manufacturing was introduced so that 1979 is not strictly comparable with later years. The effect at this level of aggregation is relatively minor.
Source: ACOST (1990, Appendix A).

begin with is the fact that UK manufacturing remains dominated by a very small number of large businesses which collectively produce three-fifths of total net output and provide slightly more than half of total manufacturing employment, yet account for less than 1 percent of total manufacturing enterprises. Conversely, the vast majority of businesses are small enterprises (96 percent of the total), employing less than 100 individuals. These account for one-fifth of national output and nearly one-quarter of total manufacturing employment.

It is apparent from Table 2.2 that in all size classes but the smallest the total number of enterprises has been in decline since 1979. The increase in the total number of enterprises has thus been generated solely by increases within the smallest size class. The increase has been especially marked after 1983 and the numbers correspond closely to the claims made in the Treasury progress report referred to in the Introduction.

Table 2.3. *Employment, net output and net output per head by size of enterprise, UK manufacturing industry, 1979–1986*

	Employment (000) 1979	Index of employment (1979 = 100)	
		1983	1986
1–99	1138	94.0	100.6
100–499	835	83.8	90.7
500–999	425	86.1	83.1
1000 plus	4087	66.6	61.6
All	6485	74.9	73.6

	Net output £m 1979	Index of net output (1980 prices) (1979 = 100)	
		1983	1986
1–99	10627	106.0	122.2
100–499	8455	95.1	115.4
500–999	4947	97.4	97.9
1000 plus	8793	78.3	81.6
All	72815	85.8	92.5

	Net output per head £000 (1980 prices) 1979	Index of net output per head (1980 prices) (1979 = 100)	
		1983	1986
1–99	9.3	112.9	121.5
100–499	10.1	113.9	127.7
500–999	11.6	113.8	118.1
1000 plus	11.9	117.6	132.8
All	11.2	115.2	125.9

Note: Net output from the census was deflated by the producer price index for all manufactured home sales (*Economic Trends Annual Supplement*, 1988, Table 118).
Source: Census of Production.

In terms of the movement of output and employment shares, a number of significant changes are evident, the most striking of these relating to the smallest and the largest groups of firms. Firms with less than 100 employees have progressively increased their share in total employment and net output since 1979. The largest group of firms, on the other hand, have experienced a shake-out in terms of their employment and output shares. Within the two middle size classes the changes are far less marked, although in both groups the number of enterprises and establishments have been in decline. Since 1979, the enterprises with between 100 and 499 employees have substantially increased both their share in employment and their share in output. Enterprises with less than 500 employees now account for slightly more than one-third of manufacturing output and 40 percent of total manufacturing employing.

It is important to note, however, that these are changing shares of a level of overall manufacturing activity which was lower in 1986 than 1979. Table 2.3 shows indices of employment, net output and net output per head in constant prices for the four size categories of enterprise. It is apparent that the growth in employment and output shares of the two smallest size groups is a result of the restoration of their employment levels to those of 1979 and of their output levels to beyond them, while the larger groups have experienced a decline over the period on both activity measures. For all groups, employment has declined faster or risen less fast than output. The result has been rising labour productivities. However, this improvement is far more substantial for those employing over 1,000 individuals than for any other group. It is, moreover, apparent that the smallest size group has declined in productivity relative to both the 100–499 and the over 1,000 size categories.

It seems at first sight paradoxical that a segment of the size distribution with declining relative productivity should be of increasing importance in absolute and proportionate terms. Leaving aside problems of productivity measurement and varying capital intensities across size of business, a number of possible explanations suggest themselves. First, to the extent that large businesses have shed inefficient plants and lines of business smaller concerns, content with lower margins, may have been able to fill the gap. Secondly, the externalization of activities which are relatively labour intensive by larger organizations may also have affected the relative productivity spread between large- and small-firm sectors. Thirdly, these aggregate comparisons may reflect aggregation biases due to different changes in small-firm shares across industries with differing productivity levels. Finally, we may be witnessing a disequilibrium phenomenon, so that as the superior productivity performance of the large firms feeds through to their competitive performance so small-firm

Table 2.4. *Market concentration in the UK manufacturing sector, 5 firm employment concentration ratios, 1980–1986*

Average 5 firm concentration ratios, largest 5 firms ranked by employment

Year	(%)
1980	45.4
1983	44.4
1984	42.2
1986	41.9

Note: Unweighted averages based on 105 3 digit industries.
Sources: Census of Production, various issues, Table 13; Dunne and Hughes (1990b).

shares may be squeezed again. The question, however, clearly merits investigation.

It seems clear that there are dramatic changes occurring at both ends of the size distribution. However, Table 2.2 makes it clear that the bulk of the changes at the bottom end occurred between 1983 and 1984. This turns out to be in large part a statistical artefact since between those years a change in the Census sampling frame resulted in an increased coverage of around 31,000 businesses employing 80,000 people (Perry, 1985). Their average employment size was thus somewhat less than 3. This must account in part for the apparent contradiction between the VAT registration data which show only a modest difference between registrations and deregistrations in the production industries and the large increase in enterprises shown in the Census data for manufacturing, and referred to in the Treasury progress report quoted in the Introduction.

To look more closely at changes at the top end of the distribution we can examine changes in patterns of concentration at both the aggregate and the disaggregated level of the 3 digit industrial group. We can begin with the latter. Table 2.4 gives the average five firm concentration ratio in terms of employment and shows a decline in market concentration since 1980, again most marked in the years 1983–1984 when census coverage changed.

Table 2.5 provides further detail on the industrial distribution of concentration ratios. It shows that the reduction in the average concentration ratio between 1980 and 1986 was the result of increases in the number of industries with employment concentration ratios of less than 50 percent and reductions in the number of industries with high ratios. However the median employment share of the five largest producers was still

Table 2.5. *The distribution of manufacturing industries by the employment share of the largest 5 employers, 1980–1986*

5 firm employment concentration ratio	Number of industries		Changes 1980–1986
	1980	*1986*	
0 < 20	16	20	+4
20 < 30	16	13	−3
30 < 40	16	23	+7
40 < 50	14	17	+3
50 < 60	14	10	−4
60 < 70	12	8	−4
70 < 80	5	4	−1
80 < 90	6	5	−1
> 90	6	5	−1
All	105	105	
Median 5 firm ratio	42	37	
Median no. plants per top 5 employers as a group	20	18	
Median plant/enterprise ratio of top 5 employers	4.0	3.6	

Source: Census of Production; Dunne and Hughes (1990b).

37 percent in 1986 so the decline in their dominance was relatively mild.

Turning to aggregate concentration Table 2.6 gives information on the shares of the 100 largest enterprises, in terms of employment, net output, establishments and sales. The largest 100 employers have shown a decline in their share of all four, a downward trend which was again most marked after 1983, when the Census coverage changed. Between 1979 and 1986 the share of the 100 largest employers in employment fell from around 37 percent to 33 percent whilst their share in net output fell only from 39 percent to 38 percent. This reflects both the increased Census coverage of small employers and the superior productivity performance of large employers.

The data leave us in little doubt about the increasing numerical importance of the small-firm sector in the United Kingdom as a whole in the 1980s, however defined, but less so in the case of manufacturing. There are nevertheless some important qualifications to note. First, it is quite clear from the Census data and the VAT statistics that the strongly growing element among the smaller businesses in manufacturing and in

Table 2.6. *Aggregate concentration in UK manufacturing industry, 1973–1986, enterprise analysis in the private sector*

(*a*) *The largest 100 employers (private sector)*

	% establishments	% employment	% sales	% net output
1979	3.5	37.3	40.4	38.9
1980	3.9	37.2	40.5	38.4
1983	4.0	36.0	41.5	39.8
1984	2.6	33.1	39.5	36.9
1986	2.4	33.2	38.8	37.7

(*b*) *The largest 100 producers in terms of net output (private sector)*

	% establishments	% employment	% sales	% net output
1979	3.3	35.7	44.7	42.2
1980	3.9	35.8	42.7	40.5
1983	4.2	35.1	43.1	41.4
1984	2.5	31.7	41.0	38.7
1986	2.5	31.8	40.9	39.1

Note: There are important breaks in the series in 1979–1980 (due to changes in the SIC on which the Census data is collected) and 1983–1984 (due to a change in the Business Register on which the sampling frame for the Census is based – this led to a large increase in the number of very small establishments and enterprises covered by the Census, see text, p. 22).

Source: Census of Production, various issues, Tables 12 and 13; Dunne and Hughes (1990b).

the economy as a whole is to be found entirely amongst the smallest of the small. Further analysis not reported in detail here shows that manufacturing establishments employing less than ten employees increased from 61.8 percent to 69.9 percent as a proportion of those employing between 1 and 99 people over the period 1979–1986. Indeed establishments employing between 20 and 99 individuals declined in numbers and in terms of actual employment in these years. Even an increase in numbers and employment between 1984 and 1986 could not prevent their employment share falling from 62.9 percent in 1979 to 59.1 percent in 1986 (Dunne and Hughes, 1990a). Secondly, a large part of the recorded increase in the 1–9 group in the period 1979–1986 undoubtedly reflects the 1983–1984 changes in the Business Register which greatly increased the coverage of the Census in the smallest size ranges. It is possible that this explanation may account for the greater part of the observed change, although it is notable that the numbers of the establishments in the 1–9 group continued to increase after 1984. Amongst the very smallest firms, then, the Census data suggests that there is an increasing rate of business formation. The emergence of increasing numbers in the 20–99 group after 1984 (reported in Dunne and Hughes, 1990a), in so far as it reflects larger start ups or growth from lower categories, rather than declines from greater size, also suggests a more dynamic relative growth performance by smaller firms. It remains the case, however, that these developments have yet to reverse the decline in activity in this group over the 1980s as a whole, and that in all greater Census size classes the trend for the number of enterprises is to decline. The developments in the 20–99 group may be regarded as of particular concern since it is within this category that we might expect to find companies managing to sustain growth beyond the start up scales of the smallest size groups. Finally, it is quite clear when we look at the upper tail of the distribution that dramatic changes in small-firm shares arise not so much from employment increases in smaller firms but from massive employment decline amongst the very largest. Even so in terms of market shares and aggregate concentration, manufacturing activity in the United Kingdom remains heavily concentrated in the hands of a few giant firms with only mild declines in large-firm dominance over the 1980s and an apparent gain in their relative productivity.

4. The size distribution in UK manufacturing in the 1980s in historical perspective

Even allowing for the various caveats discussed in the previous section the developments which have been described seem to point to a marked break with past trends. Thus in the late 1970s analysts of concentration could point to the possibility of the largest 100 firms accounting for over 70 percent of manufacturing net output by the 1990s, apparently confirming the Bolton Report's conclusion that the United Kingdom was moving inexorably to a world of diminishing small-firm business activity. Such is the nature of the time lags in the production of data and their analysis by economists that even while the ink was drying on the paper the trends they were describing (mostly based on evidence for the 1960s and earlier) were being reversed.

Table 2.7 shows the extent of this reversal in terms of small-firm shares by comparing the Bolton Committee estimates for manufacturing in 1963 with similar estimates for 1985. Two estimates are provided for the latter year, one based on businesses employing less than 200 people (which was

Table 2.7. *Shares of businesses and employment in the UK manufacturing sector by employment size of business unit, 1963 and 1985*

	% shares by employment size		
	1963	*1985*	
Business unit	Bolton definition of small < 200	< 100	< 200
Numbers of:			
Enterprises	93.8	96.1	98.0
Establishments	91.0[a]	94.2	96.9
Employment in:			
Enterprises	20.0	23.5	30.3
Establishments	31.0[a]	27.3	38.1
Local Units		32.3	45.9

Note: [a] The definition of an establishment for the purposes of the 1963 Census of Production differs from that used in 1985. In 1963 the establishment definition was closer in concept to the current one for local units used in the Business Statistics Office's Business Register. From 1985 an analysis is available for both local units and establishments. The Bolton establishment figure is therefore shown for comparison against both local unit and establishment data for 1985.
Sources: Census of Production, 1963, 1985; Business Monitor, PA 1003; Size Analysis of British Business 1987.

the benchmark used by Bolton) the other using businesses employing less than 100. This is done to allow for the effects of productivity growth between 1963 and 1985 on the implied output scale of enterprises of any given employment size. This is a point frequently overlooked in updating the Bolton results. (Productivity in manufacturing in terms of net output per head roughly doubled between 1963 and 1985.) It is apparent that on either basis the small-business sector has increased in significance since 1963, though the changes are far more limited when the effects of productivity growth are allowed for.

Interesting questions arise as to the time path on which these changes occurred, whether 1979 marks in any sense a significant departure from trends, and whether the small-business sector's share in the long run mirrors shifts in the top end of the distribution in terms of long-run developments in concentration. Tables 2.8 and 2.9 and the associated Figures 2.1–2.3 and 2.4–2.6 shed some interesting light on these questions. Table 2.8 and Figures 2.1–2.3 report on long-run developments in the shares of establishments of different sizes in UK manufacturing, while Table 2.9 and Figures 2.4–2.6 look at enterprise developments. Before discussing them it is worth emphasizing the limitations which the data sources impose on comparisons of this kind. First, the industrial coverage of the Census changes over time as the scope of manufacturing activities as defined for Census of Production purposes is refined. Second, the definition of the individual reporting units (establishments/plants, and enterprises) has also changed over time, becoming more, or less, inclusive in successive periods. Nevertheless for the kind of broad analysis attempted here the long-run trends are unlikely to be seriously misleading. A rough attempt has been made to adjust for the 1983–1984 Census coverage so that two sets of data are reported for the years 1984–1986. In 1984 31,000 businesses were added to the Census population employing on average 2.6 people (Perry, 1985). In that year we have therefore subtracted these numbers from the bottom end of the size distribution (i.e. the assumption is they all employed less than ten employees.) In succeeding years it was conservatively assumed that there was no increase in their average size, and that a number died each year at the rate of mortality found to apply to new start ups. This too is a conservative assumption since the 31,000 firms are unlikely to be all new start ups and therefore could be expected to survive on average for a longer period in the size distribution.

Figure 2.1 shows the changing shares in employment of manufacturing establishments employing less than 200 and less than 50 people respectively since the 1920s. The long-run downward trend remarked upon by Bolton is at once apparent, as is its reversal in the early 1970s. The share of establishments employing less than 50 rose from a low of 11 percent in 1963 to 19 percent in 1987 (18 percent on an adjusted basis), with the bulk of the changes occurring between 1973 and 1981. Changes since then have been much more slight. The same is true for plants employing less than 200. Figure 2.2 shows these changes mirrored in terms of the numbers of establishments in manufacturing over the same period, with the change in Census sample coverage showing up dramatically in the series relating to plants employing less than ten people. It was clearly this change, alongside other increases in the smallest of small businesses, which was driving the overall change in establishment numbers in the mid-1980s. Once again the recovery in small-scale activity dates from well before 1980. In this case the recovery begins in the late 1960s. In view of changes in Census definitions of an establishment it would be dangerous to time changes too precisely or put much weight on year to year changes. The broad trend is, however, clear. Figure 2.3 goes beyond the data on numbers and shares to look at actual employment. Here a striking result emerges. It is quite clear that employment in plants employing less than 200 workers has been in steady slow decline since the early 1950s, and that

Table 2.8. Number of establishments, employment and employment shares in small establishments in UK manufacturing industry, 1924–1987

	Employment and employment shares				Numbers of establishments		
	All establishments (000)	Establishments employing less than 200 (000)	Establishments employing less than 200 (%)	Establishments employing less than 50 (%)	All establishments (000)	Establishments employing less than 200 (000)	Establishments employing less than 10 (000)
1924	5115	2257	44	–	163	160	–
1930	5179	2238	43	19	168	164	93
1935	5409	2375	44	19	148	144	77
1948	6871	2538	37	16	108	103	52
1951	7382	2576	35	–	102	96	45
1954	7537	2500	33	14	97	91	44
1958	7781	2498	32	14	93	85	35
1964	7960	2436	31	12	90	82	33
1968	7870	2280	29	12	92	–	35
1970	8033	–	–	–	88	–	–
1973	7616	2090	27	11	94	88	47
1977	7280	2151	30	13	108	102	59
1979	6926	2065	30	14	107	101	60

1980	6495	2069	32	15	109	103	60
1981	5778	1957	34	17	108	103	61
1982	5361	1891	35	18	102	98	56
1983	5079	1841	36	18	102	98	53
1984	5059 (4979)	1912 (1832)	38 (37)	19 (18)	136 (105)	131 (100)	90 (59)
1985	4976 (4906)	1900 (1829)	38 (37)	19 (18)	143 (116)	138 (111)	98 (71)
1986	4878 (4818)	1914 (1854)	39 (39)	20 (19)	146 (123)	142 (118)	102 (79)
1987	4874 (4823)	1885 (1834)	39 (38)	19 (18)	146 (126)	141 (121)	103 (83)

Note: The series are only roughly comparable over time because of changes in Census definitions and industrial coverage. The most important recent breaks in continuity are shown by a gap. For the period 1984–1987 numbers in brackets show the effects of an adjustment for changes in Census sample coverage in 1983/1984 (see text, p. 27 for details). In 1987 the establishment was replaced by the "business" as the basic Census reporting unit, and "business" has been interpreted as corresponding to an establishment in compiling this table. This is a reasonable approximation for the smallest "business."

Sources: HMSO (1971); Prais (1976); *Census of Production: Historical Statistics; Census of Production,* various issues.

Table 2.9. *Enterprise concentration, and employment and net output shares by size of enterprise, UK manufacturing, 1909–1987*

| | Enterprise concentration | | | | Employment and net output and employment shares, by size of enterprise | | | | | |
| | Share of largest 100 enterprises in net output (%) | Share of largest 100 enterprises in employment (%) | Average levels of market concentration ratios (%) | All enterprise employment (000) | Employment in enterprises employing less than | | Employment share of enterprises with less than 200 employees (%) | Employment share of enterprises with less than 100 employees (%) | Net output share of enterprises with less than 200 employees (%) |
					200 (000)	100 (000)			
1909	16.0	—	—	—	—		—	—	—
1924	22.0	—	—	—	—		—	—	—
1930	—	—	—	—	—		—	—	—
1935	24.0	—	34.9[c]	5409	2078		38.0	—	35.0
1948	22.0[a]	—	31.2[d]	—	—		—	—	—
1951	27.0[b]	—	38.3	—	—		—	—	—
1954	—	—	33.9	—	—		—	—	—
1958	32.0	—	36.9[c]	7649	1812		24.0	14.0	20.0
1963	37.0	—	41.6	7846	1543		20.0	13.5	16.0
1968	41.0	—	45.6	—	—		—	15.8	—
1970	41.0	—	44.8[f]	—	—		—	—	—
1973	42.0	38.0	—	7268	1506	1109	20.7	17.2	17.1
1977	41.2	36.7	—	6683	1552	1175	22.5	17.1	18.7
1979	42.2	37.3	45.6	6485	1498	1138	23.1	17.5	19.5
1980	40.5	37.2	45.4[e]	6104	1485	1146	24.3	18.8	21.5
1981	40.6	36.4	—	5431	1408	1101	25.9	20.3	22.0
1982	41.0	36.5	—	5119	1368	1078	26.7	21.1	22.6
1983	41.4	36.0	44.4	4859	1351	1069	27.8	22.0	22.8
1984	38.7	33.1 (33.7)[i]	42.2[h]	4828 (4748)[i]	1465 (1385)[i]	1130 (1050)[i]	30.3 (29.2)[i]	23.4 (22.1)[i]	24.7
1985	38.3	33.2 (33.7)	—	4843 (4773)	1471 (1401)	1140 (1070)	30.4 (29.4)	23.5 (22.4)	25.3
1986	39.1	33.2 (33.6)	41.9	4775 (4715)	1456 (1396)	1146 (1086)	30.5 (29.6)	24.0 (23.0)	24.7
1987	38.1	31.0 (31.3)	—	4673 (4622)	1455 (1404)	1138 (1087)	31.1 (30.4)	24.4 (23.5)	24.5

Notes: The series are only roughly comparable over time because of changes in Census definitions and industrial coverage.
[a] Data refers to 1949.
[b] Data refers to 1953.
[c] 3 firm employment concentration ratios for 98 industries.
[d] 3 firm employment concentration ratios for 57 industries.
[e]–[h] 5 firm employment concentration ratios for varying samples of comparable industries.
[i] Data in brackets are adjusted to allow for differences in Census sampling after 1983.
Sources: Prais (1976); HMSO (1971); *Census of Production: Historical Statistics*; *Census of Production*, various issues; Clarke (1985); Hart and Clarke (1980).

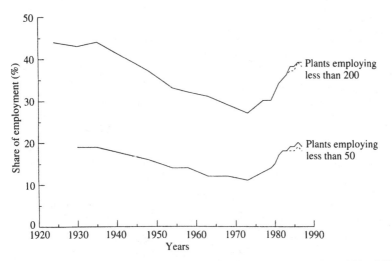

Figure 2.1   Shares of employment in UK manufacturing plants, 1924–1987.
Source: Table 2.8.
Note: – – – adjusted for change in Census coverage of small plants in 1984.

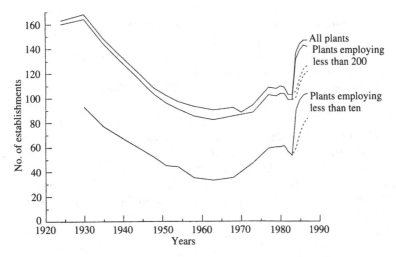

Figure 2.2   Numbers of UK manufacturing plants, 1924–1987.
Source: Table 2.8.
Note: – – – adjusted for change in Census coverage of small plants in 1984.

the declining shares of these plants prior to the Bolton Report reflected
that fact, combined with a growth in overall manufacturing employment.
The collapse in employment in the sector from 1970 and especially from

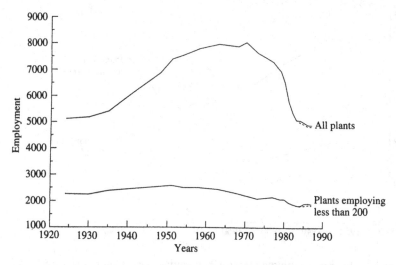

Figure 2.3   Employment in UK manufacturing plants, 1924–1987.
Source: Table 2.8.
Note: – – – adjusted for change in Census coverage of small plants in 1984.

1979 led to an increase in employment share, despite falling employment in those plants employing less than 200 workers.

Table 2.9 and Figures 2.4 and 2.5 paint a similar picture for small-enterprise employment shares and employment totals. The recovery in shares predates 1970 and is the result of stable or falling employment in small enterprises and a collapse in manufacturing employment in total. This is reflected in Figure 2.6 by decline and then collapse in the employment share of the 100 largest employers from the early 1970s onwards. Changes in large-firm dominance in terms of net output are far less marked. Thus Figure 2.6 also shows relative stability in aggregate concentration since 1970, whilst employment concentration in individual markets (shown in Figure 2.6(c)) has also stabilized since that date, and if anything declined since 1980.

It is worth noting that these long-run trends in concentration find an echo in recent studies for the Federal Republic of Germany (Fritsch, 1993) whilst similar results for small-firm shares in the United States and other Western European countries have also emerged, although there are differences in the extent and timing of the resurgence (Loveman and Sengenberger, 1991; Dunne and Hughes, 1990a). All of this suggests underlying forces at work beyond those attributable to particular time-specific policy stances in individual countries. A discussion of the nature of those forces and variations in their impact across countries and

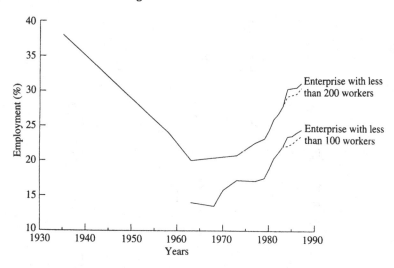

Figure 2.4   Employment shares by size of enterprise, 1935–1987.
Source: Table 2.9.
Note: − − − adjusted (see text, p. 27).

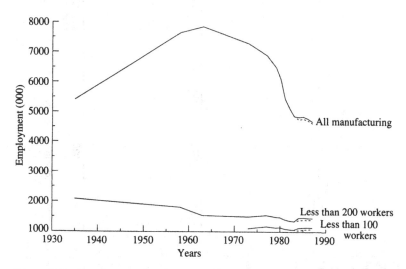

Figure 2.5   Employment by size of enterprise in UK manufacturing, 1935–
1987.
Source: Table 2.9.
Note: − − − adjusted (see text, p. 27).

industries would, however, take us far beyond the confines of this
chapter.[4]

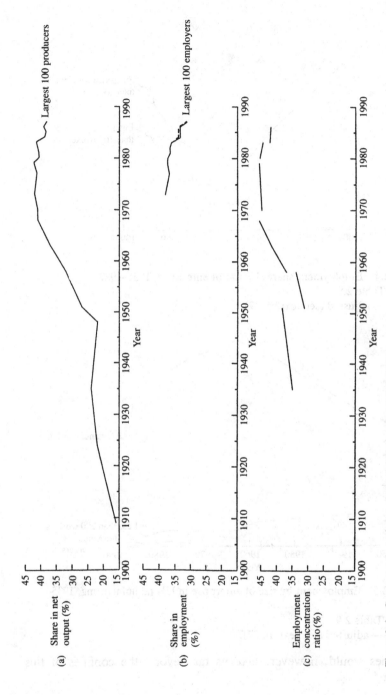

Figure 2.6 Concentration of manufacturing net output, 1909–1987.
Source: Table 2.9.
Note: — — — see text, p. 27.

5. Conclusion

This chapter has argued that new business formation in the 1980s in the United Kingdom has led to a significant increase in the number of businesses in the service sectors, but to a much less significant increase in manufacturing. Official analyses based on the raw Census of Production data and on movements in small-firms' shares have been misleading guides to changes in the scale of small-business activity in manufacturing, the former because of changes in Census coverage of small businesses and the latter because the changes in shares reflect stability or decline in employment in small businesses combined with major employment losses by larger businesses. The latter have in turn raised their productivity at a faster pace than smaller firms since 1979. Even so, the changing fortunes of the small- and large-firm sectors when measured in terms of shares of output and employment predate the 1980s by a considerable margin. They have their roots in the late 1960s and early 1970s. Such increases as have occurred in the numbers of small businesses in manufacturing have been of the very smallest sizes. The number of businesses employing over 20 people actually fell in the first half of the decade. A central problem for policy if this sector is to hold the key to the future is, then, not so much how to generate new business start ups but how to grow the best of them to maturity (ACOST, 1990).

There are of course, as always, a number of caveats which must be borne in mind in interpreting the results reported in this chapter. The first is that there are a number of ways in which the comparability of the data over time could be improved. It is doubtful, however, if this would dramatically alter the broad conclusions reached. Second the analysis has been at an extremely aggregated level. A disaggregation of small-firm activity by industrial group may well yield a picture of quite different relative fortunes between, for instance, high-tech and other sectors. Finally an analysis of the significance of small businesses in purely quantitative terms may understate their performance in qualitative terms such as their role in innovative activity. It is as well, however, to at least get the quantitative picture right.

Notes

This chapter arises from the research program into the Determinants of the Birth Growth and Survival of Small Businesses at the Small Business Research Centre. The Centre is supported under the ESRC Small Business Initiative by contributions from the ESRC, Barclays Bank, the Commission of the European Communities (DG XXIII), the Department of Employment and the Rural Development Commission. This support is gratefully acknowledged. The views expressed do not necessarily reflect those of the sponsoring organizations.

1 The discussion in this section draws on data presented in Dunne and Hughes (1990a) and Keeble (1989), which contain a fuller discussion of the VAT data in the case of Keeble and extended discussion of the uneven geographical distribution of rates of business formation.
2 These and related issues of business service growth are currently the subject of a research project at the Small Business Research Centre Cambridge, under the direction of David Keeble in collaboration with Peter Wood of University College London.
3 The following discussion draws on ACOST (1990, Appendix A) which reports the results of a survey of small-business statistics for the United Kingdom carried out by Paul Dunne and the author.
4 For a discussion of the changing macroeconomic circumstances of the 1970s and their link with the evolution of particular systems of production see Glyn, Hughes, Lipietz and Singh (1990), and for an argument that we are witnessing a fundamental shift away from mass-production technologies to small-scale production systems, see Piore and Sabel (1984). Storey and Johnson (1987) provide a useful international survey of empirical estimates of the changing role of small firms and their impact on employment generation.

References

ACOST (1990) *The Enterprise Challenge: Overcoming Barriers to Growth in Small Firms*, London: HMSO.
Bolton (1971) *Small Firms: Report of the Committee of Inquiry on Small Firms* (Cmnd 4811), London: HMSO.
Clarke, R. (1985) *Industrial Economics*, Oxford: Basil Blackwell.
Dunne, P. and A. Hughes (1990a) "Small Businesses: An analysis of recent trends in their relative importance, and growth performance, in the UK with some European comparisons," Small Business Research Centre, Department of Applied Economics, Cambridge, *Working Paper*, 1.
(1990b) "Large Firms, Small Firms and the Changing Structure of Competitive Industry," forthcoming in C. Driver and J. P. Dunne (eds.), "Structural Change in the UK Economy," Department of Applied Economics, *Occasional Paper*, **58**, Cambridge: Cambridge University Press.
Fritsch, M. (1993) "The Role of Small Firms in West Germany," Chapter 3 in this volume.
Glyn, A., A. Hughes, A. Lipietz and A. Singh (1990) "The Rise and Fall of the Golden Age," in S. Marglin and J. Schor (eds.), *The Golden Age of Capitalism: Reinterpreting the Post War Experience*, Oxford: Clarendon Press.
Graham, N., M. Beatson and W. Wells (1989) "1977 to 1987: A Decade of Service," *Employment Gazette* (January) 45–54.
Hart, P. E. and R. Clarke (1980) *Concentration in British Industry 1935–75*, Cambridge: Cambridge University Press.
HMSO (1971) *Small Firms: Report of the Committee of Inquiry on Small Firms*, London: HMSO.

HM Treasury (1989) *Economic Progress Report*, **204** (October) 7–10.

Howells, J. (1989) "Externalisation and the formation of New Industrial Operations: a neglected dimension in the dynamics of industrial location," *Area*, **21**, 289–299.

Hughes, A. (1989) "Small Firms, Merger Activity and Competition Policy," in J. Barber, S. Metcalfe and M. Porteous (eds.), *Barriers to Growth in Small Firms*, London: Routledge.

Keeble, D. (1989) "Small Firms, New Firms and Uneven Regional Development in the UK," Small Business Research Centre, Cambridge, mimeo.

Keeble, D. and E. Wever (1986) "Introduction," in D. Keeble and E. Wever (eds.), *New Firms and Regional Development in Europe*, London: Croom Helm, 1–14.

Loveman, Gary and Werner Sengenberger (1991) "The re-emergence of Small-Scale Production: An International Comparison," *Small Business Economics*, **3** (March) 1–38.

Morris, J. L. (1988) "New Technologies, flexible work practices, and regional sociospatial differentiations: some observations from the United Kingdom," *Environment and Planning, D, Society and Space*, **6**, 301–319.

OECD (1985) "Employment in Small and Large Firms: Where Have the Jobs Come From?," *OECD Employment Outlook* (September) 64–82.

Perry, J. A. (1985) "The Development of a New Register of Businesses," *Statistical News*, **70** (August).

Piore, M. J. and C. F. Sabel (1984) *The Second Industrial Divide: Possibilities for Prosperity*, New York: Basic Books.

Prais, S. J. (1976) *The Evolution of Giant Firms in Britain*, Cambridge: Cambridge University Press.

Rowthorn, R. E. and J. Wells (1987) *Deindustrialization and Foreign Trade*, Cambridge: Cambridge University Press.

Shutt, J. and R. Whittington (1987) "Fragmentation Strategies and the Rise of Small Units: cases from the North West," *Regional Studies*, **21**, 13–24.

Storey, D. J. and S. Johnson (1987) *Job Generation and Labour Market Change*, London: Macmillan.

Wood, P. (1990) "Small Firms' Business Services and Flexibility," Small Business Research Centre, Cambridge, mimeo.

3 The role of small firms in West Germany

Michael Fritsch

1. Introduction

The discussion about job generation in the small-business sector in other countries (for an overview see Storey and Johnson, 1987) has had a considerable impact on research in the Federal Republic of Germany (FRG). It has thrown doubt on the common attitude that small firms are "marginal firms" with relatively poor prospects for the future, and it has induced hope for a new source of additional employment. Unfortunately, relatively little data permitting judgments about the contribution of the small-business sector to economic development is available in West Germany; at least there is far less than in Great Britain or the United States. This applies especially for microdata that is needed for a detailed analysis of job dynamics in different size classes. Nevertheless, there has been considerable progress in this field in recent years, and the picture is much clearer now than it was some time ago.[1]

This chapter aims to investigate the importance of the small-business sector for employment in West Germany and to summarize the results of recent empirical research about the contribution of small firms to the job-generation process. Do small firms create a more than proportional share of new jobs? Section 2 sketches the size of the small-business sector; section 3 describes the long-run trends in the size distribution, focusing on the change over the last few decades. Section 4 reports evidence on the importance of size for market success and the relative contribution of surviving plants compared to entries and exits to employment in the different sectors based on data for individual plants. Section 5 contains a few remarks on characteristics of the small-business sector in Germany and the policy impact; section 6 summarizes the results and draws conclusions. All the empirical evidence presented here is limited to the non-agricultural private sector.

2. The size of the small-business sector

The annual (or even more frequent) official statistics for the FRG neglect a considerable part of the small-business sector, namely, craft firms. The most reliable and comprehensive data about employment of plant and by firm size are gathered by the statistical offices at intervals of 10 to 20 years as a Census of Business (*Arbeitsstättenzählung*). The available data from these Censuses go back as far as 1882 (for plants) and 1907 (for firms). The last census was taken in 1987, and only some of the results have been published thus far. A second relevant data base has recently been developed using information from social insurance statistics. It is limited to the level of plants and contains quarterly information about the number of employees and other aspects including skill level, age, and the individual's position within the firm from 1975. The data base covers nearly all private plants (only pure self-employment firms are missing) and more than 90 percent of private sector employment.[2] Comparisons of results from the two data bases reveal differences that need further clarification, but at least the information on size structure is relatively consistent.[3]

According to the 1987 census, firms with fewer than 100 employees accounted for more than half of all non-agricultural private sector employment and more than one-third worked in firms with fewer than 20 employees; 28.5 percent of the workforce was employed by firms with 1,000 or more employees (see Table 3.1). It should be noted here that the official statistics define "firm" as the smallest legal unit of employment; this implies that the concentration within the economy is underestimated by these figures because they do not reflect interfirm links (e.g. capital shares, cooperation, dependencies). In terms of plant size distribution, small plants account for somewhat more employment than firms, more than two-thirds of all workers are in plants with fewer than 200 employees; only 1.41 percent are in plants with 1,000 or more employees. "Plant" here means the smallest local unit of employment.

Table 3.1 also shows the size structure for the two large economic sectors manufacturing and services.[4] As can be seen, the concentration of employment is considerably lower in the service sector, which means that many services are small-scale activities that can be successfully operated by smaller units.

3. Long-run trends in the distribution of employment by firm size

Based on Census statistics Figure 3.1 shows the development of the firm-size structure for all non-agricultural private sectors in Germany from 1907 to 1970. From the beginning of comprehensive Census statistics up to 1970 the concentration of employment in large firms more or

Table 3.1. *The distribution of employment by firm size and by plant size in the FRG, 1987, percentage shares[a]*

Size class (employees)	All Sectors		Manufacturing		Services	
	Plants	Firms	Plants	Firms	Plants	Firms
1–4	15.0	13.3	5.7	5.3	23.4	21.1
5–9	13.1	11.6	8.2	7.6	17.6	15.5
	(28.1)	(24.9)	(13.9)	(12.8)	(41.0)	(36.6)
10–19	10.9	9.4	9.4	8.7	12.1	9.9
	(39.0)	(34.3)	(23.3)	(21.6)	(53.1)	(46.5)
20–49	11.7	9.5	11.5	10.2	11.8	8.8
	(50.7)	(43.8)	(34.3)	(31.8)	(65.0)	(55.3)
50–99	8.4	6.6	9.1	7.6	7.9	5.5
	(59.1)	(50.4)	(43.4)	(39.4)	(72.9)	(60.8)
100–199	8.6	6.6	9.9	8.0	7.5	5.3
	(67.7)	(57.0)	(53.3)	(47.3)	(80.4)	(66.0)
200–499	11.2	8.8	13.6	10.6	9.1	7.0
	(78.9)	(65.8)	(66.9)	(57.9)	(89.4)	(73.0)
500–999	7.0	5.9	8.9	7.1	5.3	4.7
	(85.9)	(71.6)	(75.8)	(65.0)	(94.7)	(77.7)
1000 and more	14.1	28.5	23.8	35.0	5.3	22.3
	(100)	(100)	(100)	(100)	(100)	(100)

Note: [a] Cumulated values in brackets. Only non-agricultural private-sector employment.
Source: Own calculations on the basis of *Statistisches Bundesamt* (1990).

less steadily increased; between 1907 and 1970, the gini-coefficient for the concentration of non-agricultural employment in firms rose from a value of 0.531 to 0.727 (see Stockmann, Dahm and Zeifang, 1983, p. 119).[5] This trend applies by and large to all non-agricultural sectors, and an even stronger tendency towards larger units during this time period is indicated at the plant level (see Figure 3.2).[6] The increasing concentration of employment in firms and plants has led to a relative decrease in employment in very small units and to a rising share for the relatively large units

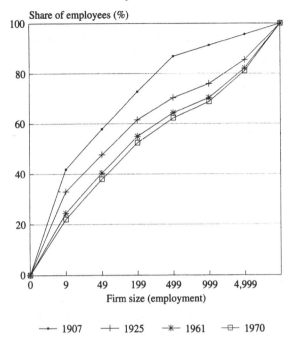

Figure 3.1   Change in firm-size structure, 1907–1970, all sectors.

while the employment share of medium size categories has remained fairly constant (i.e. the curves in Figures 3.1 and 3.2 tend to be more or less parallel in this size class).

The figures at the firm level only partly reveal the increasing concentration of economic power. Until the Second World War a great number of legalized cartels evolved in Germany and government during this period was in favour of large units. After 1945 some very large firms were split up and policy tended to be somewhat more restrictive in allowing a concentration of economic power. Many types of formerly legal cartels were prohibited, which may also have reduced the "hidden" concentration (that is not reflected in firm-level data).

The year 1970 marked a fundamental change in the economic development and the economic conditions of the FRG. It was the end of a long period of prosperity beginning with the introduction of the German Mark in 1949 (*Währungsreform*), that is often characterized as a period of "reconstruction." Presumably, the rising share of large-firm employment during this period was mainly due to economic prosperity, with a consequent realization of scale economies: when demand grew, firms grew too! In the late 1960s, the West German economy experienced its first serious

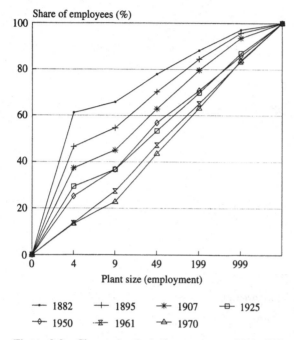

Figure 3.2   Change in plant-size structure, 1882–1970, all sectors.

recession since the Second World War. Compared with the reconstruction period, the years following (up to the time of writing) witnessed a
considerably higher degree of turbulence in the macroeconomic environment and a strong need for structural adjustment. A great part of this
turbulence was caused by the drastic upvaluation of the German Mark at
the end of the 1960s and by the oil crises during the 1970s. Other
influences that enforced structural change were a shift in the demand
structure away from manufacturing towards services and increasing competition from developing countries. At the end of the 1960s the share of
manufacturing employment was at its peak, and declined in subsequent
years.

What has happened to the size structure of West Germany private
sector firms since then? Has there been a shift towards smaller units? Is
there an extraordinary contribution of small firms to employment
growth, as claimed for several other countries? Until the recent development of the social-insurance statistics and the publication of initial
results from the 1987 Census of Business there existed no really reliable
foundation for statements about changes in firm-size structure during the
last two decades, for the earliest available Census data were from the year

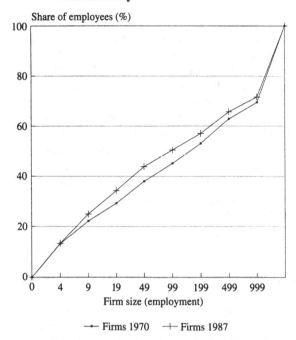

—•— Firms 1970   —+— Firms 1987

Figure 3.3   Change in firm-size structure, 1970–1987, all sectors.

1970. Figure 3.3 shows a comparison of the firm-size structure in the FRG from 1970 to 1987, based on the results of the Census of Business. As can be seen, the long-term trend towards larger firms seems to have reversed in this period. Keeping in mind that overall employment increased by roughly 700,000 in these years, this picture should be compatible with the hypothesis that small firms generated a disproportionately higher percentage of new jobs in the FRG. Another possible explanation for the rising shares of small firms in the economy as a whole could lie in the shift of employment from manufacturing to services, where average firm size is significantly lower (see Table 3.1).

Figure 3.4 compares firm-size structure in the years 1970 and 1987 for those two big sectors: services and manufacturing. It shows opposing trends: an increasing concentration in the service sector and a decreasing concentration in manufacturing! Although concentration increased in both sectors during the 1961–1970 period, the trend reversed in manufacturing alone. Figure 3.5 shows the 1970–1987 change in employment broken down by different size classes and sectors, suggesting a very simple explanation for the overall trend. There is an increase in employment among firms with up to 49 employees and a decrease among firms with 50 or more employees. The differences in the pattern of change within the two sectors are quite interesting. As can be seen from Figure 3.5, service employment gained in all size classes with the highest increase arising in the largest size category, where employment in manufacturing declined most drastically.[7] The manufacturing firms with 1,000 or more employees lost 21.3 percent of their 1970 employment. From 1970 to 1987 the number of jobs in manufacturing decreased by 2 million (16.1 percent of 1970 employment), and the service sector gained about 2.7 million jobs (33.2 percent of 1970 employment). Obviously, the decline of employment in the manufacturing sector, especially the employment losses of the large firms, led to a reduction in average firm size, whereas the rise of service employment was connected with firm growth which resulted in a higher share by large firms. Increasing demand for the output of a sector may also induce a rise in the number of entries. Because new firms very often start small, this may also contribute to an explanation of the lower average firm size in the service sector.

The extent to which the development of the firm-size structure is simply due to a change in the sectoral composition of the West German economy can be estimated on the basis of a shift approach. Table 3.2 compares the observed size structure in 1987 with a hypothetical size structure due to the effect of sectoral change that is estimated by keeping the intrasectoral employment shares of the size categories (differentiating between 22 sectors) constant at the level of the 1970s. As can be seen from Table 3.2 the estimated size structure for all sectors is very close to the observed size structure; in fact the observed share of small-firm employment is slightly *lower* than estimated, with a maximum difference of 3.4 percent in the lowest size category. According to these figures, the main reason for the increasing share of small-firm employment in the FRG is simply the change in the sectoral composition of employment during this period. In manufacturing the observed size structure has a higher share of employment in small firms, which is due to the fact that the losses of employment were mainly in the large-firm sector. The observed share of small-firm employment in services is lower than the estimated share, indicating more than proportionate growth of the large firms.

Looking at the plant level, the same sectoral trends in the development of the size structure can be found. A remarkable difference from the firm level is that the size structure for the economy as a whole remains more or less unchanged.[8]

4.   Evidence on the level of individual plants

The comparison of size structures does not tell us much about the success or the failure of firms in different size categories because increasing

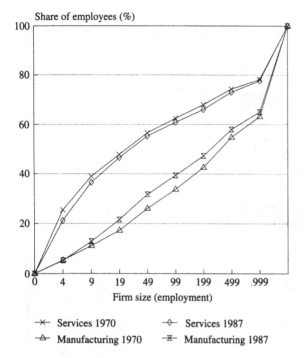

Share of employees (%)

Firm size (employment)

- ─×─ Services 1970   ─◇─ Services 1987
- ─△─ Manufacturing 1970   ─✕─ Manufacturing 1987

Figure 3.4   Change in firm-size structure, 1970–1987, services and manufacturing.

shares in the employment of small firms could be simply due to labor-shedding by large firms. It also does not say much about the effects that are connected with exits and entries. To judge the relative success of economic units within particular size categories, one needs longitudinal data for individual firms or plants.

The most comprehensive longitudinal analyses of the development of West German plants in different size classes using such microdata have been undertaken by Cramer (1987) for the period 1977–1985 and by König and Weisshuhn (1990) for the period 1980–1986. Both studies are based on social insurance statistics and both come to the conclusion that there is no clear trend towards smaller plants *within* the different sectors. Figure 3.6 is based on data provided by König and Weisshuhn (1990). It shows total employment change and the change due to survivors and to entries minus exits in the different size categories for manufacturing and for services, respectively.[9] As can be seen from these figures, the small survivor plants with up to 19 employees make a positive contribution to employment in both sectors while the net development of survivors in the

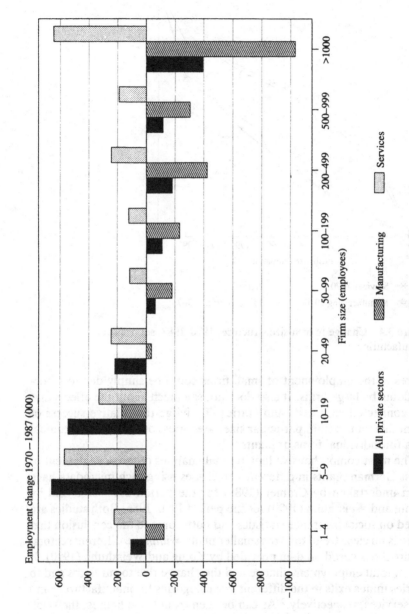

Figure 3.5 Employment change, 1970–1987, by firm size, absolute figures.

Table 3.2. *Observed and estimated firm-size distribution, 1987, percentage shares, cumulated values in brackets*[a]

Size class (employees)	All Sectors		Manufacturing		Services	
	Estimated	Observed	Estimated	Observed	Estimated	Observed
1–4	16.7	13.3	5.3	5.3	27.9	21.1
5–9	10.5	11.6	6.0	7.6	14.8	15.5
	(27.2)	(24.9)	(11.3)	(12.8)	(42.7)	(36.6)
10–19	7.5	9.4	6.1	8.7	9.0	9.9
	(34.7)	(34.3)	(17.4)	(21.6)	(51.7)	(46.5)
20–49	8.5	9.5	8.6	10.2	8.5	8.8
	(43.2)	(43.8)	(26.0)	(31.8)	(60.2)	(55.3)
50–99	6.6	6.6	7.3	7.6	5.7	5.5
	(49.8)	(50.4)	(33.3)	(39.4)	(65.9)	(60.8)
100–199	6.7	6.6	8.1	8.0	5.4	5.3
	(56.5)	(57.0)	(41.4)	(47.3)	(71.3)	(66.0)
200–499	9.0	8.8	11.6	10.6	6.3	7.0
	(65.4)	(65.8)	(53.0)	(57.9)	(77.6)	(73.0)
500–999	6.0	5.9	8.1	7.1	3.9	4.7
	(71.4)	(71.6)	(61.1)	(65.0)	(81.5)	(77.7)
1000 and more	28.6	28.5	38.9	35.0	18.5	22.3
	(100)	(100)	(100)	(100)	(100)	(100)

Note: [a] Cumulated values in brackets. Only commercial private-sector employment.
Source: Own calculations on the basis of *Statistisches Bundesamt* (1990).

other size categories is negative. The employment losses in the surviving plants show a clear size trend, with the net loss being relatively high in the upper size categories. As can be seen from Figure 3.6 exits and entries make a significant contribution to employment change, especially in the lower size classes. The net contribution of exits minus entries is negative in manufacturing and positive in services throughout all size categories. The births and deaths of plants is obviously an important factor in explaining employment change.

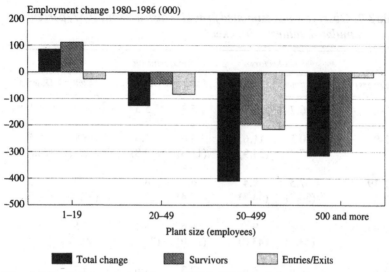

Figure 3.6   Components of change, 1980–1986, manufacturing.

Investigations into the determinants of job development in West German industrial plants during the 1980–1986 period (Fritsch, 1990a) lead to the conclusion that there is no general advantage for small firms and that a tendency for the expansion of small survivor firms is mainly due to the relatively high proportion of start ups in the lower size categories. In fact, estimating the relationships between size (number of employees), sales and job development as specified in Figure 3.7a and applying path analysis shows a significant impact of size on sales as well as on the number of jobs. The standardized path-coefficient for the relation between sales change and employment change has a value of about 0.42; the coefficients for the impact of size 1980 on sales and employment are both around 0.3.[10] If a variable for "age" is included, as shown in Figure 3.7b the "size" variable loses its significance and its explanatory power goes over to the age variable. The standardized path-coefficient for the relation between "age" and "size" is about 0.47.[11]

Other studies[12] for the FRG confirm these results, at least in so far as none indicates that small firms were significantly better off than large firms. Expressed differently: small firms were not worse off than large ones, though they were during the reconstruction period after the Second World War. To be small is not an advantage, but it must not be a disadvantage. There is room for small firms, especially for new firms to be successful and to create additional employment.[13]

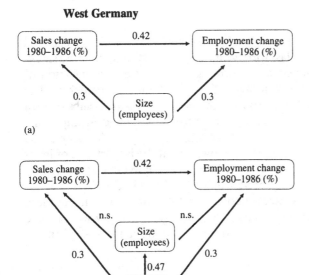

Figure 3.7   Relations between size, age, sales, and employment change.

5.   Characteristics of the West German small-firm sector and the policy impact

As has been shown in empirical investigations, German small firms face special problems in respect of access to external finance, and in addition pay higher interest rates for capital, which may be partly due to their higher probability of bankruptcy and the special difficulties financial institutions experience in evaluating the quality of small businesses.[14] Small firms pay lower wages, and working conditions are worse compared to those of larger firms. This may account for the fact that it is very unusual for an employee in the FRG to leave his workplace in a large firm (which is also relatively safe) for a job in a small firm. Though the number of new firms per year increased during the last decade, there is no broad tendency to start one's own business as has been stated for other countries.

Most policy programs in the FRG have a more or less strong bias towards large firms. There have always been special programs to promote small-firm development and it can be assumed that these programs have had some positive impacts; but it is very unclear how far these small-firm programs compensate for the large-firm bias of other policies. If comparisons of resources available to small firms are made with the large-firm sector, the advantage to the large-firm sector is highly significant.

The justification for measures aimed to help small firms has changed considerably during the last forty years. In the construction period small-firm policies were aimed at preventing too great a concentration of economic power and promoting independent entrepreneurship. The policy mainly operated by a variety of non-selective financial subsidies. In the last decade many programs were introduced aimed at improving innovation among small firms and assisting new high-technology-based firms. Unfortunately, very little is known about the importance of inno-vations in small firms compared to large firms in West Germany. It is estimated, that the number of new high-tech firms in the FRG is about 120 per year; if one takes account of the fact that only a fraction of these firms will survive their first years and that only a very few will become really large, their job-generating potential is quite limited (see Fritsch, 1990b for details).

6. Concluding remarks

There is no "dramatic" job generation by small firms in West Germany. As was shown in this chapter, the decrease in average firm size for the economy as a whole can more or less completely be explained by the change in sectoral composition. Maybe the long-term trend of employ-ment concentration by large firms has only paused during the 1970–1987 period analyzed here. Because the data do not take account of the variety of interfirm linkages, one might possibly discover further concentration by using another definition of the economic unit. In fact, since the announcement of the West European Single Market many West German firms are looking for partners in other European countries to cooperate with, so the trend seems to be in favor of big businesses again. Neverthe-less, small firms constitute an important integral part of the German economy and especially new firms are a source of giving economic growth new impetus.

Many people expect small and new firms to play a major role in the economic recovery of East Germany after the introduction of a market economy there (see Chapter 9 in this volume). It is much too early to judge whether these expectations will be fulfilled. But it is already evident that the unification of East and West Germany has been accompanied by numerous mergers, acquisitions and branch-plant foundations by West German firms in the East. So the surprise should not be too big if German unification induces an increase of average firm size and some further concentration of economic power.

Notes

I would like to thank Rainer Magnan for computational assistance and David Audretsch for valuable suggestions upon an earlier draft.

1 For an overview of work done by 1986, see Hull (1987), Fritsch and Hull (1987), Storey and Johnson (1987) and Weimer (1990).
2 Not included are the self-employed, family workers, and those working fewer than the minimum number of hours required for compulsory insurance contributions. The data base is described in König and Weisshuhn (1990, pp. 118–122).
3 The 1987 Census of Business included more small businesses than the social insurance statistics did. This difference is probably due to the fact that the social insurance statistics do not cover the self-employed. It may also be partly due to different definitions of "plant."
4 "Manufacturing" here includes mining and construction. Non-profit activities are excluded from the service sector.
5 Stockmann, Dahm and Zeifang (1983) report on their efforts in collecting the data and adjusting them for several changes in sectoral classification schemes; however, they do not mention whether they corrected for the changes in the geographic demarcation of Germany during this period. After losing the First World War the German Reich became considerably smaller in 1918 and the Federal Republic that was set up after the Second World War contains only a part of the German Reich in the borders of the year 1925. To adjust firm-size structure correctly to the geographical changes, it would be necessary to single out sites in former German territory for each firm back to the year 1907. Severe data problems would allow only for some kind of rough approximation in this respect. Even if Stockmann, Dahm and Zeifang (1983) did not adjust the data at all to the changing geography of Germany, it seems unlikely that this inaccuracy could be responsible for the rising employment shares of the large firms reported in Figure 3.1. On the contrary, it is quite imaginable that a shrinking of the national market due to loss of territory led to some reduction of average firm size because large multiregional firms experienced a more than proportionate decrease of employment. There was a Census taken in 1950 which did not report firm size. The data from the Censuses of 1961 and 1970 are based on the same geographical area.
6 The figures for the years 1882, 1895, 1907, and 1925 were taken from Stockmann, Dahm and Zeifang (1983, p. 121). The demarcation of the German Reich did not change between 1882 and 1907; the data for 1950 and following years are on a constant geographical base. Although the geography underlying the 1882–1907, and 1925, and the 1950–1970 figures may not be exactly comparable, the trend towards large-plant employment is very clear.
7 The relatively high employment gain of the large service firms indicates that there must be high economies of scale in parts of the service sector.
8 Cramer (1990) has analyzed the change in plant-size structure in the 1977–1988 period on the basis of social insurance statistics. Applying a shift approach as used here to account for the effect of sectoral change Cramer finds

that the observed share of small-plant employment is about 1 percent higher than estimated. The Census data for the 1970–1987 period do not show such an increase of small-plant employment.

9 Note that these figures do not show the employment change in different size categories (as Figure 3.5 did) but the employment change of plants of a certain size in 1980 (survivors and exits) and 1986 (new plants), respectively. Entries during the period which did not survive until 1986 are not covered.

10 The standardized coefficients are a measure of the relative importance of the analyzed relationships. They can take a value between -1 and $+1$, with the sign indicating the nature of the relationship (positive or negative); a value of 0 means that the variables are perfectly independent.

11 The variable for "age" was a dummy with the value "1" if the plant was younger than six years old in 1980 and the value "0" if the plant was more than six years old. Because the values of the path-coefficients vary within certain limits dependent on the version of the entire model (which has 16 variables) only rough values are given here. The empirical basis are data on more than 3,000 West German firms; see Fritsch (1990a) for details. Probably the influence of the age variable on growth would be weaker if one could control for the survivor bias in the sample. Unfortunately the data set provides no information about death rates.

12 Cramer (1987) and (1990), Dahremöller (1987), Acs and Audretsch (1989), Schwalbach (1989).

13 Quite similar analyses by Evans (1987a, 1987b) for samples of US firms show different results with respect to the size–growth relationship. Evans states that small-firm survivors have higher average growth rates and that the probability for survival is positively correlated with firm size. By including a variable for the age of firms and a variable for the product of age and size, Evans comes to the conclusion that age also contributes to the explanation of growth as well as the probability of firm failure (which is higher for young firms) *with the influence of the size variable remaining statistically significant*. This result holds for estimations within industries and the size–growth relationship proves to be quite robust against corrections for the selection of firms out of the sample.

14 For a detailed exposition of possible reasons why the access to external capital bears special problems for small firms and some empirical results, see Fazzari, Hubbard and Petersen (1988).

References

Acs, Zoltan J. and David B. Audretsch (1989) "Job Creation and Firm Size in the U.S. and West Germany," *International Small Business Journal*, 7, 9–22.

Cramer, Ulrich (1987) "Klein- und Mittelbetriebe: Hoffnungsträger der Beschäftigungspolitik," *Mitteilungen aus der Arbeitsmarkt- und Berufsforschung*, 20, 15–29.

(1990) "Der Trend zu kleineren Betrieben: Ergebnisse einer Auswertung der Beschäftigtenstatistik für die Bundesrepublik Deutschland," in Johannes Berger, Volker Domeyer and Maria Funder (eds.), *Kleinbetriebe im wirtschaftlichen Wandel*, Frankfurt and New York: Campus, 19–33.

Dahremöller, Aexl (1987) *Existenzgründungsstatistik – Nutzung amtlicher Daten-quellen zur Erfassung des Gründungsgeschehens*, Stuttgart: Poeschel.

Evans, David S. (1987a) "The Relationship between Firm Growth, Size, and Age: Estimates for 100 Manufacturing Industries," *Journal of Industrial Economics*, **35**, 567–581.

  (1987b) "Tests of Alternative Theories of Firm Growth," *Journal of Political Economy*, **95**, 657–674.

Fazzari, Steven M., R. Glenn Hubbard and Bruce, C. Petersen (1988) "Financing Constraints and Corporate Investment," *Brookings Papers on Economic Activity*, 141–195.

Fritsch, Michael (1990a) *Arbeitsplatzentwicklung in Industriebetrieben – Entwurf einer Theorie der Arbeitsplatzentwicklung und empirische Analysen auf einzelwirtschaftlicher Ebene*, Berlin and New York: De Gruyter.

  (1990b) "Wachstumsmotor junge Technologieunternehmen? Zu Besonderheiten der Beschäftigungsentwicklung von jungen Technologieunternehmen im Verarbeitenden Gewerbe der Bundesrepublik Deutschland," *Internationales Gewerbearchiv*, **38**.

Fritsch, Michael and Christopher J. Hull (1987) "Empirische Befunde zur Arbeitsplatzdynamik in großen und kleinen Unternehmen in der Bundesrepublik Deutschland – Eine Zwischenbilanz," in Michael Fritsch and Christopher J. Hull (eds.), *Arbeitsplatzdynamik und Regionalentwicklung*, Berlin: Sigma, 175–195.

Hull, Christopher J. (1987) "Job Generation in the Federal Republic of Germany – A Review," in David J. Storey and Steve Johnson (eds.), *Small and Medium Sized Enterprises and Employment Creation in the EEC Countries*, Report for Commission of the European Communities, DG V, Brussels.

König, Andreas and Gernot Weisshuhn (1990) "Changes in Enterprise Size and Employment Levels in the Branches of the Federal Republic of Germany 1980 and 1986," in Ronald Schettkat and Michael Wagner (eds.), *Technological Change and Employment*, Berlin and New York: De Gruyter, 111–132.

Schwalbach, Joachim (1989) "Small Business in German Manufacturing," *Small Business Economics*, **1**, 129–136.

Statistisches Bundesamt (1966) *Arbeitsstättenzählung vom 6. Juni 1961, Nichtlandwirtschaftliche Arbeitsstätten, Unternehmen und Beschäftigte 1961, 1950, 1939*, Stuttgart and Mainz: Kohlhammer.

  (1989) *Einführung in die methodischen und systematischen Grundlagen der nichtlandwirtschaftlichen Arbeitsstättenzählung*, Stuttgart: Metzler-Poeschel.

  (1990) *Arbeisstätten, Unternehmen und Beschäftigte 1987, 1970, 1961, 1950*, Stuttgart: Metzler-Poeschel.

Stockmann, Reinhard, Guido Dahm and Klaus Zeifang (1983) "Konzentration und Reorganisation von Unternehmen und Betrieben. Empirische Analysen zur Entwicklung der nichtlandwirtschaftlichen Arbeitsstätten und Unternehmen in Deutschland 1875–1970," in Max Haller and Walter Müller (eds.), *Beschäftigungssystem im gesellschaftlichen Wandel*, Frankfurt and New York: Campus, 97–177.

Storey, David J. and Steve Johnson (1987) *Job Generation and Labour Market Change*, London: Macmillan.

Weimer, Stephanie (1990) "Federal Republic of Germany," in Werner Sengenberger, Gary Loveman and Michael Piore (eds.), *The Reemergence of Small Enterprises: Industrial Restructuring in Industrialized Countries*, Geneva: International Labor Organization.

4 Has the role of small firms changed in the United States?

Zoltan J. Acs and *David B. Audretsch*

1. Introduction

Almost exactly one decade ago David Birch revealed some startling findings from his long-term study of US job generation. Despite the prevailing conventional wisdom at that time, Birch (1981, p. 8) reported that "whatever else they are doing, large firms are no longer the major providers of new jobs for Americans." Rather, Birch claimed to have discovered that most new jobs emanated from small firms.

Birch's findings triggered a storm of controversy that has only intensified with the beginning of a new decade. There are at least three major debates underlying this controversy. First, at the time Birch announced his results the preoccupation of the literature in industrial economics, the field most directly associated with studying markets, was with identifying the extent of concentration in markets and its effects on economic performance. The long-term trend had been clearly identified as an increased concentration in economic activity both at the aggregate as well as at the market level. For example, the percentage of total US manufacturing assets accounted for by the largest 100 corporations increased from about 36 percent in 1924, to 39 percent after the Second World War to over 50 percent by the end of the 1960s, causing F. M. Scherer to conclude (1970, p. 44) that, "Despite the [statistical] uncertainties, one thing is clear. The increasing domestic dominance of the 100 largest manufacturing firms since 1947 is not a statistical illusion."

Consistent with the trend towards increased concentration was the shift in economic activity away from small firms and towards large enterprises. Table 4.1 shows that the small-firm share of employment decreased substantially in every major sector of the economy during the post-war period. Perhaps most striking was the decrease in the share of employment accounted for by small firms of nearly one-quarter in the manufacturing sector between 1958 and 1977. Given the state of knowledge in

55

Table 4.1. *Small-firm share of employment, %, 1958–1977[a]*

	1958	1977	Change[b]	Ratio[c]
All industries	55.1	52.5	−2.6	95
Minerals	62.2	44.3	−17.9	71
Construction[d]	85.7	82.1	−3.6	96
Manufacturing	37.1	29.0	−8.1	78
Wholesale trade	94.1	83.1	−11.0	88
Retail trade	72.5	62.3	−10.2	86
Services	84.0	75.6	−8.4	90

Notes:
[a] Small firms are measured as those enterprises with fewer than 100 employees. Self-employment is not included.
[b] Measured as the 1977 small-firm employment share minus the 1958 small-firm employment share.
[c] Measured as the 1977 small-firm employment share divided by the 1958 small-firm employment share, multiplied by 100.
[d] Because no data are available for 1958, 1972 data have been substituted.
Source: US Department of Commerce, Bureau of the Census, *Enterprise Statistics* (1958 and 1977).

industrial economics, it was thus not readily apparent how to reconcile Birch's claim that 80 percent of the new jobs were created in small firms with the empirical evidence pointing towards an ever-increasing concentration of economic activity.

A second debate emerged regarding the exact methodology, application and interpretation of the underlying data used to make inferences in the job-generation studies (Armington and Odle, 1982; Storey and Johnson, 1987; FitzRoy, 1989; Brown, Hamilton and Medoff, 1990). As Brown, Hamilton and Medoff (1990) point out, job generation may be a deceptive measure because many of the newly generated jobs subsequently disappear. That is, without consideration of the number of job disappearances, focusing solely on the amount of job generation emanating from small firms is misleading the results in an overstatement of the amount of economic activity actually stemming from small firms (Storey, 1990).

A third debate involving anecdotal evidence has emerged in the popular press. For example, *The Economist* reports that, "Despite ever-larger and noisier mergers, the biggest change coming over the world of business is that firms are getting smaller. The trend of a century is being reversed. Until the mid-1970s, the size of firms everywhere grew; the numbers of self-employed fell. Ford and General Motors replaced the

carriage-maker's atelier; McDonald's, Safeway and W. H. Smith sup-
planted the corner shop. No longer. Now it is the big firms that are
shrinking and small ones that are on the rise. The trend is unmistakable –
and businessmen and policy-makers will ignore it at their peril."[1]

The purpose of this chapter is to provide the first systematic analysis of
the manner in which the firm-size distribution and role of small firms has
shifted from the late 1970s to the mid-1980s. Because the results from this
analysis are essentially empirical in nature, Section 2 describes the major
data sources which are used and points out their main advantages and
disadvantages. A special emphasis is placed on making a comparison
among several well-established data bases, in order to examine the ro-
bustness of the results.

In Section 3 the relative role of small firms in the US economy is
examined. The extent to which this role has evolved over time is analyzed
in Section 4. The manufacturing sector is the specific focus of Section 5. In
Section 6 a summary and conclusions are provided. While there is no
compelling evidence suggesting that the overall firm-size distribution has
changed for the entire economy, both the sales and employment
measures suggest that *manufacturing* activity has shifted away from large
firms and towards smaller enterprises. This shift has been even more
dramatic in a sub-sector of manufacturing, known as the metalworking
industries. Flexible technologies are apparently being substituted for
mass-production technologies in the metalworking industries, providing
one possible explanation for this observed shift. In any case, this chapter
makes it clear that, while firm and establishment size have been increasing in the service and finance sectors, they have been decreasing in
manufacturing.

2.   Data sources and measurement issues

Prior to 1976, there was no US government agency responsible for
collecting and disseminating statistics on all enterprises inhabiting the full
spectrum of the firm-size distribution. Most notably, firms at the small
end of the size distribution tended to be omitted from data bases. Various
agencies of the US government, such as the Census Bureau of the US
Department of Commerce, did and do publish statistics on small enterprises (firms), but only at five-year intervals, and then not for all
industries.

While certain US government agencies do publish data by establishment-size class on a regular basis, such as the employment data base of
the US Bureau of Labor Statistics (BLS), there is no attempt made to link
each establishment to its parent firm. Thus, while the BLS data shed

considerable light on the performance of establishments over time, they are not helpful for identifying the firm-size distribution and how it shifts over time.

In response to its dissatisfaction with the lack of knowledge about the full spectrum of American business, the US Congress established the Office of Advocacy of the Small Business Administration in 1976. Four years later, the Congress passed the Economic Policy Act of 1980, which mandated the president to submit to Congress an annual report on the state of small business, and authorized the creation of the Small Business Data Base (SBDB).

In order to fulfill its congressional mandate of disseminating statistics on the state of small business and its relationship to the entire size-distribution of enterprises and establishments, the Office of Advocacy turned to the Dun and Bradstreet corporation. The SBDB is derived from the Dun and Bradstreet (DUNS) market identifier (DMI). The essential building block and unit of observation in the SBDB is the establishment, which is defined as a particular economic entity operating at a specific and single geographic location. While some establishments are legally tied to parent firms through either a branch or subsidiary relationship, other establishments are independent and therefore are, in fact, firms (enterprises) in their own right. In cases of multiproduct firms, or where the establishments operate in different industries or even sectors, each establishment is classified according to its appropriate 4 digit standard industrial classification (SIC) industry. By linking the establishments by ownership to their parent firms, each establishment is then classified by the size of the entire firm, and not just by its own size.

The US Enterprise and Establishment Microdata (USEEM) files of the SBDB provide biennial observations on about 4.5 million US business establishments over the period 1976 to 1986. This covers a changing business population of nearly 20 million establishments. Each record includes the establishment location in terms of state and county, employment, the primary and secondary industry, the starting year, sales, organizational status and legal connection to other establishments, and the employment of the entire firm, if the establishment belongs to a multi-establishment enterprise.

Establishments are generally referred to as plants in manufacturing, but not in non-manufacturing. The distinction between the firm and its constituent establishment is particularly crucial in manufacturing. Although over 96 percent of manufacturing firms in 1984 comprised establishments within a single industry, about 72 percent of employment in manufacturing was in firms with establishments in at least two different industries (Starr, 1987).[2]

Storey and Johnson (1987) argue that because the underlying data have been assembled by a commercial organisation whose principal purpose is to provide credit rating information, the reliability of the data is probably enhanced. They point out that the data are not based on confidentiality but rather on publicly available information (for a fee). In addition, Dun and Bradstreet has a commercial incentive to provide data that are both current and accurate. Similarly, the reporting establishments themselves have an incentive to provide accurate information to a credit rating company.

Nonetheless, the Dun and Bradstreet data have been subjected to serious criticism. Perhaps one of the most significant weaknesses in the DUNS data is missing branch records. Because the Dun and Bradstreet files are compiled on the basis of credit rating, branches and subsidiaries of multi-establishment firms that are unlikely to require credit independently from the parent firm are often not recorded. In one of the first applications of these data, Birch (1981) dealt with this discrepancy by recalculating the total enterprise employment from the aggregation of the employment recorded in each affiliated establishment. By contrast, Armington and Odle (1982) recalculated the employment level of each affiliated establishment from the reported enterprise employment level. As Storey and Johnson (1987) note, the effect resulting from attempts to reconcile this discrepancy between the aggregation of establishment data and enterprise data was that Birch tended to understate the extent of employment in multi-establishment firms, while Armington and Odle tended to overstate it.

A second problem with the Dun and Bradstreet data is their chronic underrepresentation in industries where there is a propensity for the establishments not to apply for credit. There are also certain other dynamic weaknesses with respect to non-updated records in the data base. As Jacobson (1985) found, in a few cases firms and establishments are not included in the data base until several years after they have been established. This leads to a slight understatement of the number of new business units, particularly in rapidly expanding industries, such as certain types of services, and in new industries, such as microcomputers and software-related industries.

In order to correct for at least some of these deficiencies in the DUNS data, the Brookings Institution in conjunction with the Small Business Administration and the National Science Foundation restructured, edited, and supplemented the USEEM with data from other sources.[3] In particular, a "family tree" is constructed for each firm, identifying each branch and subsidiary. These family trees are then used to reconcile the organizational status and employment figures between member estab-

Table 4.2. A comparison of employment statistics among the SBDB, BLS, and Census data bases

	Small Business Administration (SBDB)			Bureau of Labor Statistics			Bureau of the Census		
	1980	1986	% change 1980–1986	1980	1986	% change 1980–1986	1980	1986	% change 1980–1986
US total	82,070,988	91,180,151	11.10	74,487,000	83,332,000	11.87	74,276,927	82,467,724	11.0
Agriculture	811,161	944,517	16.44	NA	NA	NA	289,843	412,010	42.1
Mining	1,127,950	1,136,989	0.80	1,025,000	792,000	−22.73	996,007	847,143	−14.9
Construction	4,748,128	5,011,112	5.54	4,469,000	4,960,000	10.99	4,473,551	4,658,669	4.1
Manufacturing	24,417,344	22,875,373	−6.32	20,361,000	19,186,000	−5.77	21,151,842	19,141,756	−9.5
Transportation	5,872,312	6,160,075	4.90	5,156,000	5,286,000	2.52	4,631,152	4,884,297	5.5
Wholesale trade	5,498,665	6,261,744	13.88	5,281,000	5,853,000	10.83	5,215,520	5,724,864	9.8
Retail trade	15,010,569	17,142,789	14.20	15,292,000	17,878,000	16.91	15,045,287	17,549,841	16.6
Finance	5,736,238	7,098,778	23.75	5,162,000	6,305,000	22.14	5,278,404	6,370,787	20.7
Services	18,848,622	24,548,774	30.24	17,741,000	23,072,000	30.05	17,195,327	22,818,357	33.0

NA = Not available.
Sources: US Small Business Administration, Office of Advocacy, Small Business Data Base, USEEM file (1988); US Department of Labor, Bureau of Labor Statistics, *Employment and Earnings* (March 1981 and March 1987); US Department of Commerce, Bureau of the Census, *County Business Patterns, US Summary* (1980 and 1985 issues).

lishments of multi-establishment enterprises. The employment figures for the entire enterprise are compared to those reported by the individual establishments. Any discrepancy arising between the employment reported for the entire firm and the aggregation of all the individual establishments is then corrected either by increasing the total amount of employment attributed to the entire enterprise to be consistent with that reported by the individual establishment, or else by imputing proxy branch establishments to represent affiliates implied by the employment reported by the enterprise (Armington and Odle, 1983).

It should thus be emphasized that the SBDB data have been adjusted by the US Small Business Administration to clean up the raw data in the original DMI files. Several important studies have compared the SBDB data with analogous measures from the establishment data of the US Census of Manufactures (Boden and Phillips, 1985; Acs and Audretsch, 1990), and from the establishment and employment records of the BLS data (Brown and Phillips, 1989). Such comparisons have generally concluded that the SBDB data are remarkably consistent with the other major data bases providing observations on establishments and enterprises.

To provide at least a simple comparison of the consistency of the SBDB data with two of the other major data bases, the BLS and Bureau of the Census' *County Business Patterns*, Table 4.2 indicates the employment according to primary business sectors in 1980 and 1986. Certain sectors, such as services, finance, retail and wholesale trade, and manufacturing provide fairly consistent employment levels for 1980 and 1986. Considerable less consistency exists in the employment patterns reported in these three data sources in the agriculture and mining sectors. However, the sector most clearly focused on in this chapter, manufacturing, shows a marked similarity in employment trends across the three data bases.

3. The extent of small firms and establishments: a static view

Using the SBDB data base described in the previous section, Table 4.3 shows the size distribution of firms and establishments, measured by employment, for 1986. Each number indicates the percentage of the total sector employment included in the respective firm- and establishment-size class. For example, in the entire economy 5.39 percent of all employment is accounted for by firms with fewer than five employees. Similarly 6.46 percent of employment occurred in establishments with fewer than five employees.

There are four important observations to make from Table 4.3. First, the employment shares of the smaller firm-size classes generally exceed

Table 4.3. *The size distribution of employment, %, for US firms and establishments, 1986*[a]

					Number of employees							
	1–4	5–9	10–19	20–49	50–99	<100	100–499	<500	500–999	1000–4999	5000–9999	10,000 and over
All industries												
Firms	5.39	6.23	6.68	9.60	7.17	35.01	14.69	49.76	5.25	12.32	5.65	27.10
Est.	6.46	7.72	10.69	16.98	12.41	54.27	23.22	77.49	7.12	11.22	2.43	1.74
Agriculture												
Firms	16.69	16.18	12.21	13.19	7.48	65.74	13.27	79.01	3.79	6.63	0.94	9.63
Est.	18.10	16.97	13.21	19.75	10.08	78.11	14.21	92.32	3.55	3.58	0.56	0.00
Mining												
Firms	3.72	4.28	5.60	7.78	5.39	26.76	10.56	37.33	4.32	10.17	9.04	39.15
Est.	5.13	5.80	9.03	16.75	11.77	48.48	23.94	72.42	8.35	17.14	2.09	0.00
Construction												
Firms	14.89	13.09	13.95	17.71	10.58	70.23	15.23	85.46	3.17	5.08	1.57	4.71
Est.	15.57	13.69	15.03	23.78	13.07	81.14	14.16	95.45	1.86	1.90	0.80	0.00
Manufacturing												
Firms	1.30	2.40	3.59	6.95	6.31	20.55	14.78	35.34	5.63	13.48	5.78	39.78
Est.	1.64	2.93	4.63	10.35	11.46	31.00	32.02	63.02	11.55	16.92	4.57	3.94
Transportation												
Firms	2.41	3.61	4.72	7.22	5.17	23.12	10.43	33.55	3.81	11.60	6.28	44.76
Est.	3.39	5.18	8.47	15.95	12.60	45.59	26.58	72.17	8.00	13.84	2.85	3.13

Wholesale trade												
Firms	8.04	11.70	12.40	15.23	9.16	56.52	13.93	70.46	3.46	7.59	2.96	15.54
Est.	10.56	15.67	20.62	21.36	10.79	79.00	14.44	93.44	2.92	2.29	0.64	0.71
Retail trade												
Firms	8.32	9.83	9.01	12.49	8.28	47.92	11.11	59.03	3.60	7.38	3.94	26.05
Est.	10.02	12.08	16.37	24.42	13.93	76.82	17.88	94.69	2.75	1.99	0.31	0.26
Finance												
Firms	5.53	4.95	5.56	8.28	6.24	30.56	13.93	44.49	5.70	15.55	9.84	24.42
Est.	7.25	8.33	18.17	17.06	9.01	59.82	17.09	76.90	6.64	12.87	2.86	0.73
Services												
Firms	4.89	5.20	5.63	7.88	6.81	30.41	18.72	49.13	7.27	16.56	6.95	20.10
Est.	5.67	6.08	7.31	15.58	13.59	48.23	24.12	72.35	8.19	15.45	2.57	1.45

Note: [a] The figures indicate the share of employment in each sector accounted for by firms and establishments within each respective size class. The data exclude government employment.

Source: US Small Business Administration, Office of Advocacy, Small Business Data Base, USEEM file, version 8 (1988).

that of the corresponding establishment-size classes. This is because employment in those establishments which are a branch or subsidiary of a multi-establishment enterprise are classified according to the entire employment of the enterprise for the firm-size distribution but not for the establishment-size distribution. However, for the larger firm- and establishment-size classes, the employment shares of the firms tend to exceed that of the establishments. This is because these firm-size classes include the employment of many smaller establishments.

Second, the employment shares in certain sectors, such as wholesale trade and construction, tend to be relatively similar between the firm and establishment measures. In other sectors, such as manufacturing and transportation, this differential is much greater, which indicates a greater presence of multi-establishment enterprises.

Third, Table 4.3 shows that the 1986 share of employment accounted for by firms with fewer than 500 employees, one of the standard benchmarks used to measure small firms, was 49.76 percent. Similarly, the employment share of firms with fewer than 100 employees, which is the standard alternative measure, was 35.07 percent. In manufacturing, 35.34 percent of employment was in firms with fewer than 500 employees, and 20.55 percent in firms with fewer than 100 employees.

Finally, there clearly exists considerable variation in the role that small firms play across the various sectors of the economy. For example, in construction, over 85 percent of employment is accounted for by small firms. By contrast, in transportation, only about one-third of workers are employed in small firms.

4. A dynamic view

Employment growth is not constant across either different sectors of the economy or across different size classes within each sector. Table 4.4 compares establishment employment growth rates between 1976 and 1978, between the SBDB and BLS data bases. Such a comparison enables at least some indication of consistency in results. The two data sources identify considerable consistency in the overall growth rate for the entire economy. Further, the employment growth rates in establishments with fewer than 500 employees are virtually identical. Both data bases indicate that the growth rates of smaller establishments exceeded that of establishments with at least 500 employees.

However, there are also several substantial differences between the establishment growth rates recorded in these two different data bases. For example, the overall growth rates in the manufacturing and transportation sectors vary considerably between the SBDB and BLS. Most strikingly, the SBDB records a growth rate in employment of 3.17 percent in manufacturing, while the BLS indicates that employment shrank by 5.85 percent. Despite these differences, one important result emerges in both data bases. The employment growth of small plants in manufacturing was clearly greater than that of large plants over this time period.

That the small-establishment growth rates exceeded that of larger establishments need not 'imply that this was also the case for firms. Because many establishments are tied to multi-establishment firms, such a trend among establishments could, in principle, result in no such trend, or even an opposing trend among firms. Table 4.5 thus compares the small-firm share of employment growth among the manufacturing, service, and finance sectors between 1976 and 1986. While employment grew by almost one-third for the entire economy over this time period, firms with fewer than 500 employees accounted for 57 percent of this growth. In the manufacturing sector, the employment growth of 6 percent was considerably less. However, 110 percent of this growth emanated from small firms. This implies that all of the employment growth in manufacturing came from the small firms, while their larger counterparts actually reduced employment over this period. Services and finance were the fastest growing sectors between 1976 and 1986. Unlike for the entire economy and for manufacturing, the rate of growth of small firms was considerably less than that of large enterprises.

These trends portraying the dynamic roles of small and large firms across the main sectors of the economy are confirmed in Table 4.6, which reveals the share of employment growth occurring in each sector accounted for by each firm-size class. While large firms accounted for nearly half of the employment growth in the finance and service sectors, and over 40 percent for the entire economy, there was nearly an 11 percent decrease in manufacturing. Most strikingly, about two-thirds of the employment growth in manufacturing came from firms with fewer than 20 employees.

The growth rate differentials between large and small firms has not left the firm-size distribution unaffected. Table 4.7 shows how small-firm employment shares have evolved over time for the major sectors of the economy. Between 1976 and 1986 the employment share of manufacturing firms with fewer than 500 employees increased by slightly less than two percentage points. How can this relatively minor shift in the firm-size distribution be reconciled with the markedly differential growth rates exhibited between the small- and large-firm size classes? This seeming paradox is attributable to the low overall growth rate in manufacturing. Although all of the employment increase in manufacturing was

Table 4.4. Employment growth rates, %, according to establishment size class[a]

	Total, all size classes	Number of employees per establishment/reporting unit					
		<10	10–19	20–99	100–499	<500	500 and over
All industries							
SBDB	21.66	12.87	25.84	35.43	20.17	24.83	11.95
BLS	18.15	20.20	23.69	26.97	24.03	24.29	2.27
Mining							
SBDB	15.20	48.98	33.77	16.32	1.87	16.55	11.80
BLS	19.09	52.15	50.27	33.03	16.66	30.14	−5.39
Construction							
SBDB	13.71	6.88	22.55	26.58	1.73	15.26	−11.35
BLS	18.27	11.06	20.99	30.16	23.37	21.63	−22.58
Manufacturing							
SBDB	3.17	16.97	20.26	17.70	1.49	8.97	−5.42
BLS	−5.85	14.31	9.35	5.36	−2.91	1.33	−14.83
Transportation							
SBDB	14.87	21.02	38.72	20.07	−1.64	12.80	20.61
BLS	8.25	29.89	26.70	33.45	18.96	26.58	−11.58

Wholesale trade						
SBDB	26.05	21.34	26.89	22.93	31.29	24.57	51.59
BLS	17.37	24.84	16.18	16.56	17.44	18.33	5.25
Retail trade						
SBDB	22.43	−1.03	20.66	38.35	67.88	27.51	−28.44
BLS	23.54	6.33	14.79	31.28	51.47	27.23	4.43
Finance						
SBDB	34.40	26.21	12.36	48.87	29.51	29.87	52.06
BLS	32.82	21.70	30.97	32.80	36.21	31.26	37.37
Services						
SBDB	44.39	25.11	49.09	58.77	40.18	45.06	42.66
BLS	42.71	33.14	42.33	41.92	51.67	42.68	42.83

Note: [a] The data exclude agriculture, forestry and fishing.

Sources: SBDB–US Small Business Administration, Office of Advocacy, Small Business Data Base, USEEM file, version 9 (1989); BLS–US Department of Labor, Bureau of Labor Statistics, unpublished data prepared under contract for the US Small Business Administration (1988) adapted from Brown and Phillips (1989).

Table 4.5. *Employment growth and small-firm share of growth by sector, 1976–1986ª*

	Employment growth rate (%)	Small-firm share (%)
All industries	32.36	57.23
Manufacturing	6.00	110.00
Services	69.09	53.75
Finance	71.15	51.74

Note: ª A small firm is defined as an enterprise with fewer than 500 employees. The small-firm share is the percentage of employment growth accounted for by small firms.
Source: US Small Business Administration, Office of Advocacy, Small Business Data Base, USEEM file, version 9 (1987).

Table 4.6. *Share of employment growth, % by firm size, 1976–1986*

Number of employees in firm	All industries	Manufacturing	Service	Finance
1–19	26.23	64.85	20.76	21.24
20–99	17.43	41.46	15.93	16.15
100–499	13.57	4.60	17.06	14.35
500+	42.77	−10.91	46.25	48.26
Total	100.00	100.00	100.00	100.00

Source: US Small Business Administration, Office of Advocacy, Small Business Data Base, USEEM file, version 9 (1987).

attributable to small firms, the overall change in employment was sufficiently low as to result in only a minor shift in the firm-size distribution.

Just as the manufacturing sector exhibited a slight but clear tendency towards small firms during this time period, a noticeable shift in economic activity towards large firms clearly took place in services and finance. As a result of these offsetting trends, the firm-size distribution, as measured by employment, remained relatively constant over this time period for the entire economy.

Although not indicated in Table 4.7, the same trends emerge when the small-firm measure of 100 employees is used. For example, the share of

Table 4.7. *Small-firm employment shares, %, by sector, 1976–1986ª*

	All industries	Manufacturing	Service	Finance
1976	49.65	33.39	52.29	45.59
1978	49.23	32.87	53.60	51.11
1980	50.48	32.02	51.37	51.36
1982	49.82	33.58	51.23	49.87
1984	49.10	35.33	50.47	48.53
1986	50.32	35.24	49.13	44.49

Note: ª Small firms are defined as enterprises with fewer than 500 employees.
Source: US Small Business Administration, Office of Advocacy, Small Business Data Base, USEEM file, version 8 (1987).

employment accounted for by firms with fewer than 100 employees in the entire economy fell slightly from 36.31 to 35.01 percent. In manufacturing, the share of employment accounted for by firms with fewer than 100 employees rose slightly, from 18.88 percent in 1976 to 20.50 percent in 1986.

5. The manufacturing sector

As explained in the introductory Chapter 1, a particular emphasis in this book is the manufacturing sector. We have just identified in the previous section that, based on the measure of firm employment, a noticeable, although slight, shift occurred in manufacturing activity, away from large enterprises and towards small firms. However, Table 4.8 shows that when an alternative measure, firm sales, is used, the trend towards smaller firms becomes considerably more dramatic. In 1976 firms with fewer than 500 employees accounted for just over one-fifth of manufacturing sales. Within a decade, the small-firm sales' share had risen to well over one-quarter. Similarly, the sales' share of firms with fewer than 100 employees rose from 11.6 percent in 1976 to 14.8 percent in 1986.

The Survey of Manufactures of the Bureau of the Census can be used to examine the extent to which plant size has increased or decreased within each manufacturing industry. Table 4.9 reveals the percentage change in plant size, measured both by employment and value added, which serves as a measure of output. The level of aggregation is at both the 2 digit SIC major industry level, as well as at the less disaggregated 3 digit SIC industry level for a sub-sample of manufacturing commonly known as the

Table 4.8. *Small-firm sales' share, %, in manufacturing, 1976–1986*

	Small firms with fewer than 100 employees	Small firms with fewer than 500 employees
1976	11.6	20.4
1978	10.2	18.7
1980	12.3	21.8
1982	12.1	21.4
1984	14.0	24.5
1986	14.8	25.8

Source: US Small Business Administration, Office of Advocacy, Small Business Data Base, USEEM file (April 1988).

metalworking industries. Table 4.9 shows that the number of employees per plant declined by about 18 percent in manufacturing between 1979 and 1984. Over the same period, the value added per plant also declined by 12 percent. With a single exception, in the tobacco industry, the mean plant employment size declined in every 2 digit SIC major manufacturing industry. The simple correlation of 0.70 between the employment and value added measures indicates that the results are consistent between the output and employment measures.

Because Carlsson (1989, 1990), Dosi (1988), and others have argued that the implementation of flexible technology has led to a reduction in the importance of scale economies and subsequently to a decrease in plant and firm size, the metalworking industries[4] present an especially important sub-sector of manufacturing. In fact, in all but one of the 3 digit industries included in the metalworking sector, guided missiles and space vehicles, mean plant employment decreased. Similarly, the average plant output also declined in most of the metalworking industries.

Table 4.10 indicates that not only has the size of manufacturing plants become smaller, but that the firm-size distribution in the metalworking industries has undergone a marked shift in economic activity away from large enterprises and towards small firms. The sales' share of firms with fewer than 100 employees increased from 15.6 percent in 1976 to 22.5 percent in 1986. Similarly, the share of sales accounted for by firms with fewer than 500 employees increased from 30.1 percent to 39.7 percent over this time period. The small-firm share of sales in the metalworking industries thus increased by between one-third and one-half within one decade, depending upon the measure of small firms used. By contrast, the small-firm shares of sales for all manufacturing firms, shown in Table 4.8, increased only by about 20 percent.

Table 4.9. *Changes, %, in average plant size, 1979–1984*

SIC Code	Industry group and industry	Employment	Value added (in 1979 prices)
2	All manufacturing industries	− 0.178	− 0.118
20	Food and kindred products	− 0.091	0.181
21	Tobacco products	0.044	0.311
22	Textile mill products.	− 0.142	0.006
23	Apparel, other textile products	− 0.121	0.041
24	Lumber and wood products	− 0.155	− 0.005
25	Furniture and fixtures	− 0.166	− 0.024
26	Paper and allied products	− 0.067	0.026
27	Printing and publishing	− 0.118	− 0.062
28	Chemicals, allied products	− 0.126	− 0.058
29	Petroleum and coal products	− 0.154	− 0.672
30	Rubber, misc. plastic products	− 0.199	0.014
31	Leather, leather products	− 0.211	− 0.015
32	Stone, clay, glass products	− 0.174	− 0.173
33	Primary metal industries	− 0.338	− 0.291
341	Metal cans, shipping containers	− 0.152	− 0.184
342	Cutlery, handtools and hardware	− 0.260	− 0.216
343	Plumbing, heating except electrical	− 0.173	− 0.068
344	Fabricated, struc. metal products	− 0.240	− 0.227
345	Screw machine products, bolts, etc.	− 0.215	− 0.090
346	Metal forgings and stampings	− 0.230	− 0.104
347	Metal services, n.e.c.	− 0.086	− 0.084
348	Ordnance and accessories, n.e.c.	− 0.127	− 0.063
349	Misc. fabricated metal products	− 0.267	− 0.215
351	Engines and turbines	− 0.384	− 0.304
352	Farm and garden machinery	− 0.390	− 0.375
353	Construction, related machinery	− 0.455	− 0.483
354	Metalworking machinery	− 0.273	− 0.300
355	Special industry machinery	− 0.221	− 0.202
356	General industrial machinery	− 0.220	− 0.178
357	Office and computing machines	− 0.277	− 0.094
358	Refrigeration and service machines	− 0.138	− 0.031
359	Misc. machinery exc. electrical	− 0.173	− 0.236
361	Electric distributing equipment	− 0.222	− 0.155
362	Electrical industrial apparatus	− 0.282	− 0.214
363	Household appliances	− 0.121	− 0.024
364	Electric lighting, wiring equipment	− 0.098	− 0.103
365	Radio, TV receiving equipment	− 0.267	0.325
366	Communication equipment	− 0.057	0.115
367	Electronic components, accessories	− 0.111	0.067
369	Misc. electrical equipment, supplies	− 0.287	− 0.003

Table 4.9. (cont.)

SIC Code	Industry group and industry	Employment	Value added (in 1979 prices)
371	Motor vehicles and equipment	− 0.280	− 0.082
372	Aircraft and parts	− 0.204	− 0.290
373	Ship, boat building, repairing	− 0.213	0.071
374	Railroad equipment	− 0.556	− 0.636
376	Guided missiles, space vehicles	0.235	0.310
379[a]	Transportation equipment, n.e.c.	− 0.078	0.233
380	Instruments, related products	− 0.154	0.044

Note: [a] SIC industry 379 also includes SIC industry 375 (Motorcycles, bicycles, and parts).
Source: US Department of Commerce, Bureau of the Census, Annual Survey of Manufacturers (various years).

Table 4.10. Small-firm sales' share, %, in the metalworking industries, 1976–1986

	Small firms with fewer than 100 employees	Small firms with fewer than 500 employees
1976	15.6	30.1
1982	17.2	30.2
1984	21.4	36.8
1986	22.5	39.7

Source: Acs and Audretsch (1990, p. 114).

What accounts for this shift in economic activity within the metalworking sector towards smaller plants and firms? One explanation has been given by Carlsson (1989, 1990), Dosi (1988), and Acs and Audretsch (1990, Ch. 6) – the implementation of new, flexible technologies. From the Industrial Revolution until the early 1970s the technology generally applied throughout the metalworking industries promoted mass production. Beginning in the 1930s, the transfer machine was at the core of this technology. Transfer, or station-type machines are comprised of a number of smaller machines or work stations. Each of these work stations is used for a distinct operation, such as drilling or milling, and is organized in a coordinated manner enabling a workpiece automatically to be put in place at one work station and then automatically transferred to the next work station. The greater the extent to which the machines could be designed for and applied to specialized functions, the more effective was the mass production of standardized products.

With the advent of numerically controlled (NC) machines in the late 1940s, the potential emerged for reversing what Dosi (1988) terms as a technological trajectory favoring large-scale production. NC machines enable the application of computers instead of manual labor to guide the operations of machine tools. Using NC machine tools, firms have been able to replace conventional automated production with flexible manufacturing systems. The main advantage a flexible manufacturing system has over mass production is the ease with which it can be reprogrammed, rendering the overall system of production substantially more flexible than is possible with transfer machines.

Carlsson (1989) explains how NC machine tools enhance three different types of flexibility – operational, tactical, and strategic. Operational flexibility enables a firm to vary its sequencing and scheduling according to need. Tactical flexibility allows fine-tuning in a firm's product mix, rate of production, and modifications in design. Strategic flexibility determines the ability of a firm to anticipate long-term changes in the product and environment.

Numerous researchers, such as Shepherd (1982) have argued that the adoption of NC machine tools may have led to a decrease in the minimum efficient scale (MES), and therefore, to a reduction in plant size, at least in some industries. Similarly, *The Engineer* has noted how adoption of NC machinery may have promoted the viability of smaller plants: "It is generally acknowledged that one NC lathe can displace four conventional machines; or one NC machinery center three conventional. First cost may be multiplied by three, but the number of operators is significantly reduced."[5]

The marked shift towards smaller firms and plants in the metalworking sector of manufacturing is consistent with the hypothesis posed by Dosi (1988, pp. 1155–1156): "As an historical example, I suggest we are currently observing, at least in the industrial countries, a process of change in the size distribution of plants and firms that is significantly influenced by the new flexibility-scale trade-offs associated with electronic production technologies ... in mass-production industries the higher flexibility of the new forms of automation is likely to allow the efficient survival of relatively smaller firms (as compared to the past)."

That there has been a trend towards smaller establishments and firms in manufacturing during the last decade is clear from the statistical evidence. However, it is less certain whether this trend is the result of existing firms and establishments "descaling" and becoming smaller, or whether it is due to the formation of new establishments and firms.

Table 4.11. *Entry and exit for establishments, by size of firm, thousands, 1980–1986[a]*

	Aggregate			Manufacturing			Services			Finance		
	Small	Large	Total	Small	Large	Total	Small	Large	Total	Small	Large	Total
1980	4,093	386	4,479	379	69	448	856	67	924	301	37	338
1986	4,485	480	4,965	413	68	480	1,052	92	1,144	350	62	412
Gross entry	2,274	239	2,513	177	29	205	589	52	641	198	36	234
Exit	-1,881	-146	-2,027	-143	-30	-173	-392	-28	-421	-150	-11	-160
Net entry	393	93	486	33	-1	32	196	24	220	49	25	74
Gross entry rate	0.555	0.619	0.561	0.467	0.420	0.458	0.688	0.776	0.694	0.658	0.973	0.692
Exit rate	0.460	0.378	0.452	0.377	0.435	0.386	0.458	0.418	0.456	0.498	0.297	0.473
Net entry rate	0.096	0.241	0.108	0.087	-0.014	0.071	0.229	0.358	0.238	0.163	0.676	0.219

Note: [a] The entry (exit) rate is defined as number of entrants divided by the number of establishments in 1980. The net entry rate is defined as the net change (entries minus exits) in the number of establishments between 1980 and 1986 divided by the number of establishments in 1980. A "small" firm is defined as an enterprise with fewer than 500 employees. A "large firm" is defined as an enterprise with at least 500 employees.
Source: US Small Business Administration, Small Business Data Base.

Because, as has already been shown, there was only minimal growth in manufacturing since 1976, it might be suspected that the firm-size distribution has shifted for the first and not the second reason.

Some light can be shed on this issue by again employing the SBDB data. Table 4.11 classifies establishment entry and exit between 1980 and 1986 according to firm size across the major sectors of the economy. Gross entry refers to the number of new establishments founded during this period, and exits are defined as the number of establishments disappearing. In addition, the gross entry rate is measured as the number of entrants divided by the number of establishments in 1980. The exit rate is similarly defined as the number of exits divided by the number of establishments in 1980. Comparing the extent of net entry, or net entry rates, among the manufacturing, service, and finance sectors, one would conclude that there was relatively little new-establishment formation in manufacturing. In fact, establishments entering subsequent to 1980 represented a little less than one-half of all the establishments in existence in 1986. Because of the equally high rate of exit from manufacturing, there was only a slight net increase in the number of plants, and yet the ownership of manufacturing plants, and presumably therefore their organizational production structures, had changed to a considerable extent.

A second point to be emphasized is that the entry patterns of small establishments did not mirror those of their larger counterparts. The gross entry rate was greater for small manufacturing establishments than for large ones, while the exit rate of large establishments exceeded that of small establishments. The net entry rate was thus actually negative for large establishments, while it was positive for small ones. By 1986, there were about 9 percent more manufacturing establishments owned by small firms but 1.4 percent fewer establishments owned by large firms. By contrast, the net entry rates were greater for the large than for the small establishments in both the service and finance sectors. There is thus at least some evidence suggesting that, in the manufacturing sector, the shift in the firm-size distribution during the 1980s was attributable to a considerable extent to the entry of new businesses and not largely due to a "downsizing" of existing large ones.

6. Conclusions

The results of this chapter clearly identify that, when the employment measure is used, no noticeable shift in the size distribution of firms occurred in the US economy between 1976 and 1986. However, when the sales measure is used, a slight trend towards smaller firms emerges. By contrast, within the manufacturing sector a pronounced shift in economic activity away from large firms and towards small enterprises has taken place. While this trend is less apparent using the employment measure, it is considerably stronger when the sales measure is used.

A detailed analysis of the exact factors precipitating this shift within the manufacturing sector is clearly beyond the scope of this chapter. One explanation nevertheless suggests that the application of new technologies, such as flexible manufacturing techniques, may have reduced the importance of scale economies in recent years. In the metalworking industries, where flexible technologies have been most widely introduced, the shift away from larger plants and firms and towards smaller enterprises is more pronounced than elsewhere in manufacturing. Consistent with this explanation is the observation that the shift towards smaller firms is to a considerable extent attributable to the establishment of new firms which are apparently replacing old ones.

One issue which has not been addressed by this chapter is that raised by Brown, Hamilton and Medoff (1990), among others: Is the shift towards smaller firms desirable or undesirable? What are the welfare implications? While our results shed little light on these questions, they do make it clear that these questions are certainly relevant and deserve attention in future research.

Notes

We wish to thank Bruce Phillips of the United States Small Business Administration for generously providing us with some of the material which is contained in this paper and Jiangping Yang for his computational assistance. All errors and omissions remain our responsibility.

1 "The Rise and Rise of America's Small Firms," *The Economist* (January 21, 1989) 73–74.
2 This calculation was based on Table 1 of the 1984 *Enterprise Statistics*, published by the Bureau of the Census of the US Department of Commerce.
3 For further explanation of the development and editing of the USEEM file, see US Small Business Administration (1986 and 1987), Harris (1983), Brown and Phillips (1989).
4 The metalworking, or engineering, industries include non-electrical machinery, electrical machinery, transportation equipment, and instruments. The 3 digit SIC industries covered by the metalworking industries can be found in Table 4.9.
5 "Switching the Focus to the Buyer," *The Engineer* (May 17, 1984) 24–26.

References

Acs, Zoltan J. and David B. Audretsch (1990) *Innovation and Small Firms*, Cambridge, MA: MIT Press.

Armington, Catherine and Marjorie Odle (1982) "Small Business – How Many Jobs?," *The Brookings Review*, 1 (Winter) 14–17.

(1983) "Weighting the USEEM Files for Longitudinal Analysis of Employment Growth," Working Paper, 12, Business Microdata Project, The Brookings Institution (April).

Birch, David L. (1981) "Who Creates Jobs?," *The Public Interest*, 65 (Fall) 3–14.

Boden, Richard and Bruce D. Phillips (1985) "Uses and Limitations of USEEM/USELM Data," Office of Advocacy, US Small Business Administration, Washington, DC (November).

Brown, Charles, James Hamilton and James Medoff (1990) *Employers Large and Small*, Cambridge, MA: Harvard University Press.

Brown, H. Shelton and Bruce D. Phillips (1989) "Comparison Between Small Business Data Base (USEEM) and Bureau of Labor Statistics (BLS) Employment Data: 1978–1986," *Small Business Economics*, 1 (4), 273–284.

Carlsson, Bo (1989) "The Evolution of Manufacturing Technology and its Impact on Industrial Structure: An International Study," *Small Business Economics*, 1 (4), 21–38.

(1990) "Small-Scale Industry at a Crossroads: U.S. Machine Tools in Global Perspective," in Zoltan J. Acs and David B. Audretsch (eds.), *The Economics of Small Firms: A European Challenge*, Boston: Kluwer Academic, 171–193.

Dosi, Giovanni (1988) "Sources, Procedures, and Microeconomic Effects of Innovation," *Journal of Economic Literature*, 26 (3) 1120–1171.

FitzRoy, Felix (1989) "Firm Size, Efficiency and Employment: A Review Article," *Small Business Economics*, 1 (1), 75–80.

Harris, Candee S. (1983) *U.S. Establishment and Enterprise Microdata (USEEM): A Data Base Description*, Business Microdata Project, The Brookings Institution (June).

Jacobson, Louis (1985) *Analysis of the Accuracy of SBA's Small Business Data Base*, Alexandria, VA: Center for Naval Analysis.

Scherer, F. M. (1970) *Industrial Market Structure and Economic Performance*, Chicago: Rand McNally.

Shepherd, William G. (1982) "Causes of Increased Competition in the U.S. Economy, 1939–1980," *Review of Economics and Statistics*, 64 (4), 613–626.

Starr, Ed. (1987) "Small Business in Manufacturing," paper prepared for the US Small Business Administration, Washington, DC (July).

Storey, David J. (1990) "Firm Performance and Size: Explanation from the Small Firm Sectors," in Zoltan J. Acs and David B. Audretsch (eds.), *The Economics of Small Firms: A European Challenge*, Boston: Kluwer Academic, 43–50.

Storey, David J. and Steven Johnson (1987) *Job Generation and Labour Market Changes*, London: Macmillan.

US Small Business Administration (1986) *The Small Business Data Base: A User's Guide*, Washington, DC (July).

US Small Business Administration, Office of Advocacy (1987) *Linked 1976–1984 USEEM User's Guide*, Washington, DC (July).

5 Recent developments in the firm-size distribution and economics of scale in Dutch manufacturing

Roy Thurik

1. Introduction

In the editors' introduction to the first issue of *Small Business Economics: An International Journal* the following questions were raised: "After several decades where smaller firms provided the bulk of employment generation, two important question are: (1) What has been the impact on the size distribution of firms? and (2) What is responsible for the shift towards an increased importance of smaller-scale enterprises?" (Acs and Audretsch, 1989, p. 3). These are the two questions I want to study in this chapter, using recent data material from Dutch manufacturing industry. Before dealing with these two questions I shall first devote Section 2 to a description of the Netherlands and its manufacturing industry from an international perspective; OECD and Eurostat data material will be used. Secondly, in Section 3 I shall give a very general account of the role of small and medium-sized business in the Netherlands using material from the Research Institute for Small and Medium-Sized Business (RISMB) in Zoetermeer, the Netherlands. Empirical evidence points to an increasing share of small and medium-sized enterprises (SME) across practically all 2 digit (ISIC) manufacturing industries (1978–1986) as well as a lower aggregate (2 digit) productivity growth for SME than for large enterprises (1981–1988).

The two major questions of the chapter are dealt with in Sections 4 and 5. A detailed analysis of developments in the Dutch manufacturing size distribution is the subject of Section 4. Employment data from four size classes and 16 (2 to 3 digit) industries for the period 1978–1989 provide the basis for the finding that average firm size declines till 1986 and appears to drift upward again afterwards, and that the small-business share generally increases until 1987. There are several causes for the increase of small-business presence in an economy. One of them, a productivity advantage of small firms, is investigated in Section 5 for a selection of (3 to 4 digit) industries. Such an advantage is indeed observed for the period 1974–1986. A simple cost model is used to capture this advantage in terms of a reduction of scale economies.

A productivity growth which is higher for medium-sized than for large enterprises for a large number of (3 to 4 digit) industries is also reported in Section 5. The reconciliation of the observed higher aggregate productivity growth for large enterprises than for SME of Section 3 with the disaggregated result of Section 5 will be discussed briefly in the concluding Section 6. Finally, some attention is devoted to why scale economies should decrease over time.

2. Dutch manufacturing: an international comparison[1]

I shall first compare the Netherlands to the three major industrialized countries in the world, the United States, Japan and West Germany and to a European country of comparable size, Denmark, using some basic dimensions. We see from Table 5.1 that the Netherlands is a very small country in terms of surface, the United States is more than 220 times as large, but less so in terms of population: the US population is less than 17 times as large. The result is a very densely populated country. In terms of employment the Netherlands lags behind, with a participation rate of about 35 per cent, mainly due to a low participation of women. The Dutch GDP amounted to 175 billion US dollars in 1986, which results in a domestic labor productivity which is somewhat less than that of the United States and Germany, but above that of Japan and Denmark. Gross investments lead to an investment rate (gross investments divided by GDP) which is far below that of Japan, but above that of the United States. Imports and exports are important. The sum of the value of yearly imports and exports is about equal to that of the national GDP, whereas this sum is a mere 33 percent of national GDP in the United States. There was a positive trade balance in 1986.

When looking at data of share and growth of manufacturing employment in the five countries we see remarkable similarities. Table 5.2 shows that the employment share of manufacturing dropped in all five countries from 1974 to 1986. We also see that Germany has a strongly developed manufacturing industry. Manufacturing employment declined in the period from 1974 to 1986 for all countries at a yearly rate ranging from −2.0 percent in the Netherlands[2] to −0.1 per cent in Japan. European countries showed positive growth rates over the more recent period of 1984–1987.

The share and growth of manufacturing GDP is given in Table 5.3. Here we also note a declining share of manufacturing for all countries, although the GDP of manufacturing at constant prices grew consistently

Table 5.1. *International comparison of the Dutch economy, 1986*

	United States	Japan	Germany	Netherlands	Denmark
Area (NL = 100)	22431	891	595	100	103
Population					
(millions)	241.6	121.5	61.1	14.6	5.1
(NL = 100)	1658	834	419	100	35
Density per km²					
(NL = 100)	7	93	70	100	34
Employment[a]					
(millions)	118.9	61.8	25.7	5.2	2.6
(NL = 100)	2303	1197	498	100	50
Employment/Population	0.492	0.509	0.421	0.354	0.506
Gross domestic product					
(GDP)					
(10⁹ US$)	4191	1958	890	175	82
(NL = 100)	2389	1116	507	100	47
GDP (US$)/Employment					
(NL = 100)	104	93	102	100	93
Gross fixed capital					
formation (GFCF)					
(10⁹ US$)	741	541	174	35	17
(NL = 100)	2103	1535	493	100	48
GFCF (US$)/GDP (US$)					
(NL = 100)	88	138	97	100	103
Imports					
(10⁹ US$)	430	147	221	88	27
(NL = 100)	491	168	252	100	30
Exports					
(10⁹ US$)	291	226	267	95	26
(NL = 100)	306	238	282	100	28

Note: [a] Employment is in number of persons engaged. Productivity indicators thus depend upon share of part-time labor.

between 1974 and 1986. The declining manufacturing share is an illustration of the considerable output growth of services as a result both of the contracting out of producer services and of the demand for new consumer services.[3] The Dutch manufacturing productivity growth of an average yearly rate of 3.6 percent in 1974–1986 is caused by technological progress, zero or low wage growth, and again the contracting out of "service parts" of production.[4] The average yearly labor productivity change in manufacturing in the period 1974–1986 is 3.0 percent for the United States, 5.8 for Japan, 2.6 for Germany and 2.5 for Denmark. In the more recent period of 1984–1987 the labor productivity growth rate of the United States and Japan remained high (4.3 and 5.1 percent, respectively), but that of the European countries dropped to 0.8 percent for Germany, 0.5 for the Netherlands and −1.7 for Denmark.

Table 5.2. *Employment in manufacturing*

	United States (%)	Japan (%)	Germany (%)	Netherlands[a] (%)	Denmark (%)
Share of manufacturing in the national economy[b]					
1974	21.3	26.9	36.3	24.5	23.2
1986	16.4	24.0	32.2	19.3	20.6
Average yearly change 1974–1986	− 0.4	− 0.1	− 0.3	− 2.0	− 0.3
Average yearly change 1984–1987	− 0.6	− 0.2	0.8	1.5	1.7

Notes:
[a] The Dutch data refer to man years, that of the other countries to persons engaged.
[b] Private and public sector.

Table 5.3. *Gross domestic product[a] in manufacturing*

	United States (%)	Japan (%)	Germany (%)	Netherlands (%)	Denmark (%)
Share of manufacturing at current prices					
1974	23.4	33.6	36.1	25.0	18.1
1986	19.8	29.2	32.2	19.0	17.2
Average yearly change manufacturing at 1980 prices 1974–1986	2.6	5.7	1.3	1.6	2.2
Average yearly change manufacturing at 1980 prices 1984–1987	3.6	4.9	1.6	2.0	0.0

Note: [a] GDP at market prices equals sum of value added at market prices in all private and public sectors.

Looking at the composition of the manufacturing industry in Table 5.4 we see that the Netherlands is strong in foods (ISIC 31) and chemicals (35), but weak in textiles (32) and investment equipment (38). Germany is strong in this last segment of manufacturing, which puts her in a favorable position in view of Eastern Europe's extensive needs in this area.

3.   SME in Dutch manufacturing[5]

Small (less than 10 employees) and medium-sized (between 10 to 100 employees) enterprises play a relatively modest role in Dutch manufacturing as shown in Table 5.5.

About 97 percent of all manufacturing enterprises belonged to SME in 1986. Outside manufacturing, this percentage ranges from 97.3 percent in the service industries, where large-scale banking and insurance companies heavily influence the figure, to 99.9 percent for garages and repairs. The modest role of SME in Dutch manufacturing is more evident when looking at labor volume, output and value added shares. Table 5.5 shows that the labor volume percentage of manufacturing SME is 40, that of output is 31 and that of value added 33. These shares are significantly below those of the other seven industries which are distinguished in Table 5.5 and which make up the entire private sector (agriculture excluded) in the Netherlands. Manufacturing is also a large-scale industry in terms of average labor and average output per enterprise. It is shown in Table 5.6 that average labor volume per enterprise is approximately 20 man years in manufacturing whereas the second largest is transportation with just over 10 man years. Average output in manufacturing is 6.2 million Dutch guilders of 1988 and again transportation is second largest with 1.8 million Dutch guilders. SME plays a modest role in manufacturing. The question now is whether manufacturing also plays a modest role in total Dutch SME. Table 5.6 shows that the answer is "no." Nearly one-third of total SME output in the Netherlands in 1990 is generated by manufacturing. This is caused by the fact that, although SME plays a minor role in manufacturing, manufacturing as a whole plays a dominant role in total Dutch private output. Nearly 50 percent of output in the private sector is generated by manufacturing.

The manufacturing data are summarized in Table 5.7. I added the share of exports in output for the three size classes to show that in a small, open and technologically advanced economy like the Netherlands the export share of small enterprises is already considerable (23 percent). The export share of SME grew from about 29 percent in 1980 to 36 percent in 1988 (with a forecast of 39 percent in 1991), whereas that of large firms remained constant at about 60 percent. Some 50 percent of these SME exports is destined for the directly neighboring countries like Belgium and Germany. 90 percent is shipped to EC countries. The export share of small firms is less than that of large firms, for obvious reasons.[6]

Table 5.4. *Composition of manufacturing industry, employment shares, 1986*

ISIC		United States	Japan	Germany	Netherlands	Denmark
31	Food, beverages and tobacco	8.7	10.9	9.7	16.7	18.2
32	Textile, wearing apparel and leather	10.3	7.1	7.1	4.9	8.1
33	Wood (products), furniture	6.7	n.a.	4.2	3.5	7.1
34	Paper (products), printing, publishing	11.6	2.4	4.5	9.8	9.9
35	Chemicals, coal, rubber, plastics	10.2	3.8	12.2	12.5	8.8
36	Non-metallic mineral products	3.1	4.6	3.8	3.2	4.3
37	Basic metal industries	3.9	3.4	8.3	3.1	1.1
38	Fabricated metal, machinery, equipment	43.2	46.7	49.2	36.3	40.2
39	Other manufacturing industries	2.2	21.3	1.1	10.1[a]	2.3
		100.0	100.0	100.0	100.0	100.0

Note: [a] This share includes that of "social workshops." Otherwise it would be about 4%.

However, small enterprises usually gain from the export efforts of large enterprises because of their subcontracting activities. In terms of the share of number of enterprises involved in exporting merchandise there is also a striking difference between small and large: 87 percent of large enterprises was involved in exporting as opposed to 26 percent of SME in 1989.[7] The latter percentage has grown steadily, however. It was 22 in 1981.

When looking at the development of output volume for a recent period with forecasts for 1990 and 1991 made by RISMB we see that the growth rates of SME and large enterprises hardly differ (see Table 5.8). Output growth in the recession and early recovery years, 1981–1986, has been systematically higher for large enterprises than for SME. The employment growth for SME is higher than that of large enterprises for the entire

Table 5.5. *Percentage share of SME (less than 100 employed) per industry, 1990, estimates*

	Number of enterprises[a]	Labor volume[b]	Output[c]	Value added[d]
Manufacturing	97.0	40	31	33
Construction	99.3	77	70	75
Wholesale trade	99.3	77	71	73
Retail trade	99.8	68	64	64
Hotel & catering	99.8	88	86	84
Garages & repairs	99.9	96	96	96
Transport	98.5	62	49	54
Services	97.3	47	39	35

Notes:
[a] 1988.
[b] Labor volume is expressed in man years.
[c] Output equals value of sales minus purchasing value of sales of merchandise. This means that output generally equals sales (including net inventory formation, excluding purchasing value of sales of merchandise) in manufacturing and sales minus purchasing value in retailing.
[d] Value added at factor costs.

Table 5.6. *Further industry data[a]*

	Labor volume per enterprise (man years)	Output per enterprise[a] (10^6 Dutch guilders)	Share in SME output (%)	Share in total output (%)
Manufacturing	20.2	6.2	31	49
Construction	9.4	1.6	17	11
Wholesale trade	7.9	1.4	17	11
Retail trade	4.8	0.3	7	5
Hotel & catering	4.0	0.4	4	2
Garages & repairs	5.1	0.5	4	2
Transport	10.4	1.8	7	6
Services	7.0	0.8	13	14
			100	100

Note: [a] The "per enterprise" data refer to 1988 and the "share" data to 1990 (estimates).

Table 5.7. *Dutch manufacturing, 1988*

	Small	Medium	Large	Total
Number of enterprises (×1000)	35.3	8.3	1.3	44.9
Labor volume (×1000 man years)	92.4	265.0	547.1	905.0
Output (10⁹ Dutch guilders)	15.1	64.3	199.2	278.6
Exports (% of output)[a]	23	38	59	52

Note: [a] Indirect exports through intermediaries included.

Table 5.8. *Percentage development in labor and output volume in Dutch manufacturing*

		1981–1986[a]	1987	1988	1989[c]	1990[c]	1991[c]
Labor[b]	SME	−1.0	2.5	0.5	3.0	2.0	1.5
	Large	−2.0	0.0	0.5	0.0	1.0	0.5
Output	SME	1.0	2.5	4.5	4.0	4.5	4.5
	Large	1.5	1.0	5.0	3.5	4.5	4.5

Notes:
[a] Yearly average.
[b] Labor years.
[c] Estimates.

period considered. The employment growth in manufacturing SME in 1989–1991 is remarkable. For 1989, for instance, SME employment rose, with about 11,000 man years. A further increase, with about 13,000 man years, was foreseen for the years 1990 and 1991 together. Labor growth is consistently below output growth for the entire period for both SME and large enterprises.

This points to general productivity growth which appears to be stronger for large than for small firms. Output generally equals sales in manufacturing which is an insufficiently adequate measure for productivity in manufacturing because developments in the purchasing value of (raw) materials are neglected as well as the degree of contracting out activities. Value added would obviously be a better measure for productivity developments. Some aggregate data on value added developments with a discrimination over size classes are given in Table 5.9.[8]

We can compute from Table 5.9 that SME productivity growth is above that of large enterprises in 1983 (2.5 percentage points difference), 1985 (1 percentage point), 1986 (1 percentage point) and 1988 (0.5 percentage

Table 5.9. *Percentage development in labor and value added[a] in Dutch manufacturing*

		1981	1982	1983	1984	1985	1986	1987	1988
Labor[b]	SME	−4.0	−5.0	−3.0	0.5	1.5	5.0	2.5	0.5
	Large	−3.0	−4.5	−5.0	−2.5	2.0	1.0	0.0	0.5
Value added	SME	−4.0	−2.0	1.5	3.5	4.0	5.5	2.5	5.0
	Large	2.5	−1.5	1.5	6.5	3.5	0.5	3.0	4.5

Notes:
[a] At factor costs at constant prices.
[b] Labor years.

point). SME productivity growth is below that of large enterprises in 1981 (5.5 percentage points difference), 1984 (6 percentage points) and 1987 (3 percentage points). There is no systematic yearly productivity growth differential between SME and large enterprises. However, annual SME productivity growth is about 1 percentage point lower on average in the period 1981–1988![9]

The above developments may be caused by a shifting composition of the share of small vs large enterprises across the whole manufacturing industry.[10] As for the SME share of Dutch manufacturing across its major parts I have data on GDP and labor volume according to 2 digit ISIC (see Table 5.10). In 1986 SME is strong in wood, wood products including furniture (84.3 percent of GDP), other manufacturing (68.2 percent), textile, wearing apparel and leather (52.8 percent) and non-metallic mineral products (50.8 percent). From Table 5.4 in the preceding section we know that these are exactly the industries with a low contribution to the entire manufacturing industry. One can also look at the development of the SME share over time. Ignoring basic metal industries, we see that SME is getting stronger in all parts of the manufacturing industry in terms of labor volume share and in all but one (paper, paper products, printing, publishing) in terms of GDP. In the basic metal industries SME loses ground, but its share is in any case negligible.

Before turning to a detailed (2 to 3 digit) analysis of recent development in the manufacturing firm-size distribution (four size classes) in Section 4, I will first compare manufacturing and non-manufacturing sectors. Percentage employment share of SME (less than 100 employed) is the only measure which is available for both manufacturing and non-manufacturing sectors for a recent period of time. Unfortunately the employment share of firms with fewer than 500 employees is not available in the

Table 5.10. *Percentage share of SME (less than 100 employed) across manufacturing industries*[a]

ISIC	GDP[b] (1980 prices)		Labor volume	
	1978	1986	1978	1986
3 Total manufacturing	29.6	30.1	36.1	39.9
31 Food, beverages and tobacco	25.9	31.4	39.7	41.6
32 Textile, wearing apparel, leather	43.6	52.8	43.6	59.8
33 Wood (products), furniture	78.2	84.3	78.2	86.2
34 Paper (products), printing, publishing	40.8	39.0	43.6	46.5
35 Chemicals, coal, rubber and plastics	10.6	14.1	17.2	20.2
36 Non-metallic mineral products	48.2	50.8	48.8	62.7
37 Basic metal industries	4.4	4.1	4.9	4.6
38 Fabricated metal, machinery, equipment	30.0	30.7	31.8	37.9
39 Other manufacturing industries	41.6	68.2	58.8	71.2

Notes:
[a] Production Statistics of the Central Bureau for Statistics, Voorburg, the Netherlands and elaborated by the Research Institute for Small and Medium-Sized Business, Zoetermeer, the Netherlands.
[b] Value added at factor costs.

Netherlands. The lack of this share prevents the comparison with development in the major industrialized countries where this share is usually available. In the Netherlands there are only about 650 firms in the entire private sector with more than 500 employed. Secrecy conditions impede the publication of this share on a 3 digit level which is the regular intermediate source for data on a higher level of aggregation. Table 5.11 provides the data for manufacturing, four non-manufacturing sectors and the entire private part of the Dutch economy. There is an upward movement of SME employment share for manufacturing, construction and to a lesser extent for transport. A downward movement is observed for trade. The time series for services shows no clear trend, nor does that of the total Dutch private sector. Then, obviously, the SME employment share in all

Table 5.11. *Percentage share of SME (less than 100 employed) for manu-*
facturing and non-manufacturing sectors

	Manufacturing	Construction	Trade[a]	Transport	Services	Total private sector
1980	36.6	72.5	79.0	58.3	48.8	58.1
1981	36.4	72.7	79.2	58.3	48.4	57.9
1982	36.3	73.6	79.5	58.5	47.9	57.7
1983	36.8	74.7	79.3	59.0	47.8	57.9
1984	37.5	74.7	78.6	59.8	48.5	58.1
1985	37.3	76.0	77.7	58.5	47.7	57.5
1986	38.3	75.9	77.3	59.4	46.6	57.7
1987	38.9	76.8	76.8	60.6	48.0	58.1
1988	38.9	77.5	76.7	61.2	48.2	58.3
1989[b]	39.6	77.5	76.7	61.3	47.4	58.3
1990[b]	39.8	77.4	76.5	61.6	47.4	58.3
1991[b]	40.1	77.1	76.3	61.4	47.6	58.3

Notes:
[a] Trade is wholesale, retail, hotel & catering and garages & repairs.
[b] Estimates.

four non-manufacturing sectors together fell in the period 1980–1991. As
a matter of fact, it diminished slowly but monotonously from 67.7 percent
in 1980 to 65.8 percent in 1991.

4.   Recent development in the manufacturing firm-size distribution[11]

It is often suggested that the share of small firms in Western economies
has risen recently. The preceding section contains some Dutch evidence.
Carlsson (1989) found empirical evidence for this proposition in manufacturing, and engineering industries in particular, in several Western
industrial countries.[12] Elsewhere similar findings are reported.[13] The
purpose of this section is to investigate the development of the Dutch
firm-size distribution for manufacturing industries for the years 1978–
1989. This will be done in more detail than in Table 5.10. The basic
question of this section is how the change of the firm-size distribution can
be measured using simple indicators. The question why it might change is
dealt with in Section 5. This section is organized as follows: in Section 4.1
the data from Dutch industries are discussed. In Section 4.2 two measures
of the firm-size distribution are described and average results for the
industries are tabulated. The general development of the manufacturing
firm-size distribution from 1978 until 1989 is discussed in Section 4.3.

After a closer look at the turning point in the average firm size for the separate industries, Section 4.4 shows conclusions.

4.1 Data

The data from the Dutch industries are derived from two files of the Netherlands Central Bureau of Statistics, "Statistics of Enterprises" and "Statistics of Man-years and Gross Wages," respectively. The first file contains the number of firms with 1 to 10 employees[14] (group 1), 10 to 50 employees (group 2), 50 to 100 employees (group 3) and 100 and more employees (group 4) of 16 manufacturing industries for the years 1978–1989. The second file contains the number of employees corresponding to the same groups and industries, but unfortunately only for the years 1978, 1981, 1984 and 1987.[15] Both data files were elaborated by the Research Institute for Small and Medium-Sized Business. The 16 industries are given in Table 5.12, where their number of firms[16] and employees are also tabulated. These 16 industries cover 58.8 percent of the total number of firms in manufacturing including those without employees (approx. 45,700) and 99.4 percent of the total number of firms excluding those without employees (approx. 27,000) in 1987. The industries cover 92.9 percent of total labor volume (approx. 933,300 million man years) in manufacturing in 1987.[17]

4.2 Measuring the firm-size distribution

We compare the firm-size distribution for each of the 16 industries using measures of the location and shape of the firm-size distribution. For describing the shape of the firm-size distribution we use the skewness of the distribution f of the number of employees per firm, A:

$$f(a_i) = f_i = \frac{\text{Number of firms in group } i}{\text{Total number of firms}} \text{ for } i = 1,..,4 ,$$

where a_i is the average number of employees per firm in group i. The moments of A can now be written as $E[A^k] = \sum_i f_i a_i^k$. The skewness measure is computed as follows:

$$SKEW = \frac{E[(A - \mu)^3]}{\sigma^3} \text{ with } \sigma^2 = E[(A - \mu)^2] \text{ and } \mu = E[A].$$

The variable μ is used to describe the location of the firm-size distribution and equals the average number of employees per firm in an industry. A decreasing value of μ points at an increasing importance of small-sized firms. A high value of $SKEW$ points at a right-skewed

Table 5.12. *Description of manufacturing industries*

ISIC	Industry	No. of firms[a]	No. of empl. ×1000[a]
31	Manufacture of food, beverages and tobacco products	6974	161
321	Manufacture of textiles	814	38
322	Wearing apparel, except footwear	1143	21
323/4	Manufacture of leather, footwear and other leather products	542	9
33	Manufacture of wood products, including furniture	3540	44
341	Manufacture of paper and paper products	282	25
342	Printing, publishing and allied industries	2637	65
351/2	Chemical industry and manufacture of artificial and synthetic filaments and staple fibres	562	85
355/6	Manufacture of rubber and plastic products	569	25
36	Manufacture of building materials, earthenware, glass and glass products	1240	37
381	Manufacture of fabricated metal products, except machinery and transport equipment	5100	93
382	Mechanical engineering	2033	85
383	Electrical engineering	474	109
384	Manufacture of transport equipment	1539	71
385	Instrument engineering	597	12
39	Other manufacturing industries	477	7

Source: Central Bureau of Statistics and Research Institute for Small and Medium-Sized Business.
Note: [a] Number of firms and employees refer to 1978.

distribution.[18] This indicates a high share of small firms in terms of employment. An increasing value of *SKEW* means that a greater share of employment is shifted to the smaller firms. Although a low μ and a high *SKEW* both point at a great importance of small-sized firms, the developments of μ and *SKEW* are not necessarily opposite. Both μ and *SKEW* will be incorporated in this study because μ and *SKEW* measure different aspects of the firm-size distribution. In Table 5.13 the averages of μ and *SKEW* over the period 1978–1989 are presented. The variables $\Delta\mu$ and $\Delta SKEW$ are the absolute changes of μ and *SKEW* from 1978 and 1989. A negative value of $\Delta\mu$ and a positive value of $\Delta SKEW$ point to a growing share of smaller firms. We see that this combination ($\Delta\mu < 0$ and

Table 5.13. *Values of mean and skewness*[a]

ISIC	$\bar{\mu}$	$\Delta\mu$	$\%\Delta\mu$	$\overline{SKEW}$	$\Delta SKEW$	$\%\Delta SKEW$
31	24.0	2.4	10.0	4.5	− 0.0	− 0.6
321	42.1	− 19.9	− 36.4	2.5	1.0	48.9
322	17.8	− 9.9	− 42.8	3.8	0.8	22.7
323/4	16.3	− 3.4	− 17.6	3.6	0.7	23.9
33	11.9	− 2.0	− 15.7	5.4	0.6	11.7
341	82.7	− 3.1	− 3.5	1.1	− 0.1	− 5.5
342	21.5	− 4.4	− 18.0	4.2	0.8	22.1
351/2	151.8	11.2	7.2	1.4	− 0.2	− 15.0
355/6	37.3	− 9.9	− 21.7	3.0	0.5	20.2
36	31.2	− 1.8	− 5.5	3.5	0.4	12.5
381	18.9	0.5	2.5	4.4	− 0.1	− 3.3
382	36.5	− 11.9	− 26.5	2.9	0.6	23.1
383	173.5	− 138.6	− 52.6	2.4	1.0	58.6
384	48.4	− 3.2	− 6.5	3.7	0.2	4.8
385	15.9	− 7.0	− 34.1	4.8	1.7	40.3
39	15.7	0.9	6.0	4.7	0.4	9.1

Note: [a] The variables $\bar{\mu}/(\overline{SKEW})$, $\Delta\mu$ ($\Delta SKEW$) and $\%\Delta\mu$ ($\%\Delta SKEW$) stand for the mean of μ ($SKEW$) in the period 1978–1989, the change in μ ($SKEW$) from 1978 to 1989 and the percentual change in μ ($SKEW$) from 1978 to 1989 respectively.
Source: Central Bureau of Statistics and Research Institute for Small and Medium-Sized Business.

$\Delta SKEW > 0$) occurs for 11 out of 16 manufacturing industries.[19] There are five exceptions to this combination, of which three have both $\Delta\mu > 0$ and $\Delta SKEW < 0$ (ISIC 321, 351/2, 381) and two have either $\Delta\mu > 0$ or $\Delta SKEW < 0$ (ISIC 341 and 39). Only in the case of chemicals (ISIC 351/2) is there a significant growth of μ (7.2 percent) and a significant decline of $SKEW$ (15 percent). I conclude that for most 2 or 3 digit industries the firm-size distribution changes in favor of small firms.

4.3 The development of the measures

In this section the development of the measures μ and $SKEW$ over the years 1978–1989 is investigated. The average value of μ and $SKEW$ over the industries are presented for these years in Figures 5.1 and 5.2, respectively. The values are weighted with the share in total employment of the 16 industries.

It is clear that the average number of employees per firm in the manufacturing industries declined during the period 1978–1989. This confirms the supposition of a generally larger share of small firms in Western manufacturing industries. We see that the decline slows down in the late 1980s and even turns into a rising curve from 1986 onwards. The development in time with respect to *SKEW* can be characterized by a general rise from 1978 till 1987 with a period of stabilization from 1981 till 1984 and by a decline from 1987 till 1989. Figures 5.1 and 5.2 both indicate that something happened around 1986.

4.4   *Developments of the separate industries and conclusions*

In this section the development of the firm-size distribution will be considered for the separate industries. This will give us a better understanding of the development of μ and *SKEW* as presented in Figures 5.1 and 5.2. In Table 5.14 we can see in which year the decline in μ changes into a rise. Of the 16 manufacturing industries two still had a declining value of μ in 1989. These two industries are textiles (ISIC 321) and instrument engineering (ISIC 385). The other industries had a turning point in the development of μ around 1986 with the exception of chemicals (ISIC 351/2) which had already seen a turning point in 1981.

I conclude that there has been a general tendency towards a lower average firm size in manufacturing industries until about 1986. After 1986, we see a general tendency for growing firm size again. I also conclude that the relative small-business presence (skewness) generally increased till about 1987. The latter result is in accordance with the 2 digit results given in Table 5.10, where an increasing share of SME is shown till 1986. The 1986 turning point may have a number of causes:

- In 1992 the 12 countries of the European Community will form a common market; this already had a strong effect in the late 1980s. The common market will probably lead to a higher degree of concentration and more similarities in the firm-size distribution across countries.[20]
- Some small firms out of the many which started in the recovery period 1983–1986 grew into higher employment-size classes in the period 1986–1989.[21] Related to this development is the additional entry of large-sized firms by acquisitions, mergers and foreign investments.[22]
- Contrary to the early 1980s the late 1980s were characterized by tighter labor markets and rising real wages. This may be advantageous for more capital intensive large firms.

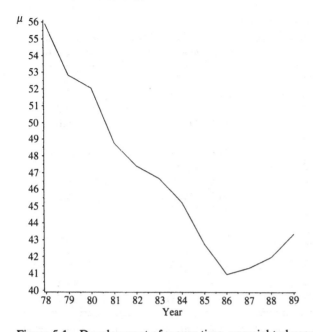

Figure 5.1   Development of μ over time, unweighted yearly averages.

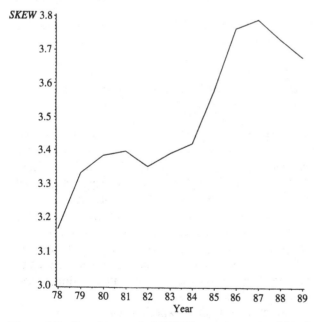

Figure 5.2   Development of *SKEW* over time, unweighted yearly averages.

Table 5.14. *Occurrence of a turning point in* μ

ISIC	$\mu(1978)$	μ_{min}(year)^a		$\mu(1989)$
31	24.3	22.3	(1984)	26.8
321	54.8	34.9	(1989)	34.9
322	23.2	12.9	(1988)	13.3
323/4	19.5	13.6	(1987)	16.0
33	12.9	10.7	(1986)	10.9
341	88.0	74.8	(1984)	85.0
342	24.2	18.9	(1987)	19.8
351/2	154.6	141.4	(1981)	165.8
355/6	45.8	30.1	(1986)	35.9
36	33.0	26.2	(1986)	31.2
381	19.5	17.5	(1985)	20.0
382	44.9	31.6	(1987)	33.0
383	263.4	123.1	(1988)	124.9
384	49.7	45.4	(1987)	46.5
385	20.4	13.4	(1989)	13.4
39	15.8	13.9	(1984)	16.7

Note: ^{a} The variable μ_{min} stands for the minimum value of μ in the period 1976–1987. The year between parentheses is the year in which this minimum is reached.
Source: Central Bureau of Statistics and Research Institute for Small and Medium-Sized Business.

5. Have economies of scale decreased over time in Dutch manufacturing?[23]

In Carlsson (1989, p. 21) two major reasons are given for the observed decline in firm size in most industrial countries: "The first one is deglomeration or specialization: the selling off or disinvestment of non-core businesses in order to free up scarce resources (particularly management time) to defend and nurture core business activities;" "The second reason is the emergence of new computer-based technology which improves the quality and productivity of small and medium-scaled production relative to standardized mass-production techniques which dominated for the previous 150 years." In other words: Carlsson's arguments are related to the question whether the impact of economies of scale has diminished over time in the last two decades.[24]

This section deals with an investigation whether scale economies decreased in Dutch manufacturing during the period 1974–1986. Such a decrease may be the cause of the observed tendencies towards a lower average firm size and an increased small-business presence reported in the preceding section. Clearly, there are more possible causes for the reversal of the upward trend in average firm size which occurred until the mid-1970s. Brock and Evans (1989) give five more reasons other than a reduction of scale economies:[25] development of new products and processes; greater importance of flexibility because of increasing competition; increasing labor supply and falling real wages; increasing demand for speciality products; and relaxation of entry regulations.

This section is organized as follows: in Section 5.1 the 3 digit data of the manufacturing industries are discussed. A declining average firm size is again observed. Cost ratios are given for both medium-sized and large firms in Section 5.2. In Section 5.3 a simple cost model is presented and estimated. This cost model does nothing more than to provide a concise representation of the findings based upon Table 5.16. In Table 5.16 the cost ratio (productivity) differentials between medium-sized (10 to 50 employees) and large firms (> 50 employees) is tabulated in terms of level (1980) and growth (1974–1986). The quintessence of this model is the discrimination between fixed and variable costs. Section 5.4, finally, contains some concluding remarks.

5.1 *Data*

A data set of 68 Dutch manufacturing industries for the period 1974–1986 is used. This set is mainly based on statistics officially published by the Netherlands Central Bureau of Statistics. All firms with 10 or more employees are observed; smaller firms are excluded. If possible, a partitioning into two size classes is made. This partitioning (10 to 50 employees and >50 employees) is available for 36 industries.[26] The 68 industries are given in Table 5.15. The level of aggregation is the so-called 3 digit level of the Dutch Standard Industrial Classification 1974 (SBI). The data cover about 82 percent in terms of number of employees of total manufacturing in 1986 (excluding oil refineries[27] and manufacture of petroleum and oil products). They cover 88 percent of employment, and 83 percent of value added if we consider only firms with 10 or more employees. Table 5.15 also presents the employment data of our 68 manufacturing industries. We see that in the period 1974–1986 firm size declined in 52 out of the 68 industries! In 14 industries firm size even declined by more than 30 percent, whereas in only one industry (21.5, breweries and malt houses) did firm size increase by more than 30 percent.

Table 5.15. *Description of the Dutch manufacturing industries*[a]

		Average firm size (in employees)	
SBI	Industry	Level 1980	% change 1974–1986
20.1	*[b]Slaughtering and meat processing industry	89	−17.8
20.4	Flour mills, groats and rice husking mills, etc.	88	−31.9
20.6	*Manufacture of margarine, other vegetable and animal oils and fats	285	5.8
20.7	Canning, preserving and processing of fruits and vegetables	119	−19.3
20.8	*Manufacture of bread, rusks, pastries, cakes and biscuits	39	−27.9
20.9	*Manufacture of cocoa, chocolate and confectionery	116	−5.8
21.2	*Manufacture of compounded animal stock feeds	59	5.8
21.3	*Manufacture of other food products	136	−30.4
21.4	Alcohol manufacturing and distilleries	81	20.0
21.5	Breweries and malt houses	488	35.0
21.6	Non-alcoholic beverages	128	14.6
22.1/2	Wool industry/cotton industry	171	−43.7
22.3	Knitting and hosiery industry	89	−39.9
22.5	Manufacture of carpets and rugs	92	−4.6
23.1/2	Manufacture of ready-made clothing/ contract manufacture of ready-made clothing	59	−24.2
24.1	Leather industry	41	6.2
24.2	Leatherware industry (excl. clothing)	29	1.0
24.3	Footwear industry	59	−12.2
25.3	Carpentering, parqueting industry	45	−14.7
25.4	Manufacture of wooden containers	57	−28.1
25.5	Manufacture of other wooden articles	27	−8.3
25.7	Furniture industry (excl. metal furniture)	31	−24.6
26.1	Paper and cardboard industry	332	−27.3
26.2	*Paperware industry	110	−3.4
26.3	*Corrugated cardboard and cardboard industry	95	−8.4
27.1	*Printing industry	55	−40.4
27.2	*Publishing industry	98	1.1
27.3	*Book binding industry	39	−33.1
29.1	Manufacture of fertilizers	997	−55.2

Table 5.15. (*cont.*)

SBI	Industry	Average firm size (in employees)	
		Level 1980	% change 1974–1986
29.2	Manufacture of plastics	359	9.1
29.3	Manufacture of dye-stuffs and pigments	126	−13.1
29.4/30.0	Other chemical basic industry/manufacture of artificial and synthetic yarns of fibres	710	−13.6
29.5	*Manufacture of paint, lacquer, varnish and printing ink	91	24.7
29.6	*Manufacture of pharmaceutical and antiseptic dressings	258	10.0
29.7	*Manufacture of soap; other washing and cleaning materials, perfume and cosmetics	140	13.7
29.8	Manufacture of chemical detergents, etc.	139	−14.7
29.9	*Manufacture of other chemical products.	107	−0.8
31.1	Rubber-processing industry	170	−19.6
31.3	Plastic-processing industry	63	−7.4
32.1/2	Manufacture of brick and tiles/manufacture of earthenware	65	−14.3
32.3	Manufacture of sand–lime bricks	61	7.7
32.5	*Manufacture of concrete and cement products	57	−5.6
33.1/2/4	Iron and steel industry/manufacture of steel tubes/non-ferrous metal industry	860	−6.8
33.3	*Wire-drawing and cold-rolling industry	119	0.7
34.0	*Foundries	101	−30.9
34.1	*Iron works, crushing and pressing industry	60	−2.2
34.2	*Manufacture of screws, mass products from lathes and springs	79	−23.9
34.3	*Construction of tanks, reservoirs and pipelines	44	−25.0
34.4	*Other metal construction	41	−16.3
34.5	*Manufacture of metal furniture	74	−1.5
34.6/8	*Metal-packing industry/manufacture of other metal products	71	−6.2
34.7	*Manufacture of heating and cooking apparatus (excl. electric)	133	−42.8
34.9	Forges, surface treatment	27	−24.2
35.1	*Manufacture of agricultural machinery	51	−10.3
35.2	*Manufacture of metal-working machinery	50	−24.6

Table 5.15. (*cont.*)

SBI	Industry	Average firm size (in employees)	
		Level 1980	% change 1974–1986
35.3	*Manufacture of machinery for food-processing, chemical and related industries	85	−20.3
35.4	*Lifting and other transport equipment for mining construction, building-materials and metallurgic industries	61	−20.4
35.5	Manufacture of cog-wheels, bearings and other driving gear	62	−43.4
35.6	*Manufacture of machinery and other equipment for industries n.e.s.	74	−4.7
35.7	*Manufacture of steamboilers, engines and turbines	141	−45.4
35.8	Manufacture of office machinery	788	−8.1
35.9	*Manufacture of other machinery and apparatus	65	−15.8
36	Electrotechnical industry	545	−41.9
37.1/3/7	*Manufacture and assembly of automobiles/manufacture of car parts/aircraft-construction and repair industry	791	15.5
37.2	*Manufacture of coach work and trailers	48	−1.7
37.4	Shipbuilding and ship repair industries	141	−34.5
37.6	*Manufacture of bicycles and motorcycles	103	−37.6
37.9	*Manufacture of other transport equipment	48	5.5

Notes:
a The Dutch SBI 1974 code is used for lack of a precise ISIC code on this level.
b An asterisk is given next to the industry if data are available for two size classes: 10 to 50 employees and >50 employees.

Equation (1) is based on the following assumptions. Costs consist of a fixed and a variable part represented by α and $\gamma_i Q_{it}$, respectively. The ratio of variable costs and value added, γ_i, is time-independent and industry-dependent. To this simple cost model we add a trend term, so that the fixed costs are allowed to be time-dependent (in a monotonous fashion). We add a correction for inflation assuming that the price index number of costs equals that of value added:

5.2 Cost ratios

I shall present some cost ratios to investigate whether they differ between medium-sized and large firms in level and growth rate. Costs consist of labor costs and other operating expenses,[28] because capital costs (i.e. depreciation, paid interest and a reward for capital of the owners) are not available. A "cost ratio" is defined as costs divided by value added.[29] The cost ratios of 1980, the relative change of the cost ratios in the period 1974–1986, and the employment share of small firms in 1980, are presented in Table 5.16. Data are presented for the 36 industries for which a partitioning into two size classes according to number of employees is available. These industries cover 47 percent of employment and 40 percent of value added of total manufacturing in 1986 (excluding firms with less than 10 employees and excluding oil refineries and manufacture of petroleum and oil products). Looking at the difference between the cost ratios of medium-sized and large firms, we see that in no fewer than 26 out of the 36 industries the cost ratio of the medium-sized firms is lower than that of the large firms. In the 2 digit groups 34 (manufacture of fabricated metal products) and 35 (manufacture of machinery) and ratios of almost every industry are lower for medium-sized than for large firms. This points to generally lower unit costs for medium-sized than for large firms in 1980. Looking at the growth of medium-sized vs large firms' cost ratios, we see that in no fewer than 23 out of 35 industries this growth has been less for medium-sized than for large firms in the period 1974–1986. This points to a higher productivity growth for medium-sized than for large firms. The last column of Table 5.16 shows that this growth differential occurs not only in industries where the medium-sized firm presence is either very small or very large. The reconciliation of the observed higher aggregate productivity growth for large enterprises than for SME of Section 3 with the present opposite results observed here will be discussed in the concluding section. Section 5.3 deals with the question whether the productivity growth differential between medium-sized and large enterprises can be interpreted as a reduction of scale economies.

5.3 A cost model

A simple cost model will be used for analyzing the taxonomy of scale-determined differentials:

$$K_{it} = \alpha + \gamma_i Q_{it} \tag{1}$$

where
K: (value of) costs per firm (firm averages)
Q: value added per firm (firm averages)
i, t: industry and time index, respectively.

Table 5.16. *Cost ratios in Dutch manufacturing, firm averages[a]*

SBI	1980 cost ratio			1974–1986 change of the cost ratio (%)			1980 share of small firms[b]
	K/Q	$(K/Q)_m$	$(K/Q)_l$	$\bullet$ K/Q	$\bullet$ $(K/Q)_m$	$\bullet$ $(K/Q)_l$	
20.1	0.94	0.83	0.97	19.9	22.3	19.7	0.18
20.6	0.73	0.63	0.73	1.9	c	−8.5	0.04
20.8	0.85	0.80	0.89	−5.5	1.5	−7.1	0.44
20.9	0.82	0.84	0.81	−6.1	10.4	−8.3	0.08
21.2	0.74	0.81	0.73	12.8	5.4	14.8	0.24
21.3	0.88	0.87	0.88	12.8	−14.6	16.0	0.12
26.2	0.80	0.73	0.81	0.8	−0.7	1.2	0.12
26.3	0.78	0.79	0.78	−4.9	−12.3	−3.5	0.16
27.1	0.82	0.83	0.82	−8.4	−8.3	−8.1	0.31
27.2	0.78	0.86	0.77	−4.9	−6.6	−4.5	0.14
27.3	0.79	0.78	0.80	−2.2	−8.6	1.5	0.44
29.5	0.82	0.78	0.82	−3.7	−3.9	−3.7	0.18
29.6	0.81	0.73	0.82	−11.8	−11.9	−11.7	0.06
29.7	0.85	0.86	0.85	9.5	7.8	9.6	0.09
29.9	0.89	0.72	0.92	−11.8	−7.9	12.6	0.16
32.5	0.78	0.76	0.79	−14.1	−13.9	−14.5	0.22
33.3	0.83	0.73	0.85	2.9	−18.6	4.6	0.09
34.0	0.93	0.87	0.94	−5.9	−3.3	−6.7	0.16
34.1	0.82	0.79	0.84	−11.8	−17.9	−8.7	0.32
34.2	0.89	0.79	0.92	−5.9	−27.4	1.8	0.20
34.3	0.89	0.85	0.92	−1.1	−5.3	3.4	0.40
34.4	0.92	0.88	0.95	2.0	0.7	4.9	0.47
34.5	0.87	0.91	0.86	−16.0	−37.3	−10.2	0.22
34.6/8	0.81	0.80	0.81	−8.4	−15.7	−6.0	0.26
34.7	0.93	0.92	0.93	−18.0	−3.9	−18.7	0.07
35.1	0.81	0.87	0.78	24.4	0.2	35.5	0.30
35.2	0.86	0.83	0.88	−4.7	−3.1	−5.1	0.36
35.3	0.92	0.87	0.93	2.0	2.3	2.1	0.18
35.4	0.88	0.88	0.88	1.7	3.4	1.3	0.29
35.6	0.88	0.86	0.88	−11.2	−14.1	−11.1	0.25
35.7	1.03	0.86	1.06	−4.4	14.4	−6.2	0.12
35.9	0.95	0.84	0.99	−5.9	−3.7	−6.2	0.28
37.1/3/7	0.89	0.85	0.89	26.0	−3.6	26.4	0.01
37.2	0.89	0.86	0.91	−12.1	−10.2	−13.4	0.41
37.6	0.82	0.80	0.82	4.8	1.3	6.1	0.12
37.9	0.86	0.88	0.85	−12.5	−33.4	−1.0	0.33

Notes: [a] Value added in million Dutch guilders; m and l indices for medium-sized and large firms, respectively; $\bullet$ indicates a relative change of a variable.
[b] Measured in employment.
[c] Value added has a negative value in 1974.

$$K_{it} = \alpha_0 p_{it} + \alpha_1 T p_{it} + \gamma_i Q_{it} \qquad (2)$$

where
p: price index number of value added (1980 = 1)
T: time, 1974: 0, 1975: 1, 1976: 2, etc.

This simple model allows us to investigate whether there is a general tendency for decreasing or increasing economies of scale. The scale determined differentials observed in Table 5.16 can thus now be interpreted in terms of systematic movements of economies of scale.

Dividing (2) by Q_{it} gives

$$k_{it} = \alpha_0(1/q_{it}) + \alpha_1(T/q_{it}) + \gamma_i \qquad (3)$$

where

$$k = K/Q \text{ and } q = Q/p.$$

There are decreasing economies of scale if and only if $\dfrac{d}{dT}\left(\dfrac{dk}{dq}\right) > 0$.
It is easy to show that $\dfrac{d}{dT}\left(\dfrac{dk}{dq}\right) = -\alpha_1/q^2$.

Hence, there are decreasing economies of scale if and only if $\alpha_1 < 0$. The advantage of the model is that it provides a representation of scale economies on the level of an entire sector of an economy. It allows an easy comparison between countries, sectors of industries and periods and few data are required. Some shortcomings due to its simplicity will be dealt with elsewhere.

The estimation results of equation (3) are reported in Table 5.17.[30]

For all 68 manufacturing industries the estimated coefficient $\hat{\alpha}_1$ is significantly negative.[31] For the 36 industries for which there is a partitioning according to medium-sized and large firms, the estimated coefficients $\hat{\alpha}_1$ are negative. The coefficient of the medium-sized firms is not significant, though. The all-firm results of the 36 and the 68 industries do not differ from each other. This provides confidence in the representativity of the results of our simple model applied to the different size classes of the 36 industries' sample. Looking at medium-sized and large firms separately, we see that the large firms contribute significantly to the effect of decreasing scale advantages over time. This is not surprising, because variation of scale is much higher for large firms than for medium-sized ones.[32] As already said, we prefer to present a simple model. Nevertheless, obvious drawbacks of our simple model are that capital costs are not included, cyclical fluctuations are not accounted for and the specification of the influence of time is limited to fixed costs. They will be dealt with in follow-up studies.

Table 5.17. *Estimation of cost model (3)*

Title	$\hat{\alpha}_0{}^a$		$\hat{\alpha}_1{}^a$		R^{2b}
68 industries					
all firms	0.289	(8.6)	− 0.0120	(− 5.7)	0.080
36 industries					
all firms	0.268	(7.1)	− 0.0146	(− 5.5)	0.096
medium-sized firms	0.138	(6.9)	− 0.0028	(− 1.8)	0.092
large firms	0.513	(6.1)	− 0.0287	(− 4.3)	0.072

Notes:
[a] t-values between parentheses.
[b] R^2 is the corrected coefficient of determination, calculated with the transformed dependent variable. It is the coefficient of determination belonging to the non-dummy part of the model.

5.4 Concluding remarks

This section is based upon a highly disaggregated data set of 68 Dutch manufacturing industries covering more than 80 percent of total manufacturing. It seems that the scale of production at which a firm can produce efficiently is declining in manufacturing, because in 52 out of these 68 industries firm size declined during the period 1974–1986. It would appear that this conjecture is supported by the estimation results of a simple cost model in which (non-capital) costs are divided into fixed and variable costs. The estimation results of this model demonstrate that there is a decreasing importance of fixed costs over time. This points to a reduction of economies of scale over time. A decreasing importance of scale economies would lead to a reformulation of the conventional market configuration measure: the emphasis would shift from understanding the mechanism which generates the relative share of large enterprises to that which generates absolute enterprise sizes (see Carlsson, 1989, p. 36). Because few data are required as input for our model, comparisons between countries, sectors and periods are relatively simple. Comparative studies would obviously contribute to our understanding of new market configuration measures.

6. Conclusion

In Section 3 the annual SME productivity growth was found to be about 1 percent lower than that of large enterprises in the period 1981–1988. This finding refers to the entire manufacturing industry whereas SME refers to all enterprises with less than 100 employed. The exercises in Section 5 using a simple cost model point to a reduction of scale economies over time. Moreover, cost ratios (cost excluding capital costs divided by value added) appear to increase more for medium-sized than for large enterprises in only 12 out of 35 of the 3 to 4 digit (ISIC) cases. This finding refers to the period 1974–1986 and medium-sized business has between 10 and 50 employed. The 35 industries account for about 45 percent of the total manufacturing employment of enterprises with 10 or more employees in 1986. The choice of the 35 industries is biased in the sense that a sufficient presence of both medium-sized and large enterprises is necessary to suppress secrecy problems. How can the findings of Sections 3 and 5 be reconciled? Of course, one may point at differences in variables,[33] period[34] and size classes. More important, however, is coverage in terms of industries. For instance, in the data set of Section 5 some industries are missing which are dominated by large firms (petroleum industry, ISIC 353/4) and which weigh heavily in aggregate comparisons. One should be careful in interpreting aggregate comparisons across size classes in view of the possibly largely differing size-class compositions of the underlying industries (see Table 5.10) and of the possibly largely differing competitive advantages of size classes across industries. Clearly, the decomposition of general structural shifts into industry and scale effects must be qualified. But the growing interest in size-related irregularities, together with the desire to analyze at low levels of aggregation, calls for an explicit warning if one wishes to compare different aggregation levels.

My second conclusion refers to the efforts of size-related data collection. Many man years have been involved in putting together the data sets used in this chapter. They have been put together after combination and elaboration of many officially published and other sources. Even in a wealthy country like the Netherlands with a strong data collection apparatus, a sound policy makers' concern about regulatory effects, a central economics research institute for SME, and a strong tradition in empirical economics, size-related economic analysis is frustrated by scarcity of data. Whether small-business economics will ever be a great field within the economic sciences, I don't know. I do know that it is a big field in the sense that without men and means for adequate data collection it will not develop at all.

Finally I want to devote some attention to an important question which has been left untouched so far. Why should scale economies be decreasing over time?

I shall briefly try to answer this question for the Dutch case. Explaining changes in scale economies one should distinguish between three aspects:

changes in the production process, in the type of product, and in the business environment. There are many possible economies in the production process relating to finance, planning and control, marketing and information, physical production, purchasing, etc.[35] It is generally thought that the emergence of computer-based technologies in the areas of production, administration and information has offset the advantages of large-scale production considerably.[36] Next to changes in the production process, changes took place in the demand for products. Consumer behavior is increasingly characterized by individualism leading to differentiated and fragmented markets with sometimes short life cycles. A greater variety of products and brands is also stimulated by increased cross-cultural and cross-national competition. Supply has to keep up, creating a flexible and complex production process with little room for learning effects. This leads to a transition from mass production to craft production with less chances for scale economies and greater chances for horizontal dispersion in business units. It may also lead to vertical disintegration in that fabricated materials (components, parts, semi-finished products, etc.) are bought rather than manufactured in-house and in that commercial services are contracted out.[37] The resulting deglomeration shows complicated structures of cooperating enterprises[38] with an increased reliance on suppliers and subcontractors.[39] Of the changes in the business environment detrimental to scale economies I shall mention two. First, there is considerable governmental support and subsidies for smaller enterprises in the Netherlands. For instance, there is an advanced infrastructure of technical and scientific support. Also, smaller enterprises profit from INSTIR (INnovation STimulation Regulation), a subsidy system for industrial innovations[40] and from the SME Security Scheme, a governmental tool to facilitate financing SME which absorbs part of a private bank's risk. Secondly, some quite highly-educated employees found their way to the smaller-business labor market in the 1980s. Clearly, there is a demand effect from the need for running more complex and flexible production systems.[41] But there is also a supply effect. People want to work in a small-scale environment, more so than in the 1960s when large enterprises attracted the most highly-qualified people. Still, the share of highly educated employees in SME employment is lower than that in large enterprise employment.

Notes

I would like to thank Aad Kleijweg, Wim Verhoeven and Sjaak Vollebregt of EIM, Martin Carree and René den Hertog of CASBEC and David Audretsch of WZB for comments, assistance or making data or research results available.

1 This section is based on the National Accounts of OECD, Department of Economics and Statistics, Paris, France and on the Statistical Yearbooks of Eurostat, Industry data, Luxembourg; Sjaak Vollebregt of the Research Institute for Small and Medium-Sized Business in Zoetermeer, the Netherlands, provided the tables.

2 Dutch employment decline would be less if measured in man years.

3 See Wennekers (1990), who deals with growth factors of both personal and collective services. The services' output share at current prices is overestimated due to its rising relative price caused by lagging productivity growth.

4 See RISMB (1990a). Probably also the increased cooperation between (small and large) enterprises contributed to the productivity growth. Vertical disintegration led to a more efficient allocation of productive mass. See Nijssen (1987) for a description of complementarity of small and large enterprises in manufacturing. Here also a survey is given on the post-war structural and regulatory developments in Dutch manufacturing. In RISMB (1990c, p. 41) a yearly output growth of manufacturing supplies is reported of 3.8 percent for SME and 2.5 percent for LE (1979–1986). It is also reported (p.46) that the yearly volume growth rates of commercial services to manufacturing exceeded that of manufacturing production by 1.3 percent (1977–1985). All these findings support the hypothesis that "service parts" of the production have been increasingly contracted out.

5 This section is based on RISMB (1990a) and RISMB (1990c). For a concise English version I refer to RISMB (1990b). Wim Verhoeven of the Research Institute for Small and Medium-Sized Business in Zoetermeer, the Netherlands provided many additional data and estimates.

6 See RISMB (1990a, p. 49), RISMB (1990c, pp. 272–35) and also Verhoeven (1988).

7 Excluding bakeries.

8 I would like to thank Wim Verhoeven of RISMB for making available the data.

9 The relative importance of some manufacturing industries largely explains productivity growth. LE is strong in basic industries like oil, chemicals and basic metals. These industries account for 24 percent of total manufacturing value added and 16 percent of total manufacturing employment. These industries had a LE share of about 82 percent in value added and one of about 75 percent in employment in 1988 (cf. Table 5.5, where it is shown that the LE share in the entire manufacturing section is 67 percent in value added and 59 percent in employment). These industries are favored by considerable scale economies: rising production has hardly led to any rising employment in the period 1981–1988.

10 I refer to RISMB (1990a) for a detailed discussion of separate developments in the four major parts of the manufacturing industry: foods; oil and chemicals; metals and machinery; other manufacturing.

11 This section is based on an unpublished paper co-authored by Martin Carree of the Centre for Advanced Small Business Economics at Erasmus University in Rotterdam, the Netherlands.

12 Carlsson showed that the average firm size declined in engineering industries from 1973 to 1983 for Denmark, Finland, Italy, Japan, the United Kingdom, the United States, and West Germany. The only exception was Sweden, which experienced a small rise in average firm size.

13 Acs and Audretsch (1989) report a small-firm share of sales increasing from about 30 to 40 percent for the US metalworking industries in the period 1976–1986. In Vollebregt (1990) many figures about 40 Dutch manufacturing industries are presented for the period 1974–1986. The figures show decreasing average firm size in most industries, and an average development of labor productivity which is higher for small than for large firms.

   Sato (1989) reports a small-firm employment share in Japanese manufacturing which declines from 69.9 percent in 1960 to 67.8 percent in 1969 and rises to 73.1 percent and 73.9 percent in 1978 and 1983, respectively.

   Schwalbach (1989) reports a minor decrease of small-firm share with respect to employment and sales in German manufacturing in the period 1977–1986 in the face of an overall important small-firm share in terms of number of businesses.

14 Employees are in man years.

15 In our analysis we use an interpolation of the employment figures for the remaining eight years.

16 "Firm" equals "enterprise."

17 Definitions used here may differ slightly from those in Table 5.7.

18 The value of *SKEW* can deviate strongly from the real skewness of the firm-size distribution because of the limited number of employment classes. However, in this study we are mainly interested in the development of *SKEW*.

19 The results for the engineering industries (ISIC 381–385) confirm the results of Carlsson (1989) for the Netherlands.

20 Sleuwaegen and Yamawaki (1988) discuss the effect of the formation of the European Common Market on the degree of seller concentration. They conclude that the formation of the Common Market has created a more concentrated industry structure in the national market for Belgium, France, Italy and West Germany.

21 This is in accordance with the concept of life cycles in industries. Brock and Evans (1989, p. 10) use the following formulation of this phenomenon: "If the formation and growth of small business is due to the development of new products or technologies, then history teaches us that, over time, only a handful of the firms in these new industries will survive."

22 In studies of changes in industry concentration the initial level of the concentration ratio often has a negative effect (Curry and George, 1983).

23 This section is based on the unpublished paper co-authored by Aad Kleijweg of the Research Institute for Small and Medium-Sized Business in Zoetermeer, the Netherlands.

24 See also Carlsson (1984)

25 See also Acs and Audretsch (1990, pp. 4–6).

26 A detailed description of the data set, called DUMA, can be found in Bakker and Prince (1990). The data set is also used in Prince and Thurik (1990). Next

to their empirical analysis of cyclical behavior of price–cost margins they also present some descriptive analyses on average price–cost margins by four firm concentration ratio.

27 Some of the world's largest oil refineries are in the so-called "Europort" area between Rotterdam and the North Sea coast.

28 Other operating expenses comprise, amongst others, renting and leasing of buildings and machinery, advertising costs.

29 Value added in this section equals the value of output minus purchasing value of (raw) materials. Output equals value of sales minus purchasing value of sales of merchandise. Elsewhere the so-called "other operating expenses" are subtracted from value added (see n.28).

30 After sweeping out the γ_1s with the so-called covariance transformation, estimation results are obtained with Ordinary Least Squares (OLS) on the transformed variables. The proof is straightforward (see Hsiao, 1986, p. 53).

31 "Significant" is used at the 5 percent level.

32 For this reason we think that the mere availability of data of firms with 10 or more employees is no major drawback.

33 Section 3 uses labor volume and Section 5 total costs excluding capital costs. This difference in definition of input does not fully explain the discrepancy of the finding of Sections 3 and 5. This is illustrated by Vollebregt (1990) who finds a medium-sized enterprise labor productivity growth which is about 0.5 percent higher annually than that of a large enterprise in the period 1974–1986. He uses 43 3 to 4 digit industries containing our 35.

34 A substantial part of the excess productivity growth of large enterprises over SME can be attributed to the year 1987, which has no part in the analysis of Section 5 (see Table 5.9).

35 Clearly, there are also general diseconomies of scale related to organizational complexity, internal communication, etc.

36 See Poutsma *et al.* (1987), and Nooteboom (1987) for Dutch and Carlsson (1989) for other evidence. The relation between process flexibility and the viability of small enterprises has of course been brought up by Piore and Sabel (1984) and has been tested by Acs, Audretsch and Carlsson (1990).

37 Clearly, the above trends in processes and products do not always lead to decreased economies of scale. Some markets are inherently bulky (primary goods), some fields of research are inherently advanced and capital intensive (basic technologies). Even large enterprises have difficulty surviving on these markets or investing in these fields of research and engaging in international cooperation. A general trend towards an increased presence of small enterprises due to a general decrease of scale economies caused by a general shift in products and processes may not be expected. See for instance Table 5.14, where 18 out of 68 industries are shown to have a positive firm-size growth in terms of employment, or Table 5.15, where 11 out of 35 industries are shown to have a higher cost ratio growth for medium-sized than for large enterprises.

Also, the small-business presence is assumed to depend upon the stage in the life cycle of the product market combination which results in the hypothesis of the dynamic complementarity between small and large enterprises, see

Nooteboom (1987). This hypothesis states that small and large enterprises play different roles in the process of innovation and diffusion and that the weight of these roles depends upon the stage of the life cycle.

38 Small enterprises play an important role in this cooperation process. About 70 percent of the domestic output of small manufacturing enterprises consists of supplies to other enterprises.

39 See Nijssen (1987, pp. 98–104) and Von Dewall *et al.* (1985) where relations are suggested between the degree of subcontracting and business cycle and between the degree of being a subcontractor and scale of business. See also RISMB (1990c).

40 See Van den Berg, Van Dijk and Van Hulst (1990) for an evaluation of this Dutch scheme for encouraging research and development.

41 The general SME employment growth in manufacturing from 1987 onwards will intensify this effect (see Table 5.8).

References

Acs, Z. J. and D. B. Audretsch (1989) "Editors' Introduction," *Small Business Economics*, 1(1), 1–5.

(1990) "Small Firms in the 1990s," in Z. J. Acs and D. B. Audretsch (eds.), *The Economics of Small Firms: A European Challenge*, Dordrecht, the Netherlands: Kluwer Academic Publishers, 1–22.

Acs, Z. J., D. B. Audretsch and B. Carlsson (1990) "Flexibility, Plant Size and Industrial Restructuring," in Z. J. Acs and D. B. Audretsch (eds.), *The Economics of Small Firms: A European Challenge*, Dordrecht, the Netherlands: Kluwer Academic Publishers, 141–154.

Bakker, K. and Y. M. Prince (1990) *Data Set of Dutch Manufacturing per Third Digit Industry 1974–1986*, Department of Fundamental Research, Research Institute for Small and Medium-Sized Business, Zoetermeer, the Netherlands, mimeo.

Brock, W. A. and D. S. Evans (1989) "Small Business Economics," *Small Business Economics*, 1(1), 7–20.

Carlsson, B. (1984) "The Development and Use of Machine Tools in Historical Perspective," *Journal of Economic Behavior and Organization*, 5(1), 91–144.

(1989) "The Evolution of Manufacturing Technology and Its Impact on Industrial Structure: An International Study," *Small Business Economics*, 1(1), 21–38.

Curry, B. and K. D. George (1983) "Industrial Concentration: a Survey," *Journal of Industrial Economics*, 31(3), 203–255.

Dewall, F. A. Von, C. W. Kroezen, R. J. Schmidt and C. Valk (1985) *De Relatie tussen Grote en Kleine Bedrijven in de Industrie* (The Relation between Large and Small Firms in Manufacturing), Amsterdam: Nederlandsche Middenstandsbank.

Hsiao, C. (1986) *Analysis of Panel Data*, Cambridge: Cambridge University Press.

Nijssen, A. F. M. (1987) "De Industrie" (Manufacturing), in B. Nooteboom *et al.* (eds.), *Op maat van het Midden – en Kleinbedrijf*, The Hague, the Netherlands: WRR, 77–113.

Nooteboom, B. (1987) "Doen en Laten van het MKB" (The Whereabouts of SME), in B. Nooteboom *et al* (eds.), *Op Maat van het MKB*, The Hague, the Netherlands: WRR, 17–45.

Piore, M. J. and C. F. Sabel (1984) *The Second Industrial Divide: Possibilities for Prosperity*, New York: Basic Books.

Poutsma, E., P. M. van der Staal, F. W. van Uxem, A. H. C. M. Walravens and A. B. Zwaard (1987) *Procesvernieuwing en Automatisering in het MKB* (Process Innovation and Automation in SME), Research Institute for Small and Medium-Sized Business, Zoetermeer, the Netherlands.

Prince, Y. M. and A. R. Thurik (1990) *Concentration and Cyclical Behaviour of Price–Cost Margins in Dutch Manufacturing*, paper prepared for the XVIII EARIE Conference, Lisbon (September 2–4).

Research Institute for Small and Medium-Sized Business (RISMB) (1990a) *De Sectoren in het Midden – en Kleinbedrijf* (Industries in SME), Zoetermeer, the Netherlands.

(1990b) *The State of Small Business in the Netherlands*, Zoetermeer, the Netherlands.

(1990c) *Kleinschaling Ondernemen 1990* (Small Scale Business 1990), Zoetermeer, the Netherlands.

Sato, Yoshio (1989) "Small Business in Japan: A Historical Perspective," *Small Business Economics*, 1(2), 121–128.

Schwalbach, Joachim (1989) "Small Business in German Manufacturing," *Small Business Economics*, 1(2), 129–136.

Sleuwaegen, L. and H. Yamawaki (1988) "The Formation of the European Common Market and Changes in Market Structure and Performance," *European Economic Review*, 32(7), 1451–1475.

Van den Berg, M., A. Van Dijk and N. Van Hulst (1990) "Evaluating a Dutch Scheme for Encouraging Research and Development," *Small Business Economics*, 2(3), 199–211.

Verhoeven, W. J. J. (1988) "The Export Performance of Small and Medium-Sized Enterprises in the Netherlands," *International Journal of Small Business*, 6(2), 20–33.

Vollebregt, J. A. C. (1990) *Schaalverandering in de Industrie International Bekeken. De Nederlandse Industrie Nader Beschouwd* (The Change in Firm Size in Dutch Manufacturing: An International Comparison), Research-publikatie **31**, Research Institute for Small and Medium-Sized Business, Zoetermeer, the Netherlands.

Wennekers, A. R. M. (1990) *Economics of Personal and Collective Services Growth*, Research Institute for Small and Medium-Sized Business, Zoetermeer, the Netherlands.

6 Small firms in Portuguese manufacturing industries

José Mata

1. Introduction

In the recent past, the enthusiasm for small firms and the research devoted to these issues have been growing considerably, but only a few studies have specifically investigated the determinants of small-business distribution across industries.[1] These studies were made on highly developed countries, and they found that, in one way or another, small firms had been able to develop strategies that, taking advantage of their smallness, allowed them to match their larger counterparts, which seems to confirm the widespread belief that small firms are more flexible and adapt better to adverse environments.[2]

These results do not necessarily hold for a less developed country, like Portugal. The purpose of this chapter is to investigate the determinants of small-firms' presence across Portuguese manufacturing industries, using cross-section data for 73 industries and covering the years 1982 and 1986. The topic of flexibility is specifically addressed, and it is suggested that small firms have different patterns of behavior in Portugal than in more developed countries.

Section 2 of this chapter presents a brief overview of small-firm importance in the Portuguese manufacturing industries. In Section 3, the hypotheses intended to explain small-firm intensity are put forward and, in Section 4, estimation procedures and empirical results are presented and discussed. A short conclusion summarizing the most important results, is provided in Section 5.

2. An overview of small-firm importance

An accurate picture of the importance of small firms in Portuguese manufacturing is not easy to obtain. Because most surveys examine only firms or establishments above a certain dimension, or those which meet a given criterion, most available statistical data are biased against small

110

business. In Portugal, only the Census of Manufacturing and Mining aims to cover all the establishments and firms in the manufacturing sector, and data recently released reveal that in 1984 almost one-half of the total number of firms operating in manufacturing industries employed no more than two people. More than 95 percent employed less than 50 people, and only 1 percent had more than 200. According to this source, average firm size was 18 people, and firms with fewer than 50 people were responsible for more than 30 percent of total employment in the manufacturing sector. At the time this chapter was written, data from this Census were not yet available with the desirable disaggregation, and so other sources were used.

The source used in this chapter is a yearly survey conducted by the Statistics Department of the Ministry of Employment. This survey is not a very good source for very small firms, since it does not consider firms with only self-employed people or family workers. Even though it investigates only 25 percent of the total number of firms employing less than five people that were considered by the Census, it reports more firms in almost all the other employment classes and records a greater employment figure than the Census itself. Hence, except for very small firms, it can be seen as a highly reliable source, and was used after these very small firms were excluded from the sample. In the rest of this chapter whenever "small firms" are mentioned, we are dealing with small firms with at least five people employed. A major shortcoming of using this source, however, is that reliable data are available only since 1982, which impedes long-run comparisons.

Table 6.1 depicts the size distribution of firms classified in the manufacturing sector in 1982 and 1986. In spite of this period being a period of high entry and exit (44 percent of the total number of establishments in 1986 entered after 1982, and 38 percent of the establishments in existence in 1982 were no longer in activity in 1986), the size distribution of firms in the manufacturing sector experienced little modification. Perhaps the most remarkable alteration is a slight shift towards smaller firms; those employing 1000 and more people lost four percentage points in their share of total employment, while all the other classes (except the 100–199 class, which had a small reduction) experienced an increase in their relative importance as well as in their absolute levels of employment.

The importance of small firms varies enormously across industries, as is observable from Tables 6.2 and 6.3. Small-firms' employment importance (*SFEI*), defined as the proportion of total employment for which small firms are responsible, ranges from 100 in the cooperage (33121) to less than 1 in the chipboards industry (33114). In addition, Tables 6.2 and 6.3 show Small Firm Importance (*SFI*) (the proportion of firms which are

Table 6.1. *Small-firm presence in manufacturing*

Employment classes	5–9	10–19	20–49	50–99	100–199	200–499	500–999	1000 and more	Total
1982									
Firms	4856	4266	3856	1563	881	463	159	74	16,118
Share of total (%)	30.1	26.5	23.9	9.7	5.5	2.9	1.0	0.5	100.0
Cumulative share	30.1	56.6	80.5	90.2	95.7	98.6	99.5	100.0	100.0
Employment	32,499	58,417	117,961	108,767	121,994	140,487	109,394	160,210	849,729
Share of total (%)	3.8	6.9	13.9	12.8	14.4	16.5	12.9	18.9	100.0
Cumulative share	3.8	10.7	24.6	37.4	51.8	68.3	81.1	100.0	100.0
1986									
Firms	5649	4578	4106	1583	872	492	164	60	17,504
Share of total (%)	32.3	26.2	23.5	9.0	5.0	2.8	0.9	0.3	100.0
Cumulative share	32.3	58.4	81.9	90.9	95.9	98.7	99.7	100.0	100.0
Employment	37,675	62,860	126,169	109,935	120,205	148,132	112,440	125,152	842,568
Share of total (%)	4.5	7.5	15.0	13.0	14.3	17.6	13.3	14.9	100.0
Cumulative share	4.5	11.9	26.9	40.0	54.2	71.8	85.1	100.0	100.0

Source: Ministry of Employment, and own calculations.

Table 6.2. *Industries with highest small-firm presence, 1986*

CAE	Industry	SFEI (%)	SFI (%)	Firms	Employment
33121	Cooperage	100.00	100.00	9	106
32331	Cases	76.78	95.00	140	2567
33201	Wood furniture	71.24	94.36	1241	22422
33204	Mattresses	63.75	92.59	27	549
36995	Stone products	63.75	94.72	398	6893
36924	Plaster products	58.62	87.50	8	145
34201	Printing	58.60	90.76	768	17333
33203	Shutters	56.37	91.30	23	353
36202	Glass products	55.12	92.44	119	2275
36993	Cement products	49.68	87.27	267	7698

Note: A firm is considered to be small if it has fewer than 50 employees.
Source: Ministry of Employment, and own calculations.

small), the total number of firms and employment in the industry. From these tables, it is clear that among both the industries with highest and

Table 6.3. *Industries with lowest small-firm presence, 1986*

CAE	Industry	SFEI (%)	SFI (%)	Firms	Employment
36922	Hydraulic lime	4.35	50.00	2	161
36201	Glass melting industries	4.04	65.00	40	7541
32113	Spinning, weaving and finishing of artif. and synth. fibres	3.33	39.45	327	74716
38391	Electric cables	2.99	36.36	11	3745
35133	Artificial and synthetic fibres	2.42	60.00	5	869
33113	Veneer and plywood	2.10	40.00	5	904
38431	Cars	1.91	28.57	21	9911
35511	Tires	1.82	37.50	8	3195
32151	Ropes and cables	1.63	27.27	11	3247
33114	Chipboards	0.15	12.50	8	3972

Note: A firm is considered to be small if it has fewer than 50 employees.
Source: Ministry of Employment, and own calculations.

lowest small-firm presence, one can find both very small and quite large industries.

The ten industries with the highest small-firm presence are concentrated in four 2 digit sectors. Four industries belong to the wood and furniture 2 digit sector (33), another four to the non-metal products (36) and the remaining two to the textiles, leather and apparel (32) and the paper and printing (34) sectors. The industries with lowest small-firm presence are less concentrated, each one of the five sectors represented (textiles, leather and apparel (32), wood and furniture (33), chemicals, petroleum, rubber and plastic (35), non-metal products (36) and metal products and machinery (38)) having two industries.[3]

3. The hypotheses

To explain the relative importance of small firms in different industries, I hypothesized that small-firm presence is determined by small-scale entry deterrence, international trade involvement and demand growth and instability.

With respect to entry deterrence, the small-scale aspect must be emphasized.[4] For example, where scale economies are concerned, it is well recognized now that they do not really represent an entry barrier if there are no sunk costs (see Baumol and Willig, 1981); however this is true only for entrants with a scale at least as large as the minimum efficient scale (MES). Small-scale entry will still be affected by the existence of scale economies, being more difficult the larger is the minimum efficient scale, and the higher is the cost gap between small and efficient firms. MES was measured by the proxy suggested by Lyons (1980), which has the important advantage of making an explicit appeal to an economic reasoning about the decision of opening a second plant. It does not just rely, as the traditional ad hoc measures do, on the market share of firms below a certain dimension, and therefore the criticism made by White (1982) regarding the use of proxies of MES to explain small-firm presence does not apply. As a proxy to the cost disadvantage suffered by small firms, capital intensity, measured by the capital–labor ratio (KI) was employed. The effect of these two variables is mutually reinforcing, and to take this interactive effect into account, their logarithms were actually used.

Product differentiation represents an ambiguous force. On the one hand, a differentiated market may require an additional effort in the form of advertising, R&D, etc. which, by exacerbating the scale economies and the capital requirements barriers to entry, can be particularly troublesome for small firms. On the other hand, it is also true that in such a market it can be easier to find niches in which small firms can survive, provided they are able to follow a product differentiation strategy. Product differentiation was measured by a dummy variable (ADV), which takes the value 1 if the industry is consumer oriented in Portugal and advertising intensive in Spain,[5] and by PAT, the ratio of Patents and Trademarks to Production, averaged for 1980–1981 and 1984–1985.

Small-firm presence is also expected to be related to international trade involvement. Export opportunities, alleviating the market size constraint, allow exploitation of scale economies and represent an incentive for the presence of larger firms. Besides, in the international market firms have to face an increased competitive pressure and, in such a hostile environment, small inefficient firms are less likely to survive. Finally, export activities require a minimum dimension clearly superior to the one required to compete in the national market, since the fixed costs firms must incur to acquire information are definitely greater for foreign than for domestic sales. Exports were found to be negatively related to small-firm presence in the German manufacturing industry (Schwalbach, 1989), and Machado (1989) reported evidence that export activities of Portuguese firms vary positively with their size. Due to different methodologies in data collection, data on Portuguese international trade are not directly comparable to industrial data, at least at the aggregation level we are working with. Although the actual figures for EXP (the export–production ratio, averaged for the two years before the one in study) are not accurate, one can reasonably expect them to convey some information about the true degree of openness of the industries.

Two conflicting hypotheses can be made about the relationship between industry growth and small-firm presence. Acs and Audretsch (1989b) suggested that small-firms' intensity should vary negatively with industrial growth. They did not explicitly test for the relationship between growth and small firms, but they found a positive and significant relationship between small-firm presence and a measure of "product age." Their argument is that in the earlier stages of the product life cycle, small firms face higher technological barriers, and thus are less likely to succeed. Since the growth rate decreases along the product life cycle (at least after the very beginning), their result suggests a negative effect of industry growth on small-firm presence.

Other findings, such as White (1982), suggest a positive association between growth and small-firm presence in the United States. White justifies his result by asserting that "[t]he newer the industry, the more unsettled are the conditions in the industry, the greater the uncertainties, and the more likely that small business will do well. Alternatively, a high growth rate could be seen simply as an indication of an area in which there are expanding possibilities and one in which smaller firms, capable of moving quickly, could flourish" (p. 45). The implicit reasoning in this argument is that small firms are more flexible, and that they will perform better than their large counterparts in uncertain environments or in situations which require rapid moves, a reasoning that follows the lines of Mills and Schumann (1985). According to this view, small-firm flexibility would more than offset the size disadvantage in growing markets.

Two points deserve mention here. The first is that, as Carlsson (1989) points out, there are several aspects of firm flexibility and they do not all vary negatively with firm size. The second is that even if flexibility is taken in its narrower sense, it is not something that is inherent to the smallness of size; it comes from the fact that small firms use variable factors more intensively, which allows them to vary the output level with minor cost changes, and that they have less organizational barriers to giving quick responses to detected changes in their environment.

In the Portuguese case there are some reasons to make us believe that small firms are not more flexible, and that on the contrary may be less flexible than their larger counterparts. It is commonly believed that one of the most important problems of Portuguese small firms is the quality of their management,[6] and smallness, rather than an advantage due to the absence of barriers to quick change, may be a handicap, as it may determine the relative lack of ability quickly to detect environment changes. Furthermore, Portuguese law was, until very recently, quite stringent concerning job dismissal, making labor a factor almost as fixed as capital, which at least attenuates the advantages small firms may have in changing output levels.

Flexibility is included in the empirical model via demand instability. For each industry, the logarithm of industry production was regressed on a constant and a time trend, for the six years preceding the one under observation. These regressions provided estimates for the industry growth rate and for demand instability. GR, the growth rate, is the estimated coefficient of the time trend, and as a proxy to demand instability, $1 - R^2$ of the regression was used ($INST$). Instability will have a positive, null or negative influence on small-firm presence, depending upon small firms being more, equally or less flexible than large ones. The net effect of growth can be positive only if small firms are clearly more flexible, and from the preceding arguments, it follows that a negative effect for growth and a non-positive effect for instability are expected.

4.   Empirical results

Previous works have generally employed a share measure similar to $SFEI$ either in terms of employment (Schwalbach, 1989) or sales (White, 1982;

Table 6.4. *Regression results for alternative measures of small firm, 1982*

	SFI20	SFI50	SFI100	SFEI20	SFEI50	SFEI100
CONSTANT	4.254	6.355	8.799	5.688	6.511	7.970
	(5.66)	(5.91)	(7.24)	(4.91)	(4.83)	(5.94)
LMES	− 0.611	− 0.795	− 0.849	− 1.172	− 1.190	− 1.055
	(− 5.93)	(− 6.78)	(− 5.88)	(− 9.11)	(− 8.20)	(− 6.95)
LKI	− 0.157	− 0.211	− 0.486	− 0.354	− 0.364	− 0.607
	(− 1.74)	(− 1.70)	(− 3.11)	(− 2.03)	(− 2.01)	(− 2.92)
ADV	− 0.864	− 0.817	− 0.907	− 0.603	− 0.381	− 0.365
	(− 2.22)	(− 2.69)	(− 2.81)	(− 1.77)	(− 1.51)	(− 1.19)
PAT	− 0.019	− 0.031	− 0.031	− 0.045	− 0.051	− 0.036
	(− 2.51)	(− 2.91)	(− 3.51)	(− 3.54)	(− 3.07)	(− 3.33)
EXP	− 0.003	− 0.004	− 0.006	− 0.005	− 0.005	− 0.006
	(− 2.15)	(− 2.36)	(− 3.62)	(− 2.86)	(− 2.52)	(− 2.94)
INST	− 1.141	− 0.924	− 0.861	− 1.422	− 0.854	− 0.706
	(− 2.82)	(− 1.76)	(− 1.54)	(− 2.61)	(− 1.45)	(− 1.35)
GR	− 2.750	− 1.715	− 0.572	− 3.151	− 0.646	− 0.582
	(− 1.70)	(− 0.69)	(− 0.23)	(− 1.41)	(− 0.23)	(− 0.75)
R^2(adj.)	0.35	0.33	0.35	0.47	0.41	0.39
Obs.	67	68	66	67	68	66

Notes: t-values in brackets. Critical t-values for a one-tailed test with 40 d.f. are 1.303, 1.684 and 2.425 for the 10, 5 and 1 percent significance levels, respectively.

Acs and Audretsch, 1989b) and, except for the latter, employed an *a priori* definition of small firm. There is not, however, any reason for a share measure to be better than a number measure. In the present study, several regressions were run using transformations of *SFI* as well as of *SFEI* as the dependent variable, and three different upper limits for what constitutes a small firm, ranging from 20 to 100 employees. Results of these regressions for the years 1982 and 1986 are provided in Tables 6.4 and 6.5.

SFI_i, the proportion of firms in industry i which are small, is bounded between 0 and 1, and it can also be interpreted as the probability that a firm is small, given that it operates in industry i. Similarly $SFEI_i$ can be viewed as the probability that a worker is employed by a small firm, given that he works in industry i, and is also bounded between the same limits. In these circumstances OLS, using *SFI* or *SFEI* as the dependent variable, is not an appropriate estimation method, since fitted values could lie outside the interval [0, 1], and a logit transformation is required. Applying these transformations, the error terms become heteroskedastic, even if originally they were not and, if this is the case, the models can be

Table 6.5. *Regression results for alternative measures of small firm, 1986*

	SFI20	SFI50	SFI100	SFEI20	SFEI50	SFEI100
CONSTANT	2.649	5.121	7.918	4.533	6.402	8.535
	(2.82)	(5.70)	(7.19)	(3.91)	(6.01)	(6.60)
LMES	− 0.491	− 0.582	− 0.694	− 1.036	− 0.995	− 1.014
	(− 4.35)	(− 6.39)	(− 5.34)	(− 8.50)	(− 9.57)	(− 6.24)
LKI	− 0.067	− 0.196	− 0.460	− 0.356	− 0.503	− 0.752
	(− 0.55)	(− 1.39)	(− 2.72)	(− 2.00)	(− 2.57)	(− 3.36)
ADV	− 0.865	− 0.458	− 0.486	− 0.498	(0.018)	− 0.054
	(− 3.34)	(− 2.20)	(− 1.93)	(− 1.62)	(0.08)	(− 0.17)
PAT	− 0.003	− 0.014	− 0.019	− 0.021	− 0.025	− 0.028
	(− 0.36)	(− 2.10)	(− 3.26)	(− 2.01)	(− 3.37)	(− 3.38)
EXP	− 0.004	− 0.006	− 0.007	− 0.005	− 0.007	− 0.007
	(− 1.28)	(− 2.03)	(− 2.04)	(− 1.47)	(− 2.08)	(− 2.04)
INST	− 0.011	− 0.426	− 0.641	− 0.375	− 0.610	− 0.461
	(− 0.04)	(− 1.49)	(− 1.81)	(− 0.96)	(− 1.74)	(− 1.12)
GR	− 1.873	− 2.326	− 2.335	− 2.513	− 2.040	− 1.167
	(− 1.66)	(− 2.13)	(− 1.94)	(− 1.69)	(− 1.77)	(− 0.87)
R^2(adj.)	0.21	0.31	0.35	0.43	0.43	0.37
Obs.	67	66	64	67	66	64

Notes: t-values in brackets. Critical t-values for a one-tailed test with 40 d.f. are 1.303, 1.684 and 2.425 for the 10, 5 and 1 percent significance levels, respectively.

estimated by WLS using the appropriate weights.[7] However, after the transformations required by WLS, Breusch–Pagan tests indicated that heteroskedasticity was still present, and it was decided to handle this problem by estimating coefficients by OLS and using the procedure suggested by White (1980) to correct for heteroskedasticity. Another consequence of the logit transformation is that industries with values of 0 to 1 had to be excluded, rendering us different sample sizes, depending on the upper limit for the small firm considered.

Results obtained clearly confirm the hypotheses previously made about the importance of entry barriers in explaining the importance of small-firm presence, regardless the definition adopted or the year under study.

Economies of scale were found to be consistently related to small-firm presence, the coefficients associated to *LMES* being negative and significantly different from zero and, except in one case, the same happens with *LKI*. These results suggest that small firms are indeed deterred from entry in industries where the MES is larger and where the cost disadvantage incurred by smaller firms is more important.

Given the hypothesis made about small firms' lack of flexibility, it follows that, concerning product differentiation, we would not expect that the niche effect could prevail over the entry barrier effect. In fact for both years, results show a clearly negative effect of product differentiation on small-firm presence. *PAT* coefficients are always negative and, in all cases but one, they are statistically different from zero at the usual significance levels. *ADV* is also negative and significant for *SFI* regressions, but in *SFEI* regressions its performance seems to be better with narrower definitions of small firm. It should be noted however that, in all regressions, at least one of the product differentiation proxies is statistically significant, and that in the only case in which a coefficient is positive, its t-value is quite small.

Results also confirm unequivocally the predicted effect of exports on small-firm presence, and indicate that small firms avoid export-oriented industries where they would be exposed to more intense competition, and prefer to operate in the domestic market.

Turning now to the effect of growth and instability, we observe that, once again, all the estimated coefficients for these two variables carry the expected sign, albeit that statistical significance is not as strong as for the other variables. *INST* is significant for all cases in 1982, but it is significant only for two definitions of *SFI* and one of *SFEI* in 1986. This result could be taken as an indication that small firms might have been becoming less "inflexible." However, results for the other variables, especially for *GR*, prevent such an interpretation. The negative effect of growth appears to be much more unambiguous in 1986, suggesting that small firms did not substantially improve their ability to operate in the most dynamic industries.

Although results for each one of these two variables may not be so strong as they are for the other variables, they confirm the general impression about the small firms' relative lack of flexibility. In other studies, authors generally found that, in one respect or another, small firms had the ability to develop strategies that allowed them to attenuate or compensate their inherent size disadvantage. Industries with higher growth rates were found to be attractive to smaller firms (White, 1982; Schwalbach, 1989), product differentiation failed to be significant in acting as a small-firm deterrent (White 1982; Baldwin and Gorecki, 1985) and was even shown to be a reason for small-firm success (Bradburd and Ross 1989); Acs and Audretsch (1989b) found that innovative strategies were used by American small firms to maintain their viability. In the present study, no indication of such capability was ever found.

Our results generally become worse as we go to broader definitions of small firm, especially concerning the advertising, growth and, to a certain extent, instability variables. This is not surprising, since as we enlarge the small-firms' group, larger enterprises are being included, and in these firms those characteristics that determine the relative lack of flexibility of smaller firms are becoming less present. These are questions related to quality of management, and it is not surprising that from a certain dimension upwards, these problems may be attenuated.

5. Conclusion

This chapter studied the determinants of small-firm presence in Portuguese manufacturing industries. It was found that entry barriers, namely economies of scale and product differentiation, exerted a negative influence on small-firm intensity, and that small firms avoided export oriented industries, where they would be exposed to more intense competition. Results also show that small firms in Portugal are preferentially located in more stable and settled industries, which confirms that they have not, in the recent past, had the flexibility attributes that are usually said to characterize small business.

The different roles that small firms seem to have been playing in Portugal and in more developed countries raise some doubts on the *generalized* optimism that has been prevailing with respect to small businesses. Recognition that small firms may play different roles in different countries is particularly important to avoid importing policy conclusions derived for different contexts. For the policy maker, the above analysis suggests that more important than merely supporting small business activities would be the identification of the factors contributing to small firms' positive aspects and the promotion of small-firm development. These reflections may prove to be equally useful for other countries than Portugal, namely for relatively less developed countries such as most Eastern economies.

Appendix: sample and sources

Our sample consists of 73 industries from the Portuguese manufacturing sector, meeting the requirements of availability of information and excluding all the "miscellaneous" industries, all those judged to be essentially of local extent, and those in which the public sector has a predominant position.

Data on small-firm presence and the measure of MES here employed were directly computed from raw data from the Ministry of Employment. Capital intensity data are estimates, available from the Ministry of Industry for 79 industries, defined with a superior level of aggregation than the one that was used in this study, and I assumed that all the sub-industries of each industry had the same capital–labor ratio. The Institute of Statistics was the source for data on Production and expenditures with Patents and Trademarks, as well as for the figures on International Trade, and for the classification of the industries according to the destiny of production (consumer–producer). Data on the Spanish Advertising–Production ratio are non-published data of an official survey on the Spanish manufacturing sector, kindly provided by J. Jaumandreu and G. Mato.

Notes

I am grateful to David Audretsch and to António Leite for helpful suggestions; however, responsibility for errors and omissions remains entirely mine. This study was partially supported by a grant provided by the Instituto Nacional de Investigação Cientifica.

1 Among them see White (1982) and Acs and Audretsch (1989b) for the United States; Baldwin and Gorecki (1985).
2 See Brock and Evans (1989) for a survey of small-business economics literature.
3 Industries without small firms were not considered when preparing Table 6.3. Five industries included in the sample had zero small-firm presence, according to the definition employed in Tables 6.2 and 6.3. They are: Sugar refineries (31182), Ferments (31214), Paper, paperboard and fibreboard (34112/3), Asbestos cement products (36992) and Steel tubes (37107).
4 See Acs and Audretsch (1989a) and Mata (1991) for empirical studies providing evidence that small- and large-scale business responds differently to entry barriers.
5 There is no available data on advertising at the industry level in Portugal. Spanish data were used based on the belief that the industries which are potentially differentiable are roughly the same in both countries.
6 Improvement of the quality of management, particularly in small firms, has been one of the priorities of Portuguese industrial policy.
7 See Johnston (1984) Chs. 10–15 or Judge et al. (1985) Chps. 18–20.

References

Acs, Z. J. and D. B. Audretsch (1989a) "Births and Firm Size," *Southern Economic Journal*, **55(2)**, 467–475.
(1989b) "Entrepreneurial Strategy and the Presence of Small Firms," *Small Business Economics*, **1(4)**, 193–213.
Baldwin, J. R. and P. K. Gorecki (1985) "The Determinants of Small Plant Market Share in Canadian Manufacturing Industries in the 1970s," *Review of Economics and Statistics*, **67**, 156–161.
Baumol, W. and R. Willig (1981) "Fixed Costs, Sunk Costs and Sustainability of Monopoly," *Quarterly Journal of Economics*, **96(3)**, 405–431.

Bradburd, R. M. and D. R. Ross (1989) "Can Small Firms Find and Defend Strategic Niches? A Test of the Porter Hypothesis," *Review of Economics and Statistics*, **71(2)** (May) 258–262.

Brock, W. and D. Evans (1989) "Small Business Economics," *Small Business Economics*, **1(1)**, 7–20.

Carlsson, B (1989) "Flexibility in the Theory of the Firm," *International Journal of Industrial Organization*, **7**, 179–203.

Johnston, J. (1984) *Econometrics Methods*, Singapore: McGraw-Hill (3rd edn).

Judge, G. *et al.* (1985) *The Theory and Practise of Econometrics*, New York: Wiley (2nd edn).

Lyons, B. (1980) "A New Measure of Minimum Efficient Plant Size in U.K. Manufacturing Industries," *Economica*, **17**, 19–34.

Machado, C. (1989) "Determinants of Foreign Market Performance by Portuguese Firms", Universidade do Minho, mimeo.

Mata, J. (1991) "Sunk Costs and Entry by Small and Large Plants," in P. Geroski and J. Schwalbach (eds.), *Entry and Market Contestability. An International Comparison Study*, Oxford: Basil Blackwell.

Mills, D. E. and L. Schumann (1985) "Industry Structure with Fluctuating Demand," *American Economic Review*, **75(4)** (September) 758–767.

Schwalbach, J. (1989) "Small Business in German Manufacturing," *Small Business Economics*, **1(2)**, 129–136.

White, H. (1980) "A Heteroskedastic-Consistent Covariance Matrix Estimator and Direct Test for Heteroskedasticity," *Econometrica*, **48**, 817–838.

White, L. J. (1982) "The Determinants of the Relative Importance of Small Business," *Review of Economics and Statistics*, **64(1)** (February) 42–49.

7 Small firms and the Italian economy: structural changes and evidence of turbulence

B. Invernizzi and *Riccardo Revelli*

1. Introduction

Available evidence shows that the relative importance of small and medium (SME) firms grew from the mid-1970s to the mid-1980s; the process may be still under way. The increased importance of SMEs is due to two parallel processes: a net inflow of new small firms and a decline in the average size (in terms of employees) of the existing firms. Several diverse factors may have contributed to the final outcome: technological changes reducing the importance of economies of scale, modifications in consumer tastes and consumption patterns, the quest for organizational flexibility and the need to lower the negative impact of cost rigidities (induced by increased uncertainty and competition in the product markets).

Small firms have always been more important in Italy than in other Western economies. Besides, the development of SMEs and the emergence of "industrial districts" has been one of the most interesting features of the industrial growth in the North-Eastern and Central regions. Section 2 is devoted to analyzing the Italian specificities and the major recent changes in the industrial structure.

The new role of SMEs and their relationship with the large firms is the subject of a flourishing literature. We try to enlarge the picture by presenting some evidence on the existence of areas of great turbulence among small firms. The focus of Section 3 is on entry and exit flows of firms, on the patterns of growth and decline and on labor mobility. Section 4 analyzes the recent behavior of wage differentials across firms' size.

2. An overview of recent developments in the Italian economy[1]

There are clear indications that the relative importance of small firms increased in the late 1970s and early 1980s; see, for instance, Contini

Table 7.1. *Employment shares by firm size (number of employees) and branch, Piemonte (North) and Puglia (South) region*

PIEMONTE

	1981			1984			1987		
Branch	<20	21–200	200+	<20	21–200	200+	<20	21–200	200+
1	0.018	0.042	0.940	0.020	0.035	0.945	0.018	0.042	0.940
2	0.151	0.339	0.510	0.177	0.341	0.482	0.213	0.394	0.393
3	0.140	0.206	0.654	0.156	0.210	0.634	0.218	0.252	0.530
4	0.231	0.368	0.401	0.257	0.355	0.388	0.304	0.352	0.344
5	0.618	0.342	0.040	0.636	0.319	0.045	0.660	0.285	0.055
6	0.648	0.209	0.143	0.679	0.178	0.143	0.702	0.177	0.121
7	0.153	0.166	0.681	0.167	0.183	0.650	0.277	0.250	0.473
8	0.283	0.114	0.603	0.275	0.105	0.620	0.338	0.108	0.554
2–4[a]	0.171	0.272	0.557	0.193	0.271	0.536	0.250	0.302	0.448
6–8[b]	0.442	0.174	0.384	0.458	0.156	0.386	0.527	0.163	0.310

PUGLIA

	1981			1984			1987		
Branch	<20	21–200	200+	<20	21–200	200+	<20	21–200	200+
1	0.422	0.578	–	0.364	0.636	–	0.143	0.275	0.582
2	0.183	0.158	0.659	0.199	0.161	0.640	0.196	0.147	0.657
3	0.283	0.197	0.520	0.309	0.200	0.491	0.354	0.222	0.424
4	0.500	0.352	0.148	0.515	0.354	0.131	0.526	0.387	0.087
5	0.701	0.277	0.022	0.738	0.240	0.022	0.748	0.236	0.016
6	0.857	0.108	0.035	0.911	0.089	–	0.894	0.101	0.005
7	0.291	0.286	0.423	0.299	0.264	0.437	0.315	0.218	0.467
8	0.439	0.334	0.227	0.412	0.292	0.296	0.503	0.222	0.275
2–4[a]	0.356	0.258	0.386	0.381	0.265	0.354	0.399	0.285	0.316
6–8[b]	0.641	0.192	0.167	0.664	0.171	0.165	0.686	0.151	0.163

Notes:
[a] Manufacturing industries (branches 2–4).
[b] Services (branches 6–8).
Branches
1: oil, supply of electricity, water and gas; 2: steel, chemicals, clay and glass; 3: metal products, machinery, office equipment, electronics, vehicles; 4: food, textiles, garment, footwear, furniture, paper and printing, rubber, plastics; 5: building industry; 6: trade and repairs; 7: transportation; 8: banking, insurance, services to firms.
Source: R&P statistics on social security files of firms.

Table 7.2. *Percentage of total value added by firm size and industry, Italy, 1973 and 1985*

Industry	1973			1985		
	sme	mme	mle	sme	mme	mle
Stone, clay, glass	31.3	14.1	54.6	39.6	17.9	42.5
Chemical	9.8	9.5	80.7	16.7	12.5	70.8
Artificial fibers	0.2	0.8	99.0	2.1	0.8	97.1
Fabricated metal products	43.0	17.7	39.3	52.9	18.3	28.8
Non-electr. machinery	28.0	17.1	54.9	35.4	18.1	46.5
Office equip., computers	0.8	0.6	98.6	1.0	0.7	98.3
Electrical machinery	11.9	8.0	80.1	17.6	10.0	72.4
Motor vehicles	3.6	2.6	93.8	7.7	5.8	86.5
Aircraft, ship building	8.2	3.9	87.9	9.8	4.1	86.1
Precision instruments	35.9	19.9	44.2	35.5	16.1	48.4
Food and kindred prod.	28.2	10.9	60.9	38.9	13.6	47.5
Sugar, beverages	16.7	12.7	70.6	22.7	12.3	65.0
Textiles	27.5	14.7	57.8	46.1	20.1	33.8
Footwear, leather	47.3	18.9	33.8	69.2	21.3	9.5
Garment	35.5	17.6	46.9	52.0	17.9	30.1
Wood, furniture	58.4	19.2	22.4	70.3	18.5	11.2
Paper, printing	26.0	12.1	61.9	30.8	13.0	56.2
Rubber, plastics	22.6	12.3	65.1	41.5	16.2	42.3
Total manufacturing	22.6	11.7	65.7	30.0	13.3	56.7

Notes:
sme: 20–99 employees
mme: 100–199 employees
mle: more than 199 employees
Source: Barca (1988, p. 45).

(1984). Tables 7.1 and 7.2 provide evidence on manufacturing industries in Italy, where the average size of manufacturing firms continued to fall throughout the 1980s (Table 7.1). The picture is unchanged if we look at the shares of value added by firms' size (Table 7.2).

2.1   *A theoretical background*

For a long time, small firms were viewed as an inferior good, bound to disappear as the process of concentration in industrial activities developed.

Steindl's approach (1945) is one example. Rents originating from innovation and latent economies of scale give some firms weapons and motives to increase market share. In the process "marginal" firms, where average cost is near price, are driven out of the market. Mainly because of capital market imperfections, being small implies a marginal position (but not the contrary); as witnessed by high infant mortality, small firms rarely grow. Steindl lists labor market imperfections and the existence of "local" product markets to explain small firms' permanence and formation. Small entrepreneurs often show "gambling attitudes" as they "accept unusually high risks at a low remuneration," because of social status of entrepreneurs but also because "they are in a position to reduce their remuneration in real terms to any amount, whereas as wage-earners they would not be able to get employment by offering themselves at a lower rate" (1945, p. 60). Some of these arguments are echoed in a very stimulating work by Wellisz (1957) on Italian manufacturing. The continued existence of small firms is made to depend on rigidities in the large firms' structure (mainly due to "firing constraints"), opening up room for peak demand subcontracting. Small firms supply "unprofitable" markets for inferior and luxury versions of manufactured goods. But, above all, they take advantage of the large labor cost differential across firms' size, due to the existence of a segmented labor market. The "negative" evaluation of small firms was also based on their low degree of capitalization and the "primitive" type of internal organization. Many of Wellisz's remarks are still relevant, but the main prediction does not seem to be confirmed by recent developments: during the prolonged stagnation following the oil shocks, the relative importance of small firms increased and appears not to have declined in the subsequent recovery.

2.2   *Development stages*

The end of the first stage of development may be placed around 1973. Its main features were the rapid increase of the relative weight of manufacturing activities compared to agriculture, the growth of the average size of industrial firms, and the increase of vertical integration. The concentration of employment and productive activities in the industrialized North-West drove migratory flows from the South, but also from the peripheral areas of the Center and North-East.

In the early 1960s, however, industrial activities began to diffuse in peripheral areas of the North-West itself (outside the metropolitan areas) and, to a lesser extent, in the North-East and Center. This phenomenon, known in the literature as a "filtering down" process, finds its explanation in the emergence of diseconomies of agglomeration and productive polarization in the highly urbanized areas, and in the improvement in communication and transport systems.

The picture begins to change after the 1973 oil shock. In the first place, the overall growth rate of the economy slows down as in the rest of the industrialized world. Secondly, the trends of division of labor and social organizations that prevailed until then change in both intensity and direction. Industrial employment declines, while service employment vigorously takes off. The average size of firms declines too, as a consequence of job-shedding by the large firms and of the rising role of small-size enterprises. Migration flows towards the North-West, the large metropolitan areas, and also towards the stronger areas of Northern Europe, come to a halt. Industrial employment continues to increase in the North-East and in some areas of Southern Italy.

These changes are too radical and abrupt to find simple explanations in terms of hypotheses of saturation of the North-West. What appears to be changing is the relation between the large enterprise and the territory in which it traditionally operates: instead of centralizing the major share of economic activities in the large urban areas, the system operates in such a way as to shift an important share of activities towards the local economies.

2.3   Recent trends in industrial organization

Industrial restructuring – in Italy as elsewhere – has been the response to technological advances, greater uncertainty in factor and product markets, fiercer competition in open economies, implying a general reassignment of roles between the organization and a market. What one observes is the reduction of plant and firm size (in terms of employment), and the increased turnover among small firms that enter and leave the market at higher pace than in the past.

The structure of vertical and horizontal integration of production has undergone important changes in the 1970s and in the 1980s: the externalization of functions has been a characterizing feature of many business firms that have decided to buy intermediate products and business services from outside firms, rather than providing them from within their own structure.

The division of labor *vis-à-vis* the increasing size of the market had been theorized two hundred years ago by Adam Smith, and almost forty years ago by George Stigler. Nowadays this process takes place also in the face of shrinking markets, but it develops along new dimensions. Two examples are provided by the networks of firms that generate externalities to the surrounding economy, and by the relations between central and peripheral areas where unskilled labor intensive operations can be subcontracted to a low-cost workforce.

Economic growth leads to a higher degree of product standardization that helps to capture the benefits of scale economies. In parallel with this, wealthier consumers demand more sophisticated products. Intermediate services respond to the need of differentiation both with regard to product characteristics (market studies, design, assistance service) and by providing an appropriate distribution system (wholesale, merchandising, transportation). Hence the increasing integration of the service sectors with manufacturing activities. The emergence of new technologies that favor small batch and customized production adds to the factors leading to the reassignment of roles between the organization and the market. Advances in information technology, the need for developing ideas and new products, all require organization forms characterized by a high degree of flexibility. The theory of the product life cycle itself suggests that innovations in the early stages of life need flexible manufacturing systems. Hence the need to redesign organizational functions in order to enhance the development of innovative products.

In periods of slow growth and uncertainty of demand, firms are exposed to the risk of finding their fixed, specialized structures severely underutilized. In these circumstances the incentive to resolve the "make or buy" option by delegating the supply of business services or intermediate goods to outside firms is strong, to the extent that these functions can be separated from the main productive process without affecting its efficiency. Thus new demand is created for intermediate products and business services, and market niches open up attracting new enterprises.

The new business organization appears to emerge in two distinct ways. The first is through the transformation of the corporation. Large organizations are developing more flexible internal structures, by decentralizing authority and giving greater autonomy to the different organizational components. A second form which the new business organization may take is by way of local or regional networks of small enterprises: such networks insure continuity and stability where any single business unit may be shortlived, and supply services which no single organization is capable of providing for itself.

The long-run trend of the division of labor in Italian industry is well

Table 7.3. *Subcontracting firms, as % of total number of firms*

	Italy		Japan
	1973	1984	1971
Food, beverages and tobacco	4.5	14.8	30.2
Textiles	18.3	54.4	75.4
Garment	18.7	43.1	71.7
Footwear, leather	8.1	30.5	64.5
Wood products	4.5	16.3	46.0
Metal manufacturing	12.0	52.9	66.0
Machinery (electronics and electrical)	11.7	28.5	75.2
Motor vehicles	12.6	30.6	77.2
Stone, clay, glass and concrete	3.7	16.5	33.7
Chemicals	6.8	20.8	38.4
Rubber products	6.4	n.a.	53.4
Paper products	5.0	12.9	43.8
Printing and publishing	10.7	36.3	51.0

Source: Italy: Mediocredito Centrale (1984); Japan: Ministry of Small and Medium Business, Japan (1973).

described by Table 7.3: the percentage of firms that operate as sub-contractors increases by three to five times in all industries between 1973 and 1984. The comparison with Japan is eloquent, and requires little explanation. Another piece of evidence is provided by Table 7.4. In 1977–1984 the ratio of value added to sales declined by almost four percentage points (from 32 percent to 28 percent) in manufacturing industries: increased purchases of services and intermediate goods contributed to the observed changes.

2.4   The development of local economies in Italy: the NEC model

A feature of the Italian economy is the diffusion and development of systems of local economies, after referred to as the NEC (for North–East–Center) model of Italian development. This process has taken place in areas that were peripheral with respect to the regions of traditional industrialization of North-West Italy, and – to some extent – also to the Southern regions of the country which became targets of projects of heavy industrialization after the late 1950s, largely subsidized by public intervention. This process has drawn the attention of many economists, sociologists and political scientists. The roots of its development have been traced back to the history of the regions that were protagonists of

Table 7.4. *Percentage of value added to sales in manufacturing industries, by firm size, Italy, 1978 and 1984*

| | Firm size (employees) | | | | | | | |
| | 11–100 | | 101–500 | | >500 | | Total | |
	1978	1984	1978	1984	1978	1984	1978	1984
Food	15.7	14.4	21.3	18.7	30.9	24.2	20.2	18.0
Textiles	38.4	29.7	36.6	30.3	38.5	40.4	37.8	31.3
Garment	39.8	33.8	40.8	35.1	43.3	34.7	41.1	34.4
Leather	30.9	26.6	32.2	28.2	29.8	29.4	31.2	27.4
Furniture	35.7	30.4	33.5	29.5	35.1	33.0	35.1	30.2
Total	25.7	23.7	29.7	26.1	34.9	29.0	28.6	25.4
Metalworking[a]	38.3	34.7	37.1	37.2	36.8	30.7	37.4	34.1
Electrical								
equipment[b]	39.6	36.0	39.3	38.2	45.1	37.0	42.5	37.1
Vehicles	39.2	36.2	36.8	33.4	33.0	31.3	33.8	32.0
Total	38.8	35.0	37.7	36.9	37.9	32.9	38.1	34.4
Primary metal	26.5	20.7	27.2	23.0	29.9	22.8	28.5	22.5
Chemical	27.3	26.5	29.7	24.4	22.0	16.9	24.2	19.6
Paper	29.7	26.7	31.6	25.7	29.7	27.9	30.2	26.9
Total	27.5	25.0	29.1	24.2	24.6	19.1	26.0	21.2
Clay, glass	41.8	35.4	42.4	35.7	38.8	41.5	41.1	36.5
Printing	46.2	43.8	47.3	40.3	46.7	40.3	46.7	41.3
Total								
manufacturing	30.9	28.5	33.3	30.4	32.6	27.8	32.2	28.8

Notes:
[a] Fabricated metal products, machinery (except electrical), office equipment and electronics.
[b] Electrical equipment and supplies, precision instruments.
Source: Mediocredito Centrale (1987, p. 46).

the NEC model. The NEC areas are characterized by a high density of rural villages and small towns where handicrafts have been developed since the Middle Ages. The agriculture is based on small private holdings or sharecropping. The rural milieu and the surrounding commercial towns are connected by highly developed exchanges in nature and trade between the rural regions. There are strong traditions of independent forms of work and crafts, both in the countryside and in the neighboring urban areas. The social structure is based on a system of "extended family" and neighborhood networks, with a high degree of participation in community life and interests, and solidly rooted social integration.

Vast industrial relocations have taken place in the North-Eastern and Central regions of the country since the late 1960s. Table 7.5 shows output and employment indicators of 1973 and 1981 for some significant industries. The traditionally industrialized North-West (area A) loses terrain to the NEC regions (area B) in all sectors both in terms of gross output and of employment. Area C represents the industrializing regions of the Center-South, while area D includes the backward regions of the Mezzogiorno. Both areas C and D fall within the reach of activity of the Cassa di Mezzogiorno, a government agency that provides important financial and fiscal incentives to relocating enterprises and new ventures. Our indicators show minor changes with respect to the shares of such areas.

Relocation patterns between areas A and B are very clear both in the traditional commodity sectors, as well as in some technologically advanced industries: the electrical engineering industry is particularly astounding. In a period of eight years the sector has completely changed its appearance, in terms of prevailing location, but not so much, however, employment-wise. This suggests that not only has relocation taken place at very rapid pace, but also that average productivity must have risen at a tremendous speed in the new establishments of area B compared to the pace in area A. Not surprisingly, the sectors in which area B enjoyed a comparative advantage at the beginning of the observation period (the traditional industries), are those in which relative expansion has been slower.

Italian economists and social scientists have given explanations for this process in terms of cultural, political and economic motives.[2] All the regions were traditionally heavily agricultural, with a prevalence of small private ownership of the land. The fast modernization of agriculture in the 1960s released enormous human resources and a high potential for entrepreneurial behavior. Italy thus became fertile ground for small-scale industrial ventures, which did not even require injections of outside finance, as local savings were traditionally high. Local governments were supportive of the emerging patterns of small-scale industrialization, regardless of political ideology (both Christian Democrat and Communist). Networks of complementary enterprises began to spring up, giving rise to industrial districts that generated important externalities to the surrounding economies. This process started in the course of a historical period in which the advantages of mass production were becoming less important *vis-à-vis* other, more flexible, modes of production. Such timing of events was, obviously, not a mere coincidence.

Table 7.5. *Industrial relocation, shares of gross output and employment among Italy's geographical areas*

Industry		Output 1973	Output 1981	Employment 1973	Employment 1981
Basic chemicals	A	66	65	66	59
(20)	B	19	22	17	20
	C	8	11	8	8
	D	7	2	9	12
Glass, concrete, tiles	A	24	21	23	20
(24)	B	57	60	56	58
	C	12	12	14	15
	D	7	7	7	7
Machinery	A	62	55	61	58
(32)	B	37	44	37	40
	C	1	1	2	2
	D	–	–	–	–
Electrical engineering	A	70	21	70	66
(34)	B	18	75	19	20
	C	12	4	10	13
	D	–	–	1	1
Food products	A	33	31	32	30
(41)	B	43	45	37	40
	C	20	21	25	25
	D	4	3	6	5
Garments	A	47	41	43	40
(45)	B	44	51	45	48
	C	8	7	11	10
	D	1	1	1	2
Wood products	A	36	30	32	30
(46)	B	56	62	57	60
	C	7	7	9	9
	D	1	1	2	1

Note:
Geographical areas:
A = North-West (Piemonte, Liguria, Lombardia).
B = North-East & Center (Veneto, Friuli-Venezia-Giulia, Emilia-Romagna, Toscana, Umbria, Marche).
C = Center-South (Lazio, Abruzzi-Molise, Campania, Puglia).
D = South and Islands (Basilicata, Calabria, Sicilia, Sardegna).
Source: ISTAT, surveys on value added.

One of the striking aspects of the NEC model of industrialization is the degree of product specialization often found in many local economies. For instance, 60 percent of production of women's stockings takes place in a district (Castelgoffredo) whose resident population is less than 100,000. More than half of Italy's exports of glass frames originate from the Cadore area (total population of about 35,000). Almost 80 percent of jewelry production is concentrated in three areas: Arezzo and Vicenza (two good examples of diversified industrial districts), and Valenza Po, a small town of 15,000 people where jewelry making absorbs 90 percent of local manufacturing activities. Close to 60 percent of tile manufacturing takes place in the Sassuolo area, near Bologna.

Many more examples could be provided, all underpinning the high degree of specialization characterizing many industrial districts of older and newer development. Whether there is anything special about Italy's NEC model is an open question, and it is indeed a difficult question to answer, mainly because the NEC model originated no more than thirty years ago, often much more recently than that. If one's imagination is caught by the degree of product specialization (as illustrated above), the immediate association evokes much more ancient and famous examples of industrial districts all over Europe. A second, related, question is whether the NEC model represents a transitory or "stable" form of social and industrial organization. Becattini (1962) lists the conditions under which Italian districts may survive.

3. The new role of small firms: a more complex picture

The somewhat new role of Italian small firms has been emphasized by Barca (1988), who tries to interpret the recent development of the Italian economy in the light of the model of flexible specialization (Piore and Sabel, 1984). Barca's agruments are similar to those outlined in Section 2 above. After analyzing the reorganization of large concerns, he argues that the gap between small and large firms in terms of labor productivity, wages (Table 7.6) and capital–labor ratio shrank significantly between 1975 and 1985. However, small firms still lag behind large ones in terms of machinery and equipment per employee (Table 7.7).

Barca is very cautious in predicting a continued growth of small firms' economic importance. Their major weakness is seen in a difficulty in keeping up with the pace of innovation in the production process.

Incidentally, Barca dismisses as of minor importance the "neo-Schumpeterian" view according to which small firms, because of their flexible structure and the risky attitudes of small entrepreneurs, may be

Table 7.6. *Productivity and wage differentials between small and large firms, 1973, 1980 and 1985, 2 digit manufacturing industries, Italy*

Industry	Productivity[a]			Wage[b]		
	1973	1980	1985	1973	1980	1985
Stone, clay, glass	71	74	79	68	81	83
Chemical	73	96	99	68	81	84
Fabricated metal products	84	102	97	71	89	87
Non-electrical machinery	86	89	93	67	84	90
Electrical machinery	88	100	96	75	88	87
Motor vehicles	88	118	94	63	91	98
Aircraft, ship building	91	105	92	67	87	93
Precision instruments	108	107	92	79	92	86
Food and kindred products	82	102	90	69	84	78
Sugar, spirits	89	108	104	67	89	90
Textiles	83	98	100	73	89	89
Footwear, leather	72	79	130	63	75	99
Garment	78	80	73	73	81	76
Wood, furniture	70	86	87	73	86	81
Paper, printing	73	84	75	60	70	71
Rubber, plastics	80	91	100	66	77	85

Notes:
[a] Ratio of productivity in firms with 20–99 employees to productivity in firms with more than 199 employees.
[b] Ratio of average wages in firms with 20–99 employees to average wages in firms with more than 199 employees.
Source: Barca (1988, p. 69) based on ISTAT value added survey.

more responsive to innovation opportunities. The argument is empirical and it is based on ISTAT surveys on the introduction of new technologies and organizational changes; it is obviously confined to the Italian case, where two important exceptions can be found.[3]

To these warnings it is appropriate to add some evidence pointing to the great degree of turbulence that appears to characterize the small and very small firms, quite independently from the industry where they operate. Since data on firm and workforce turnover became available only at the end of the 1970s, it is difficult to tell whether turbulence was much lower in the previous decade than we have witnessed in recent years.

Assessing the dispersion in the growth rates of small firms, the magnitude of demographic flows and of labor mobility across firms' size may

Table 7.7. *Machinery per employee in Italian manufacturing, 1978 and 1984, million lire, 1978 prices*

| | Firm's size (employees) | | | | | | | |
| | 11–100 | | 101–500 | | > 500 | | > 11 | |
	1978	1984	1978	1984	1978	1984	1978	1984
Food	13.5	18.4	14.8	19.9	16.6	18.7	14.7	18.9
Textiles	7.7	11.7	9.0	12.8	8.9	11.5	8.5	12.1
Garment	2.3	2.2	2.1	2.6	2.7	5.0	2.3	2.8
Leather	2.9	4.3	2.9	4.8	3.4	4.3	2.9	4.5
Furniture	6.2	7.5	7.8	10.2	6.6	6.7	6.5	8.1
Total	7.0	9.1	7.8	11.1	9.1	12.2	7.7	10.3
Metalworking[a]	7.2	9.6	7.3	11.1	8.6	12.3	7.6	10.8
Electrical equipment[b]	6.0	7.2	7.0	7.2	8.8	9.1	7.8	8.2
Motor vehicles	8.0	9.0	6.9	9.8	15.0	18.9	13.5	16.7
Total	6.9	9.0	7.2	9.9	11.1	13.7	9.0	11.4
Primary metal	16.1	17.9	15.9	19.9	24.3	48.8	21.3	37.7
Chemical	12.8	15.0	15.6	22.9	35.9	42.4	25.6	32.3
Paper	15.1	17.9	15.8	24.9	40.6	52.2	23.9	31.0
Total	14.3	16.5	15.7	22.4	30.9	45.6	23.6	33.8
Clay, glass	11.4	13.3	15.7	25.6	22.3	17.6	14.8	17.9
Printing	7.9	11.8	7.2	8.6	7.2	9.2	7.5	10.0
Aggregate manufacturing	8.2	10.3	9.2	13.2	15.9	20.7	14.8	16.6

Notes:
[a] Fabricated metal products, machinery (except electrical), office equipment and electronics.
[b] Electrical equipment and supplies, precision instruments.
Source: Mediocredito Centrale (1987, p. 58).

help to qualify the role of small firms and to avoid excessively optimistic views. Structural and cyclical components may partially explain the large reallocation of resources observed among small firms. Depending upon its magnitude and characteristics, the "residual" turbulence can be considered "physiological," implicitly stressing the social benefits of "trade," or "pathological," as a sign of inherent weakness.

3.1   *The birth and death of small businesses*

The subject of birth and death of firms has for many years been relatively neglected by economists. Even though never mentioned explicitly, the question of the life cycle of firms which operate in a competitive market was already present in Marshall's analysis. As Becattini (1962) reminds us, the Marshall system rested on two cornerstones: "a socio–biological principle of exchange between firms in an industry, according to which each firm goes through a life-cycle including all phases of the human organism, and the postulate of free access to the industry." As already remarked, Steindl added several qualifications to Marshall's notion of competition. Quoting Becattini (1962) again, "there will be a continuous ebb and flow between workers and small rentiers, on the one side, and the smallest firms in all industries, on the other side . . . Competition . . . will therefore be the typical form of movement of an industrial structure in which a stable core of large and medium firms coexists with a group of small firms, individually destined to fail, but socially condemned to multiply and perpetuate themselves." The elimination of the least efficient firms is due to an excess of production capacity over demand which periodically affects innovative oligopolistic industries.

During the 1970s a number of interpretations involving the supply side were also put forward. Changes in the level of vertical integration of the industry, as well as in the expenditure composition of the affluent societies, provide important explanations. As the division of labor deepens, production processes tend to destructure. New demand is created for the intermediate products and services of a firm, and opportunities and incentives open up for new firms to set up to satisfy them. The worsening of employment prospects (income and job duration) may reduce the threshold of acceptance of entrepreneurial risks, increasing the supply of "small" entrepreneurs. In fact, during the decade of prolonged stagnation 1973–1983, common to all industrialized countries, many small firms entered on the scene in both the manufacturing and the service sector.

An accurate discussion of the determinants of new firms' formation is beyond the scope of this chapter.[4] However, Tables 7.8 and 7.9 highlight important aspects of firm demography. Yearly birth rates are fairly high (10–13 percent) and are influenced by the general economic climate: in the expansion period 1978–1980 entry rates were, on average, 1.3 points higher than in the recession years 1981–1983, in 1984–1986 they began to rise again, especially in the service sector. Death rates appear to be less sensitive to changing economic circumstances, and remain in general one or two points below the birth rate (the gap between birth and death rates

Table 7.8. *Birth and death of firms in Northern and Southern Italy, 1978–1986*

	Births			Deaths		
	Annual rate	% small firms[a]	% jobs created[b]	Annual rate	% small firms[a]	% jobs destroyed[b]
Manufacturing			*Piemonte region*			
1978–80	0.135	93.6	n.a.	0.099	90.2	n.a.
1981–83	0.103	92.4	42.0	0.096	88.7	30.9
1984–86	0.122	94.1	28.0	0.102	89.3	28.6
services						
1978–80	0.138	97.3	n.a.	0.105	96.0	n.a.
1981–83	0.123	97.0	37.8	0.096	95.6	31.1
1984–86	0.135	98.3	35.7	0.105	96.4	31.2
Manufacturing			*Puglia region*			
1981–83	0.123	97.4	38.5	0.097	97.5	29.4
1984–86	0.113	96.5	38.6	0.119	91.7	41.2
services						
1981–83	0.117	99.4	39.1	0.116	99.4	36.7
1984–86	0.131	99.4	43.7	0.117	99.3	41.4

Notes:
[a] Small new firms on total new firms; the definition of "small firms" is 1–5 employees for the Piemonte region, 1–19 employees for the Puglia region.
[b] On total number of created (or destroyed) jobs.
Source: R&P statistics on social security files of firms with dependent workers.

is however greater in periods of expansion). The great majority of new firms are extremely small: out of 100 new firms, around 90 in the manufacturing sector began activity with less than six employees. The combined movement of entry and exit of new firms led to a notable increase in the proportion of small firms in 1978–1980; in the following three years the growth was more modest. The probability of survival of a new firm is also modest: around 30 percent of new firms do not survive beyond the third year of activity and, not surprisingly, the chances of early closure increase as initial size lowers.

The image of industry suggested by these observations is fairly similar to the one outlined above. A hard core of industrial firms with all the textbook prerequisites and close to the "minimum efficient size" (MES) coexists with a fringe of small marginal producers, often destined to

Table 7.9. *Infant mortality rates in 1978–1982 and in 1981–1986, manufacturing industries*

(a) *Probability of closure in the first 3 years of operation, Italy, 1978–1982*

	Clay/ glass	Fabricated metal prod.	Precision instruments	Food	Textiles	Garment
North-West	0.26	0.33	0.27	0.29	0.33	0.40
North-East	0.24	0.28	0.25	0.29	0.37	0.37
Center	0.28	0.30	0.32	0.36	0.37	0.30
South	0.30	0.39	0.21	0.35	0.22	0.37

(b) *Percentage of new firms closing in 1981–1983 and in 1984–1986, by firm's size, Torino area, manufacturing*

	Firms closing in 1981–1983 out of 100 born		Firms closing in 1984–1986 out of 100 born	
Size	Before 1978	In 1978–1981	Before 1981	In 1981–1983
0–5	27	45	38	47
6–19	18	31	25	35
20–49	18	18	21	36

Source: R&P statistics on social security files of firms.

remain such all their lives, characterized by a high degree of turbulence both in entry and exit. We can image a continuum of firm size with a threshold S to the left of which there is free entry and exit. The average life of a firm in this area is short, as there is a high risk of early death. To the right of S we find the hard core of industries, where firms will tend to settle around an optimal or semi-optimal size which varies from sector to sector. These firms have longer average life than the marginal firms.

3.2 *The role of small firms in job creation*

Evidence on the role of small firms in the job-creation process is presented in Table 7.10, which refers to firms operating in the Piemonte region (Northern Italy).[5] In the expansion period 1978–1980, while total employment in Piemonte grew by about 17,000 jobs a year, net job creation in small firms (under 20 employees) was around 30,000 a year. In the three recession years 1981–1983 a yearly average of 21,000 jobs

Table 7.10. *Piemonte region, job creation in the private sector, annual average, thousands*

	All firms	1–20 employees	Other firms
1978–1980 (expansion)			
Manufacturing	+ 11	+ 21	− 10
Services	+ 6	+ 9	− 3
Total	+ 17	+ 30	− 13
1981–1983 (recession)			
Manufacturing	− 23	0	− 23
Services	+ 2	+ 2	0
Total	− 21	+ 2	− 23
1984–1986 (moderate recovery)			
Manufacturing	− 11	+ 6	− 17
Services	− 4	+ 5	− 9
Total	− 15	+ 11	− 26
1987–1988 (expansion)			
Manufacturing	+ 1	+ 6	− 5
Services	+ 5	+ 8	− 3
Total	+ 6	+ 14	− 8

Source: R&P statistics on social security files.

were destroyed, whereas in small firms we find once again a slight positive net difference. Despite the upturn in the economy from 1984–1986, jobs in industry continued to contract (11,000 jobs a year); small firms however created about 6,000 new jobs. This implies that the firms with more than 20 employees destroyed in reality 17,000 jobs a year. Expansion reached a peak in 1987–1988 when net employment was once more positive (+6,000 jobs): small firms created about 14,000 jobs, far fewer than in the period of expansion, but nevertheless a considerable number. Employment in large firms fell by a further 8,000 confirming the reduction in the average size of firms.

A similar pattern of job creation was found in other countries (see, for instance, Loveman and Sengenberger, 1991) and sometimes used as evidence that gains in employment were going to come mainly from the small firms. The results need some "statistical" qualification: this way of presenting flows hides possible random movements around the selected size threshold, i.e. 20 employees.[6] Much more important is, however, the fact that net job creation is the result of huge flows of positive and

Table 7.11. *Employment changes as percentage of total workforce by firm size, manufacturing, Piemonte region, 1982–1988*

All firms	1982	1984	1986	1988
Total job creation	6.6	6.4	8.2	7.8
of which, due to births	3.2	1.7	2.1	1.5
Total job destruction	8.0	11.8	8.0	7.1
of which, due to closures	1.2	3.1	2.0	2.3

Small firms (1–20 employees)[a]	1982	1984	1986	1988
Total job creation	16.6	18.0	20.3	14.5
of which, due to births	6.0	5.2	6.3	3.6
Total job destruction	14.8	16.2	13.8	10.5
of which, due to closures	4.3	6.2	5.7	3.0
Employment share in firms below 20 employees	0.176	0.192	0.203	0.252
Total workforce	438,333	391,105	393,840	400,397

Note: [a] Changes as percentage of workforce in firms below 20 employees.
Source: R&P statistics on social security files.

negative size changes. In other words, the size of the small firms (and the related labor demand) is subject to wide and frequent shocks.

Table 7.11 qualifies the statement. Overall job creation and destruction amounts on average to 8 percent of the employment at the end of the year; entry and exit of firms accounts for one-third to one-quarter of the gain and losses in employment. The employment share of firms with less than 20 employees was 17 percent in 1982 and had reached 25 percent by 1988. Related to their employment, jobs created by small firms range from 15 to 20 percent; job losses average 15 percent of the relevant labor force. Simple calculation based on reported figures indicates the importance of small firms both in creating and in destroying jobs. For instance, in 1986 small firms were responsible for slightly more than 50 percent of all new jobs, for 35 percent of all lost jobs. More striking figures would obviously be obtained by looking at the service sector. Comparable figures can found in Loveman and Sengenberger (1991) and in Davis and Haltiwanger (1989). According to the latter, in the United States the opening of new factories created 20 percent of all new jobs every year and closures accounted for 25 percent of jobs destroyed (in their study Davis and Haltiwanger exclude all establishments with less than five employees).

Table 7.12. *Percentage of expanding and shrinking firms in manufacturing, Piemonte region*

	Firm's size (employees)								
Growth	0–5			6–19			20–49		
+40% < g	29[a]	21[b]	29[c]	15[a]	10[b]	19[c]	8[a]	5[b]	9[c]
+5% < g < +40%	5	6	8	24	19	28	24	15	29
−5% < g < +5%	43	41	39	14	15	17	20	20	19
−40% < g < −5%	7	11	9	32	38	27	37	47	35
g < −40%	15	21	15	15	19	9	11	13	9
Observed no. firms.	8387	8876	5222	3612	3655	2652	1138	1064	729

Notes:
a 1978–1980 expansion. b 1981–1983 recession. c 1984–1986 recovery.
g: percentage rate of employment change over 3 years.
Source: R&P statistics on social security files of firms.

3.3 Patterns of expansion and contraction of small firms

Growth profiles of small firms throw further light on the strong random components in the size of these firms. In Table 7.12 firms are classified according to their size at the beginning of each of the selected three-year periods (1978–1980, 1981–1983, 1984–1986) *and* to their employment growth rate during the period (e.g. "great expansion" in 1981–1983 stands for an employment increase of 40 percent or more between 1981 and 1983).

A surprisingly small fraction of firms exhibits a "stable" employment profile (growth rate between −5 percent and + 5 percent) in the three periods: around 15 percent in the size class 6–19 employees, 20 percent in the size class 20–49. Somewhat surprisingly, among the very small firms (1–5 employees) "stable" profiles come close to 40 percent. In this size class, the growth rate is very sensitive to small employment changes, so that the distinction between stability and growth (or decline) is not clear cut. Furthermore, since a small employment decline may result in exit from the sample, the evidence on very small firms may be affected by a truncation bias. Finally, the social security records (on which these statistics are based) do not show the "irregular" and family component of the workforce: their inclusion may significantly lower the percentage of "stable" firms.

The patterns of expansion and contraction vary with the cycle, independently of the firm's size. The percentage of firms increasing their employment is higher in the two expansion periods 1978–1980 and 1984–1986, lower in the 1981–1983 recession. The percentage of shrinking firms follows the opposite pattern. The number of stable firms, on the other hand, remained almost constant.

Table 7.13. *Birth and death rates, employment growth and turnover in expanding and declining industries, Torino area, firms below 20 employees*

Industry code		Birth rate	Death rate	Employment growth rate		Annual rate gross job turnover
				> +40%	< −40%	
330	81–83	12.1	5.4	16.1	9.0	33.0
	84–86	15.6	4.1	16.7	3.9	11.3
421	81–83	13.0	5.1	13.0	7.7	21.1
	84–86	17.1	7.2	16.2	9.0	36.1
343	81–83	12.0	6.1	11.6	11.5	24.2
	84–86	12.3	7.3	25.4	6.7	22.9
451	81–83	5.8	6.0	10.8	13.7	31.3
	84–86	9.0	10.4	9.0	6.6	43.0
322	81–83	4.6	3.8	8.1	12.5	30.9
	84–86	7.1	3.8	18.0	7.1	18.6

Notes:
Fast-growing industries
330 electronics and office equipment.
421 confectionary industry.
343 electrical equipment for the car industry and other uses.
Declining and restructuring industries
451 footwear industry.
322 machine tools for metal working.
Source: R&P statistics on social security files.

3.4   Features of rapidly growing and declining industries

Areas of great turbulence, high entry and exit rates, firms which either grow or contract dramatically and high job turnover can be found in extremely different industries, technologically advanced and traditional ones, rapidly expanding and declining ones. Table 7.13 reports some demographic and development indicators on five industries showing a very different evolution in the period 1981–1986. The attention is confined to firms with less than 20 employees, operating in the Piemonte region.

Electronics and office equipment (ISTAT code 330) experienced a fast growth of output and jobs. Rapid expansion of output and moderate job growth characterized the confectionary industry (421) and the production of electrical equipment for the car industry (343). The footwear industry (451) and the machine tools for metal working (322) underwent restructuring and rapid employment decline.

Birth of new firms is very high in the three expanding sectors (330, 421, 343) both in the 1981–1983 recession and particularly during the 1984–1986 upturn. The birth rate is lower in the other two industries but far from insignificant, considering that we are dealing with industries in rapid employment decline. The death rates, on the other hand, are very similar in four of the five industries in 1981–1983 with a minimum in sector 322, which was the one most affected by restructuring processes. In 1984–1986 the exit rate fell in electronics (330), remained steady at a low level in sector 322 and rose in the other three sectors.

The percentage of "rapidly expanding" or "rapidly contracting" firms (employment growth rate exceeding 40 percent in absolute value) is not correlated with industry-specific trends. It may be hardly surprising that over 16 percent of firms in the electronics sector have been growing for the whole period. But, unexpectedly, in 1984–1986 18 percent of the small firms in industry 322 and 25 percent of those in industry 343 experienced a large employment growth. Conversely, also in expanding industries (e.g. 343) the number of rapidly contracting firms was high. In the two sectors of decreasing employment, the frequency of dramatic job losses lessened in the second period.

Another sign of great turbulence is provided by the average annual rate of gross job turnover (ratio of created plus lost jobs in each firm to total employment). The rate is very high in all five industries (11–43 percent), irrespective of the specific industry trends and of the economic cycle.

3.5 The concentration of job creation and destruction

Another way to characterize size changes is to build concentration curves of positive and negative employment changes at the firms' level. The procedure is straightforward. We separate growing firms from declining ones and sort each set by the magnitude of associated employment changes. It can then be found, for instance, which percentage of new jobs is created by the top 5 or 20 percent more "creative" firms. In Table 7.14a further distinction is made between firms active throughout the 1981–1986 period and those born in 1981–1983, for which separate concentration curves are built. The focus is on firms with fewer than 20 employees in 1981. In branch 3, for instance, out of 100 new jobs created during the years 1984–1986 by firms *existing both in 1981 and in 1986*,

21 came from the top 5 percent fastest growing firms, 51 from the "top" 20 percent. Out of 100 new jobs created during the years 1984–1986 by firms *born in 1981–1983*, 22 were generated by the top 5 percent fastest growing firms.

There are very few differences across branches and, more surprisingly, between the 1981–1983 recession period and the 1984–1986 expansion years. The top 5 percent of growing firms already existing in the former period created about 25 percent of all new jobs, the top 20 percent accounted altogether for 50 percent of new jobs; the remaining 50 percent of new jobs were created by the other 80 percent of (slower) growing firms. The concentration of job creation and destruction is similar in the set of firms born in 1981–1983: this suggests, contrary to what is normally claimed, that the employment growth of new firms is no different from that of existing ones. As for layoffs, the 5 percent fastest contracting firms (most of which left the market during the observation period) were responsible for about 20 percent of all layoffs, with no difference between observation periods.

A question may arise as to whether the sectoral composition of branches is responsible for the observed concentration of job creation and destruction. In Table 7.14b concentration figures are displayed for the five industries presented in section 3.4 which, in a sense, represent extreme cases of employment growth and production technologies in manufacturing. A quick glance at the table reveals striking regularities in the concentration statistics, with a small variance across industries; as before, the figures refer to firms with less than 20 employees.

What emerges is a picture in which industrial sectors, whether in expansion or decline, whether using advance technologies or techniques that are considered (maybe erroneously) old-fashioned, display areas of great turbulence. Despite the apparent homogeneity of sectors, there is in reality great heterogeneity within each one. In all five industries, we find that 20 percent of the new jobs are created by the top 5 percent growing firms. Similarly 18 percent of job losses are accounted for by the fastest declining 5 percent of firms.

Davis and Haltiwanger (1989) calculated the percentage of job creation and destruction by growth rate. Their analysis is carried out on a sample of establishments stratified according to size, from which businesses with less than six employees are excluded. Firms with a very high growth rate ($g > 100$ percent) generated about 18 percent of new jobs and those which reduced their workforce drastically ($g < -50$ percent) were responsible for about 24 percent of the overall job loss (excluding loss due to closures). The remaining 82 percent of new jobs and 76 percent of

Table 7.14. *Concentration of job creation and destruction in firms below 20 employees*

(a) By branches, Piemonte region

	% jobs created by					% jobs destroyed by		
	Top 5% firms			Top 20% firms		Top 5% firms		
Branch	1981–83[a]	1984–86[a]	1984–86[b]	1981–83[a]	1984–86[a]	1981–83[a]	1984–86[a]	1984–86[b]
2	22	22	19	52	50	22	18	15
3	24	21	22	45	51	18	22	24
4	24	27	26	54	52	20	21	21
5	25	28	26	59	48	18	20	21
6	22	24	29	53	55	19	20	18
7	27	35	n.a.	55	55	18	24	22
8	23	20	14	46	49	20	11	17

(b) Five 3 digit industries, Torino area

	% jobs created by					% jobs destroyed by	
	Top 5% firms			Top 20% firms		Top 5% firms	
Industry code	1981–83[a]	1984–86[a]	1984–86[b]	1981–83[a]	1984–86[a]	1981–83[a]	1984–86[a]
330	23	17	14	55	46	14	18
421	29	13	16	57	47	21	25
343	21	33	19	51	61	16	15
451	21	18	21	58	53	25	12
322	19	13	9	49	41	21	13

Notes:
[a] Firms born before 1981.
[b] Firms born in 1981–83.
For the definition of branches see Table 7.1; for the definition of industries in part (b), see Table 7.13.

layoffs were therefore in establishments with slower rates of growth–decline.

Monducci and Picozzi (1989) classify Italian firms according to the *yearly* growth rate in the 1983–1987 period; "stable" firms are those experiencing an annual growth rate between −1 percent and + 1 percent. The percentage of "stable" firms is around 13, across size classes. On the other hand, firms displaying an "irregular" pattern of employment increases amount to 32 percent in the size class 1–20 employees; the percentage falls as the firm's size increases, down to 12 percent among large firms. Almost 50 percent of firms above 500 employees show steadily declining employment between 1983 and 1987.

3.6   *Turbulence and the variance of economic performance*

The observed turbulence in the performance of small firms is not a novelty. As can be readily seen, the distribution of positive and negative size changes (job creation and destruction) is closely related to *the variance of the growth rate*. Heteroskedasticity, i.e. a correlation between firms' size and the variance of the random component, is detected in almost every study on employment growth at the firm level, often done through a misspecified labor demand equation; see, for instance, Evans (1987); Hall (1987); Contini (1989). Mansfield (1962, p. 1034) notes that "The growth rate of a large firm can be viewed as the means of the growth rates of its smaller 'components' (e.g. plants)," so that "if the growth rates of the components (plants or otherwise) were independent, the standard deviation would be inversely proportional to the square-root of a firm's size." However, since the plants "tend to be located in the same region and have other similarities, one would expect the growth rate of such components to be positively correlated. Thus, the standard deviation would not be expected to decrease as rapidly with increases in size as the square-root formula suggests." Differences in the variance of growth *at the plant level* are not explained by Mansfield's remarks. One might then resort to technological considerations (rigidities) and to possible spillovers of economies of scale on the randomness of performance. But, in this way, the question of what determines persistence of small firms is brought back to the forefront. The impact of variance on entry is examined in Revelli and Tenga (1989).

3.7   *Labor mobility in the small firms*

A much wider labor mobility must be associated with the flows of jobs created and destroyed by firms. Since jobs differ by quality, type and income offered to the worker, each *new* job triggers a chain of moves of workers across firms; the chain ends when a vacant job is matched by an unemployed worker. This model and some of its implications are discussed in Contini and Revelli (1988) and Akerlof, Rose and Yellen (1988), who stress the role of non-monetary aspects in the worker's choice of job.

This setup brings to the forefront the *EE* type of moves, that is the job-to-job movements of workers without unemployment spells. According to Contini and Revelli (1988) out of 100 separations 60 to 70 are due to workers changing jobs; Akerlof, Rose and Yellen (1988) find somewhat lower percentages for the United States.

Workers' mobility is affected by industry, firms' size and time (cyclical) components. A discussion of these aspects falls outside the scope of this

Table 7.15. *Association and separation rates, Torino, 1981–1983, 1987*
(a) 1981–1983

		Firm's size (employees)						
	0–9		*10–49*		*50–500*		*500+*	
Manufacturing								
1981	36[s]	33[a]	18[s]	22[a]	11[s]	10[a]	11[s]	3[a]
1982	45	50	13	19	18	12	7	6
1983	35	34	14	16	11	12	7	9
Services								
1981	35	39	23	25	16	23	15	13
1982	28	35	22	21	26	21	9	13
1983	29	32	19	18	32	30	9	2

(b) 1987

	Branch 3				*Branch 4*		
<20	*20–99*	*100+*	*Total*	*<20*	*20–99*	*100+*	*Total*
40[a]	16	10	15	41	17	6	17
33[s]	16	12	15	34	21	11	19

	Branch 3+4				*Branch 6*		
<20	*20–99*	*100+*	*Total*	*<20*	*20–99*	*100+*	*Total*
40[a]	16	9	15	45	19	14	36
33[s]	18	12	16	38	24	15	33

Notes:
[a] Association rate: percentage of yearly new hires on employment at the end of the year.
[s] Separation rate: percentage of quits (or layoffs) on employment at the end of the year.
For the definition of branches, see Table 7.1.
Source: R&P statistics on social security files of firms and individual workers.

chapter; reference should be made to the growing literature on job matching. A quick examination of some empirical evidence may suffice to illustrate little known and striking aspects of worker's mobility related to the dynamics of small firms. In Table 7.15 association and separation rates in a Northern industrialized area (Torino) are broken down by year, industry and firms' size.[7]

Remarkable regularities emerge from the table and can be found in other different Italian contexts. Association and separation rates are almost insensitive to the economic cycle: almost the same estimates are obtained in deep recession (1981–1983) and strong expansion years (1987). There are sectoral differences, as *job* turnover is related to the industry composition by firms' size: association and separation are slightly higher in services than in manufacturing. However, the major difference in workers' mobility can be detected across firms' size. For instance, during one year, in manufacturing 30–40 percent of workers in firms below 20 employees quit (or were laid off) to join a new firm or enter unemployment (or to withdraw from the labor force). This percentage falls with firms' size down to less than 10 percent in the large firms' segment.

These figures may be somewhat biased because observed labor mobility is lowered by the existence of an "internal" labor market in the large firms: what surfaces as a move from one small firm to another may be hidden inside a large firm as a move from one job to another. Still the empirical evidence raises important questions. In steady state, the reciprocal of the association rate is a measure of the average job tenure: in the small firms it ranges between 2 and 3 years, in the larger firms it comes close to 10 years.[8] A picture emerges of a "thick" and "segmented" market but, in this case, it is doubtful that improved allocation of resources and welfare derive from higher density of trade.

In the small firms, the very high turnover of workers depends upon the random behavior of labor demand (or the magnitude of job creation and destruction). It is difficult to believe that experience coming from training on the job can be entirely transferred across firms. But then the frequent renewal of portions of the labor force ought to bring about productivity losses. Some of the workers may join large firms from small ones, which would then act as "early trainers" of the labor force. It remains unclear to what extent this conjectured "specialization" works. Even if it were a general feature of the Italian economy, which is doubtful in the light of the above evidence, taking the risks and the costs of training and screening "productive workers" may be beneficial for the system as a whole, but it certainly weakens the position of small firms.

Labour mobility is also related to workers' choices: for any given stock of vacant jobs the actual turnover depends on workers' judgment of their current condition. To some extent, high turnover should then reflect a vast degree of "job dissatisfaction."[9]

4 Wages and labor force composition

Barca (1988) found signs that the gap of wages paid by small and large firms shrank between 1975 and 1985. This is an important issue, as wage differentials may be related to quality of labor, skill composition (often connected to organizational forms) and productivity.

More recent evidence indicates, however, that the gap after 1985 widened remarkably. Table 7.16 shows average wages of manual and non-manual workers by firms' size, in 1984 and in 1988. To get robust results three extremely different areas were considered: Torino and Varese (Northern Italy) and Bari (Southern Italy). A section of Table 7.16 displays the incidence of non-manual workers in total workforce in the years 1984–1988. Apprentices, managers and part-time workers are excluded from these statistics.

The figures are rather impressive and remarkably regular. For instance, setting to 100 the average wage paid to manual workers by firms with more than 100 employees, in the Torino area (branch 3, metalworking, car industry, electronics) workers in firms below 20 employees were paid 89 in 1984 and 79 in 1988; workers in firms with 20–99 employees started with 99 in 1984 but dropped to 92 in 1988. Exactly the same profile can be detected for the non-manual workers (white collar), as well as in other branches and areas. Incidentally, the percentage of non-manual workers has generally increased in the period; however, there remain significant differences across firms' sizes, the very small firms still lagging behind.

Efficiency wages and working conditions have been used as arguments to explain wage differentials across firms' size. According to this view (for the Italian case, see Barca, 1988), workers in the small firms trade off benefits deriving from a more satisfactory working environment (easier human relationships, control over performance, flexible organization of labor, etc.) with monetary wages. In the large firms, the more difficult monitoring of performance calls for a higher "contractual" or fixed portion of wages, above individual productivity, in order to give appropriate incentives to individual workers.

This explanation is not very satisfactory in the light of the widening wage gap. The reduced size of large firms and the huge internal reorganizations should have lowered the monitoring difficulties; along with the declining power of unions, this should have resulted in further shrinking wage differentials.

Perhaps the appropriate explanation of the widening gap has to be found in the structural changes at the beginning of the 1980s. As large firms reorganize, workers with low qualifications and pay are first to exit:

Table 7.16. *Wage differentials and workforce composition, Northern (Torino, Varese) and Southern (Bari) Italian areas, 1984–1988*

		Branch		1984			1988		
				Non-manual workers					
Bari	3	71[a]	91[b]	66[a]	2580[d]	20245[c]	84[b]	29945[c]	2475[d]
Bari	4	64	82	60	2668	20888	72	30800	2603
Torino	3	75	94	69	71826	21546	89	32615	76781
Torino	4	72	89	69	15498	20905	86	30282	17281
Varese	4	71	87	67	7431	20120	83	28525	8746
				Manual workers					
Bari	3	79	97	72	10258	15132	87	22613	8792
Bari	4	64	73	59	19756	15748	67	22545	20359
Torino	3	89	99	79	174287	15109	92	23074	177984
Torino	4	85	93	79	49074	14349	89	21143	47192
Varese	4	83	92	77	47558	14181	87	19981	47782

Percentage of non-manual workers

	Branch	1984				1988			
		<20	21–99	99+	Total	<20	21–99	99+	Total
Bari	3	14	21	24	20	16	26	26	22
Bari	4	8	10	24	12	8	11	24	11
Torino	3	20	26	31	29	20	28	32	30
Torino	4	18	24	26	24	20	24	31	27
Varese	4	10	13	15	14	11	15	18	15

Notes:

[a] Average wages in firms with 1–19 employees as percentage of wages in c.
[b] Average wages in firms with 20–99 employees as percentage of wages in c.
[c] Average wages in firms with more than 99 employees.
[d] Total number of workers.

For the definition of branches see Table 7.1.

Source: R&P statistics on social security files of firms.

average wages are then bound to increase. Besides, in the expansion period (1986–1989), relatively high wages were almost certainly used by large firms to attract skilled workers.

Once again, market segmentation appears to be a more appropriate picture. The small firms get lower-quality workers to be placed in less productive jobs; whatever value workers place on the small-firms' environment they are ready to move as soon as a chance of change is offered. This scenario may not be universal but it certainly applies to a consistent portion of small firms.

5. Concluding remarks

In this chapter we examine the persistence of Italian small firms, which has attracted the attention of economists since the early 1950s, and their more recent growth. Explanations about the role of small firms modified along with the changing pattern of economic development. The early view, according to which small firms were bound to disappear as the markets widened, was challenged by the emergence of rather stable clusters of small firms in the North-Eastern and Central parts of Italy. As in the "industrial district," these networks of firms were often judged to be as efficient in production as larger, centralized organizations. Theories based on local factors cannot, however, explain the more recent and generalized shift towards smaller firm size. New trends in the division of labor and the increased risks connected with "fixed costs" in production should be taken into proper account.

To caution against misleading generalizations about a conjectured new role for small firms, we provide evidence about the turbulence affecting their performance. Entry and exit rates are fairly large; cohorts of entering firms are quickly reduced by high infant mortality rates. As a fraction of the relevant labor force, jobs created by small firms exceed those created by larger firms; but the same is true for job losses. Labor turnover turns out to decline with firm size, so that job tenure is significantly lower in the small firms than in the large ones. There is convincing evidence that wages differentials across firms' size have been widening since 1988. Finally, areas of great turbulence are found in extremely different industries. Since turbulence is related to the variance of economic performance, its connection with size should be investigated from a substantive point of view. So far, this issue has received only occasional attention in the literature.

Notes

1 This section is quoted almost literally from Contini (1989): we thank the author for the permission to reproduce his work.

2 Similar evidence on another important Italian region is provided by Regione Emilia-Romagna (1989).
3 For a different view and empirical results see Acs and Audretsch (1987).
4 There is a vast literature on the subject; more general results (and references) on Italy are contained in Contini and Revelli (1986) and Revelli and Tenga (1989).
5 Reference to the most important contributions can be found in Becattini (1989).
6 A more accurate argument is presented by Leonard (1986).
7 Association and separation rates are estimated from employment records of individual workers and from monthly counts of employment changes at the firm's level; the latter approach is discussed at length in Contini and Revelli (1988).
8 According to Poterba and Summers (1988) job tenure is 2.1 years in the United States.
9 Contrary to what Barca (1988) claims to be a distinguishing feature of small organizations.

References

Acs Z. J. and D. B. Audretsch (1987) "Innovation, Market Structure, and the Firm Size," *The Review of Economics and Statistics*, 4, 567–574.
Akerlof G. A., A. K. Rose and J. L. Yellen (1988) "Job Switching and Job Satisfaction in the U.S. Labor Market," *Brookings Paper on Economic Activity*, 2.
Barca F. (1988) "La dicotomia dell'industria italiana: le strategie delle piccole e delle grandi imprese in un quindicennio di sviluppo economico," Banca d'Italia, *Ristrutturazione economica e finanziaria delle imprese*, Rome.
Becattini G. (1989) "Piccole e medie imprese e distretti industriali nel recente sviluppo italiano," *Note Economiche*, 3, 397–411.
Blanchard O. and P. Diamond (1989) "The Beveridge Curve," *Brookings Paper on Economic Activity*, 1.
Contini B. (1984) "Firm Size and the Division of Labor," *Banca Nazionale del Lavoro Quaterly Review*, 151.
    (1989) "Employment Problems under Structural Adjustment: the Case of Italy," paper presented at the International Symposium on Local Employment, Tokyo (September).
Contini B. and R. Revelli (1986) "Natalità e mortalità delle imprese italiane: risultati preliminari e nuove prospettive di ricerca," *L'industria*, 2.
    (1987) "Job Creation and Job Destruction: the Italian Experience," *Labour*, 3.
    (1988) "Job Creation and Labour Mobility: the Vacancy Chain Model and Some Empirical Findings" unpublished manuscript.
    (1989) "The Relationship between Firm Growth and Labor Demand," *Small Business Economics*, 1, 309–314.
Davis S. T. and J. Haltiwanger (1989) "Gross Job Creation, Gross Job Destruction and Employment Reallocation," unpublished manuscript.

Evans D. S. (1987) "Tests of Alternative Theories of Firm Growth," *Journal of Political Economy*, **95**.

Hall, B. H. (1987) "The Relationship between Firm Size and Firm Growth in the U.S. Manufacturing Sector," *Journal of Industrial Economics*, **35**, 585–605.

Leonard J. S. (1987) "In the Wrong Place at the Wrong Time: the Extent of Frictional Unemployment", in K. Lang and J. Leonard (eds.), *Unemployment and the Structure of the Labour Market*, Oxford: Basil Blackwell.

(1986) "On the Size Distribution of Employment and Establishments," *Working Paper*, **1951**, Cambridge, MA: NBER.

Loveman, Gary and Werner Sengenberger (1991) "The Re-emergence of Small-Scale Production," *Small Business Economics*, **3**, 1–38.

Mansfield, E (1962) "Entry, Gibrat's Law, Innovation, and the Growth of Firms," *American Economic Review* (December) 1023–1051.

Mediocredito Centrale (1984) *Indagine sulle imprese manifatturiere*, vol. 1, Rome.

(1987) *Indagine sulle imprese manufatturiere*, vol. 1, Rome.

Ministry of Small and Medium Business, Japan (1973) *The Fourth Fundamental Survey on Small and Medium Enterprises*.

Monducci and Picozzi (eds.) (1989) "Struttura ed evoluzione dell'occupazione nelle imprese manufatturiere italiane (1983–1987)," *Quaderni di discussione*, ISTAT, Rome.

Pakes A. and R. Ericson (1987) "Empirical Implications of Alternative Models of Firm Dynamics," University of Wisconsin, Social System Research Institute, mimeo 8803.

Piore M. and C. F. Sabel (1981) *The Second Industrial Divide*, New York: Basic Books.

Poterba J. M. and L. Summers (1988) "Reporting Errors and Labor Market Dynamics," *Econometrica*, **54**.

Regione Emilia-Romagna (1989) "Osservatorio del mercato del lavoro," *Rapporto annuale*, Franco Angeli.

Revelli R. and S. Tenga (1989) "The Determinants of New Firm Formation in Italian Manufacturing," *Small Business Economics*, **1**, 181–192.

Steindl J. (1945) *Small and Big Business*, Oxford: Basil Blackwell.

Wellisz S. H. (1957) "The Coexistence of Large and Small Firms: a Study of the Italian Mechanical Industries," *The Quarterly Journal of Economics*, **89**, 116–131.

8 The role of small firms in Czechoslovak manufacturing

Gerald A. McDermott and *Michal Mejstrik*

1. Introduction

As Czechoslovakia enters into the uncharted waters of radical economic transformation from a centrally planned economy to a liberalized market economy, serious consideration must be given to the past and current performance and, in turn, the structure, of the industrial sectors at the firm level and to the challenges facing future prosperity. More specifically, the decreasing overall efficiency of the Czechoslovak economy, notably in manufacturing, questions the very foundations of a command economy as well as the blind, rigid economic strategy of perverse maintenance of the mass-production paradigm.

This chapter aims at offering an alternative to the often fallacious description of firm behavior in the command economy, in this case Czechoslovakia, as a strict government controlled hierarchical structure, a description inadequate as a point of departure for transition into a market economy. It is our belief that a better understanding of Czechoslovak firm behavior can be given within the context of the evolution of economies of scale production and the distorted political–economic paths followed by Czechoslovak economic leaders. Although there has been unquestionable support for the mass-production regime, large-scale firm size has not aided the performance and competitiveness of Czechoslovak manufacturing firms. Primary attention will be paid to the size of the firm and the conditions needed for creating a harmonic size structure of firms in the transitional economy.

Section 2 analyzes the diffusion of the "law of economies of scale," which was derived as a generalization of the concentration of production processes in market economies over most of the twentieth century. The "larger-is-better" attitude exclusively shaped the Czechoslovak economic policy for almost the last 45 years. We try to depict the crisis of the mass-production regime and the flexible response developed recently in market economies. The notable advantages of small firms which have bloomed in the many advanced market economies (i.e. lower MES, high job generation, significant innovation rates) indicate that small firms have the potential to play a critical role in the democratic marketization and social transformation of Czechoslovakia.

Section 3 provides an analysis of the declining productivity and competitiveness and firm-size distribution in Czechoslovak manufacturing. In particular, the evidence reveals that after 45 years of central planning Czechoslovakia is left with an extraordinarily low number of smaller firms, while preference has been given to a few giant monopolies.

Section 4 offers a qualitative analysis of the coalition structure and, in turn, the perverse behavioral consequences of Czechoslovak enterprises, which seems to go hand in hand with the high concentration of industry. Section 5 analyzes the current challenges to the transformation process in Czechoslovakia for the development of a dynamic industrial composition. We pay special attention to the critical importance of facilitating greater opportunities for the proliferation of smaller firms during the economic and social transformation of the country.

Lastly, we present our conclusions in Section 6. The evidence suggests that the former regime utterly neglected the development of a harmonic firm-size distribution, which has not aided firm performance in the Czechoslovak export manufacturing sector. The preference to large economies of scale has given rise to a corrupting coalition of economic and political monopolists of resources. Subsequently, the transformation process and, in turn the development of dynamic firm formation, faces a hostile environment.

2.   45 years of economies of scale

2.1   *The rise of mass production*

It was widely recognized that most process innovations since the Industrial Revolution involved increasing exploitation of economies of scale, generally associated with "Taylorist" or "Fordist" principles of organization and production (Chandler, 1977). Classicists, as well as Marxists, seemed to have agreed with Adam Smith in believing that large-scale production was the most efficient form of exchange, and any disruption of mass production would be regarded as wasteful, in that it would not contribute to the transformation of the property order into something higher (Piore and Sabel, 1984). The degree of concentration and plant sizes increased while products became more standardized (Blair, 1948;

Scherer, 1980). These were the main factors of efficiency and growth. Such a tendency of technological change was also reflected by Lenin at the beginning of the twentieth century (Lenin, 1916). Lenin's findings on the concentration of monopolies were further enriched and developed for socialism by Stalin and his collaborators. The Stalinist political economy of socialism and "socialist growth theories," both deeply rooted in the economies of scale paradigm, have governed the economic policy of all centrally planned economies.

As mankind crossed its first "industrial divide," industrialization became synonymous with mass production (Piore and Sabel, 1984). Mass production required large investments in highly specialized equipment and narrowly trained workers. Resources became highly particularized: a piece of modern machinery dedicated to the production of a single part could not be turned to another use. As Wheelwright (1985) emphasized, even labor was considered as indistinguishable from all other inputs, as long as scientific management was able to extract a full day's worth of energy for a full day's pay. As tasks became increasingly specialized, the required skill level was less important. In the end, this logic of mechanization strove to make human involvement in the production process superfluous.

In both East and West, mass production was seen as the technologically dynamic form, smaller, specialized production as the subordinate. Incremental process innovations, rather than ceaseless product innovations, dictated the limits of creativity. Organized labor would press for higher wages and possible modifications in the hierarchical structure of the firm, rather than considering a reform in the existing organization of production (Piore and Sabel, 1984). Ironically, leaders in socialist economies accepted the subordination of labor and the superiority of large economies of scale, reserving only bargaining over the wage fund for the possible betterment of labor. What mattered most under the mass-production regime was the consistency and reliability of each cog (Audretsch, 1989). Moreover, as the minimum size of an efficient plant became larger and larger, instability threatened the firm, internally as well as externally. In the Czechoslovak case, the emphasis on size pertained not only to particular firms but to the state controlling center as well, which could be considered as one large conglomerate (Triska, 1990). Certain responses predicated its survival.

So-called "scientific management" structures became the standard for the internal organization of firms. The essence was "command and control of effort" and the masses of raw materials and capital resources. The importance of management and stability was stressed, rather than creativity. A particular equation for production was implemented into the corporate structure, with each parameter predetermined, and a very specific use of resources was achieved. As Reich (1983) points out, detailed planning was developed to guide the firm's internal operations and could be applied generically toward other companies in the same industry:

The tools used to plan and coordinate various lines of production within a single firm could in principle be extended to encompass an entire industry. Instead of each firm's responding in isolation to economic upturns and downturns by expanding or contracting its capacity – resulting in cycles of overcapacity or undercapacity – industry-wide coordination could enable each to accommodate its investment and production plans to the plans of every other firm... Strategic planners in major firms and within the government strove to "rationalize" each industry as a whole (p. 87).

Thus, we turn to controlling external volatility, that is, the stability, continuity, and reliability that constituted the core of successful mass production.

Achieving industry stabilization was attempted in three main ways: collusion, consolidation, and government regulation. Collusion, or the creation of "pools," provided agreements either to fix price or restrict output, enabling prices to rise. This process was formally institutionalized under the direction of trade associations (Audretsch, 1989). Coordination also entailed bargaining among firms. It required expert knowledge of the needs of the industry and pending changes in supply and demand. Bargaining implied "accommodation and consensus; expertise suggested technical fact finding." In practice, these two processes were often indistinguishable from each other (Reich, 1983, Ch. 5).

The drive for stability next took the form of consolidation. Mergers, horizontal and vertical, attempted to amass larger market shares as well as stabilizing the inflow of supplies and distribution of outputs. Alfred D. Chandler (1977) has emphasized the integration of mass marketing and mass production as one of the basic organizational innovations. Also, backward integration, through inventory accumulation, was designed simply to ensure a steady supply of raw materials of the requisite quality.

As stabilization attempts through collusion and consolidation met with marginal success, industries increasingly turned toward the federal government for help. Ultimately, the government were able to provide a stable environment for planning and coordinating investments among industry participants (Reich, 1983). Firms were besieged by increasing competition within the market as well as by "democratic ferment." As Kolko (1963, p. 6) notes, government intervention was responding not necessarily to the need to control monopoly power. "It was not the existence of monopoly that caused the federal government to intervene into the economy, but the lack of it." It was a move to stabilize industry.

Over time, a network of government managed advisory boards, trade associations, and regulatory agencies was established, enabling companies and industries to coordinate investment and production, as well as pricing, both formally and informally. A "working oligopoly" partnership between government and the corporation, especially in American manufacturing industry, evolved, making industry-wide cooperation practically obligatory (Audretsch, 1989). Simply stated, collusion, yet this time aided by the federal government, was brought to a greater height. This so-called "regulation movement," which lasted through 1970, seemed to aid greatly the prominence of mass production in the United States (Audretsch, 1989). This was the world of "countervailing power," so aptly described by Galbraith (1967), where virtually every major institution in society acted to reinforce the stability needed for mass production. In fact, the unprecedented growth during this period has been attributed less to the outcome of technology than to the result of prevailing political and social forces working to provide the market stability required for the corporation to thrive (Piore and Sabel, 1984).

2.2 Czechoslovakia follows suit

Paradoxically, leading market economies strove to insulate industries from the realities of fluctuating markets. Mass production was profitable only with contrived markets that were large enough to absorb an enormous output of a single standardized commodity and stable enough to keep the resources involved in the production of that commodity continuously employed (Piore and Sabel, 1984, Ch. 3). On the other side of the coin, Czechoslovakia, along with its socialist brethren, bought the mass-production story lock, stock and barrel, following it to its logical economic as well as political extreme. Before we discuss the development of the socialist mass-production regime, it is important to note the structure of Czechoslovak industry before its annexation by Hitler in 1938.

Formed on the break-up of the Austro–Hungarian Monarchy in 1918, Czechoslovakia by the 1930s ranked as a major European industrial country, enjoying a strong tradition of craftsmen skilled in producing machinery and other manufactures and of businessmen adept in exporting these goods. Incomes were high, and the well-developed economy had succeeded in forging close financial and industrial links with the rest of Europe. Although the Second World War amputated one-third of the nation's territory and subjected the remainder to foreign domination, it did not inflict on Czechoslovakia the wholesale destruction of property, plant, and infrastructure that devastated Poland and Germany.

During the inter-war years, the importance of the industrial sector for Czechoslovakia's economy constantly increased. As early as 1921, 33.8 percent of the working population was employed in industrial occupations. Estimates indicate that by 1938 the industrial sector accounted for 65 percent of the total value of Czechoslovak production and that in 1937 it contributed 35 percent of the national income. Moreover, until 1929, the increase in Czechoslovakia's industrial production was greater than in the majority of European countries, four times greater than the increase of Germany and Austria and seven times greater than that of Britain (Teichova, 1988, p. 33).

Czechoslovakia was the only country in Central and South-East Europe where industrial development resembled that in West Europe, with the producer-goods' industries being strengthened in relation to the consumer-goods' industries. Although the share of the iron and steel, mechanical engineering, and chemical industries in Czechoslovak industrial production lagged behind that of the West European countries, the rate of growth of the producer-goods' industries in Czechoslovakia was higher than that of overall production in these countries (Teichova, 1988).

The initial rapid rise in industrial production was accompanied by moves to introduce labor-saving devices in the production process, to reduce the costs of production and to improve profit margins which gave renewed impetus to the trend to rationalization and concentration in Czechoslovak industry. However, this process had differing effects on individual branches of industry, ranging from an effective oligopolistic structure in iron and steel to widespread dispersion in the food-processing, textile, and clothing industries. We find, in fact, that Czechoslovakia had a substantial base of small and medium-sized firms. According to the 1930 Census, a total of 378,015 mining and industrial enterprises were counted. The great majority – 336,577 firms employing between one and five people – consisted of handcraft workshops or small specialist establishments, mainly in food-processing, wood, clothing, and leather industries. As Teichova (1988, p. 37) points out, this 89 percent of industrial firms used only 10.5 percent of all power produced, whereas the 41,438 establishments with six or more employees (11 percent of all industrial firms) consumed 89.5 percent of all power used by Czechoslovak industry.

Although self-employment and small firms continued to play a significant role, the overwhelming majority of Czechoslovak workers were employed in the medium-sized to large-scale enterprises. Despite the

relatively widespread distribution of medium-sized enterprises, a tendency towards concentration is visible from the opposing direction taken
by the number of enterprises and the employment figures. As Table 8.1
reveals, enterprises with more than 501 employees represented only 1.1
percent of all undertakings but employed 29.4 percent of all industrial
workers while firms with more than 250 employees accounted for 42.1
percent of total industrial employment. However, as we shall see below,
when we also take into consideration the fact that firms with less than 250
employees accounted for over 50 percent of industrial employment, the
level of concentration through the 1930s pales in comparison with the
extremely high degree of concentration and centralization established
during the forced rationalization of entire industries by the communist
regime.

Table 8.1. *Czechoslovak industrial enterprise size distribution, according
to number employed, 1930*

Enterprise employment size categories	Number and shares of enterprises		Number and shares of workers employed	
	No.	*(%)*	*No.*	*(%)*
6–20	28,612	69.0	262,326	15.6
21–50	7,020	17.0	223,538	13.3
51–100	2,905	7.0	202,617	12.2
101–250	1,833	4.4	281,144	16.8
251–500	622	1.5	213,667	12.7
501 and over	446	1.1	492,160	29.4
Total	41,438	100.0	1,675,272	100.0

Source: Teichova (1988).

As part of the process of concentration during the First Republic
(1918–1938), companies developed a pyramid corporate structure which
created opportunities for wide-ranging connections within the Czechoslovak economy itself, as well as favorable conditions for further capital
expansion in South-East Europe, via subsidy companies of Czechoslovak
banks and industry concerns. Czechoslovak businesses were compelled
by their country's geographic size and position and the level of foreign
competition to establish a competitive foreign trade profile and strong
foreign investment links. By 1937, direct and indirect West European
investment alone accounted for 68.1 percent of foreign investment. By
1933, the economic crisis, which began effectively in 1929, had driven
almost 77 percent of Czechoslovak industry to domestic and foreign

Table 8.2. *The percentage share of NMP produced by individual sectors, 1948–1983, current prices*

	1948	1960	1970	1980	1983
Total Net Material Prod.	100.0	100.0	100.0	100.0	100.0
Individual farms	1.1[a]	5.0	3.5	2.1	2.6
Private sector	33.4	1.6	0.9	0.5	0.7
Socialist sector	65.5	93.4	95.6	97.4	96.7
state owned enterprises	62.9	81.8	85.1	87.5	86.4
cooperatives	2.6	11.6	10.5	9.9	10.3

Note: [a] One man or one family.
Source: Historical Statistical Yearbook of CSSR, FSU, SNTL, Prague (1985).

cartel links through agreements between manufacturers and, later, through legislation (Pryor and Pryor, 1975).

At this point, it is important to realize that while this gradual process of concentration and centralization of industry may be relatively similar to that occurring in the West, after 1948 the communist authorities took centralization and mass production to its logical economic and political extreme. Market demand was subordinated to the will of the state center, and consequently to the whim of enterprise directors. Shortages ensued under the planned price system and, in turn, the demand necessary to absorb and support the mass-production regime was created. Similar to a "Catch-22" situation, the only way the political authorities saw fulfillment of sufficient supply was through manipulation of mass production, once again exacerbating the shortage (see below). Stabilization went hand in hand with increasing returns to scale. What better way to exploit both paradigms but to monopolize whole industries and the whole economy as well – the state center as headquarters I. In turn, Czechoslovakia applied management and organization methods within firms and over the whole market which paralleled the Western efforts at controlling the internal and external business environments, as discussed above.

Socializing the economy effectively brought industries under the control of one body of ownership – the state. Small enterprises were either liquidated or integrated into larger enterprises. During the 1950s, the private sector was almost completely liquidated, while several thousand enterprises were merged into approximately 1,400 centrally controlled firms, 60 percent of which were accounted for by the manufacturing sector (Zemplinerova, 1989b), thus stabilizing the development of the size structure of firms. As can be seen in Table 8.2 even by 1960, 93.4

percent of Net Material Product (NMP) was under state domination (for all practical purposes, cooperatives behave and are regulated like state firms). The non-farming private sector share of NMP had dropped from 33.4 percent to 1.6 percent in only the first twelve years after 1945. As the mid-1980s approached, Czechoslovakia found itself with 96.7 percent of its NMP dominated by the state sector and only 0.7 percent of NMP contributed by the non-farming private sector.

In Czechoslovakia, industry made massive investments in highly specialized equipment and narrowly trained workers. The goal was fully to exploit natural resources as well as the largest economies of scale possible for the country. "Command and control" planning became the rule of thumb, where the only serious management discussions concerned the level of inputs and outputs possible for the production equation over the medium term. Through government regulation (i.e. restrictions on ownership, absolute price control, CMEA), five-year plans were thought to be given some of the needed stability to function predictably. Detailed planning was required not simply of a firm but of the whole economy as well. Where attempts at providing internal and external stability overlapped was in this planning. The various industry ministries and the instituted planning commission planned to the last "koruna" each firm's level of investment, production, pricing, and "earnings," providing consistency of production for each firm and, in turn, a somewhat reliable "market." In reality, targets and plans were redrawn within a planning period, often succumbing to the demands of the state firms.

Concurrent with the socialization period of the 50s, with its organizational restructuring and concentration of production, the growth of organizational units gradually accelerated over time. As an attempt more easily to manage the centrally planned economy and, in turn, better to coordinate industries, economic authorities decreased the number of enterprises while increasing the size of the firms. As can be seen in Table 8.3, firms with over 2,500 employees constituted only 4.7 percent of the total number of manufacturing enterprises in 1956.[1] However, we also observe that after 1960 through to the present, this share stabilized at about 25 percent, while the share for firms of 500–2,500 employees stabilized at about 65 percent. Conversely, the share of the total number of enterprises for firms with less than 500 employees fell from 49 percent to 10.2 percent between 1956 and 1988.

As consolidation increased over the years, membership of industrial trade associations became obligatory. The associations acted as middle level management or bureaucracy, creating a network to control the distribution of resources. If an industry was not formally vertically

Table 8.3. *Enterprise-size distribution of Czechoslovak manufacturing firms between 1956 and 1988*

| | Share of total number of enterprises: employment size categories | | | | | |
| | In absolute terms | | | In relative terms (%) | | |
Year	<500	500–2500	>2500	<500	500–2500	>2500
1956	763	721	73	49.0	46.3	4.7
1960	137	523	181	16.3	62.2	21.5
1970	109	560	204	12.5	64.1	23.4
1980	80	562	218	9.3	65.3	25.4
1988	91	586	213	10.2	66.8	24.0

Sources: Historical Statistical Yearly CSSR, Prague, SNTL, Prague (1985); *Statistical Yearly* (1989).

integrated under one firm, these associations provided the conduit for informal, yet absolutely rigid, integration. As Reich (1983) noted, bargaining within government aided regulatory institutions in the United States was more of a limited exchange of information for the sake of industry coordination, and plan-bargaining between the firm and center in Czechoslovakia evolved similarly into a perverse collusion of various high level government bureaucrats, firm directors, and the regional Party bosses, where the state became dependent on the firm for coordinating information (Triska, 1990; Mlcoch, 1990) (a fuller discussion of the problems and nature of this collusion is given in Section 4 below). As plan management became more detailed and informal control of distribution more pervasive, the complex formalities of this management rivaled what Reich (1983) termed in the United States "paper entrepreneurialism." In the end, the worker was still a cog in the machine, and government regulation became a way for firm directors to manipulate the state.

The expectations associated with the law of economies of scale (with little consideration for optimal plant size) represented a technical reason for the steady increase in plant size, which led the small and functionally closed Czechoslovak economy to the artificial formation of an indivisible single plant with an economic monopoly. The hierarchical structure of the centrally planned economy generated institutional reasons for the formation of an administrative monopoly. These large firms possessed both an economic and administrative monopoly, which allowed them to act without respect to economic efficiency (Triska, 1990). As mentioned above, producers could count on state subsidies, price interventions, priority credits, tax exemptions, etc. By not reflecting actual market costs, prices revealed little objective evaluation of performance. The distorted price system of Czechoslovakia thus further complicated the empirical identification of efficiency and competitiveness by plant size in the centrally planned economy.

2.3 Crisis for the regime and adjustment in the West

Beginning in the mid-1960s, a series of disruptions began to wreak havoc on the fragile mass-production order in the West, notably in the United States. External shocks jolted the much cherished stability, while the institutional structure was incapable of accommodating the spread of mass-production technology. The much needed consistency and reliability of inputs, materials as well as labor, was greatly hampered, rapidly increasing the costs of production. The economy started to experience shortages of labor, food, and fuel, while increased global competition and deregulation exacerbated the uncertainty in the market (see Piore and Sabel, 1984, Ch. 7; Shepherd, 1982). The inflexibility of the corporation paralyzed it from adequately responding to greater competition, in turn leading to a questioning of the very nature of its production and marketing strategies. The confusion led to the break-up of mass markets for standardized products, and so reducing sufficient demand to support long-term, stable planning.

However, this instability pushed industry toward more flexible restructuring of economic agents. The stage was set for a radical, innovative response – the growth of small, flexible firms. Meanwhile, as an organizational and technological revolution was taking place in the West, Czechoslovakia actually became more totalitarian in its politics and more centralized in its floundering economics.

Blair (1948) argued that due to particular innovations and fundamental shifts in technology, the trend towards increasing size was being replaced by an opposing trend towards smaller size. He reasoned that it was the "decentralizing" effects of these new technologies which were reducing scale economies, and leading to smaller-sized plants and firms. Piore and Sabel (1984) suggest that the emergence of this new flexible technology represents, in fact, an "industrial divide" where firms and society are confronted with a choice of technological mode. In referring to the Italian example, where an increased reliance on small-scale production has resulted from underlying technological and institutional changes, Piore and Sabel (1983) argue that flexible production will tend to promote the relative viability of small firms. They argue that the flexible-production firm thrives on the same factors that are debilitating to firms applying mass-production technologies. Rather than trying to control the path and direction of markets and technological change, as is customary for mass-production firms, the flexible-production firm needs to create new market niches by continuously innovating and redesigning the product to serve changing consumer tastes.

More specifically, six major factors have been cited as underpinning the recent shift toward flexible, small firms in the United States (Acs and Audretsch, 1989a; Brock and Evans, 1989). First, increased globalization has rendered markets more subject to volatility, as a result of competition from a greater number of foreign competitors as well as from exchange rate fluctuations. This greater variability of sales may have increased the returns to "flexibility," a key advantage of smaller firms (Mills and Schumann, 1985; Acs, Audretsch and Carlsson, 1991). Second, increased labor force participation of women and the baby boom generation may have increased the supply of exactly those kinds of labor which are most conducive to small firms (Evans and Leighton, 1989). In addition, the decrease in the United States real wages during the 1970s and early 1980s may have also provided labor intensive smaller firms with a competitive edge over capital intensive larger firms. Third, the proliferation of consumer tastes, away from standardized mass-produced goods and towards stylized and personalized products, has also been a catalyst for small firms. Fourth, relaxation of entry regulation in some industries, such as telephone manufacturing and financial services, has increased the opportunities for small firms (Shepherd, 1982).

Fifth, recent technological changes, such as those that have decreased computer and reprogramming costs, may have reduced the optimal size and the minimum scale of entry (Shepherd, 1982; Carlsson, 1989). In fact, Acs, Audretsch and Carlsson (1991) suggest that the application of flexible-production technology, particularly NC machines, has tended to shift the firm–size distribution towards small firms, notably in manufacturing industries which historically have been dominated by large firms. Sixth, we appear to be in the midst of "creative destruction," Schumpeter's (1950) description of the process by which entrepreneurs develop new products and processes which remove and replace the traditions of the past. Acs and Audretsch (1989a, 1989b) show that innovative activity is a strategy which small firms have been using to enter industries and remain viable in industries in which they would otherwise experience an inherent cost disadvantage. Concurrently, Carlsson (1989) argues that many firms, large and small, have divested themselves of activities of entities which they do not consider to be part of their "core" business.

2.4 *Implications of small-firm dynamics*

Market economies appear to be producing new technological and organization innovations which allow a much greater flexibility of production in terms of (a) acceptable variance of inputs and outputs (defined in terms of the number of cost-effectively produced homogenous items per unit of time), (b) acceptable variances of product varieties, and (c) a decreased minimum scale of efficiency. Dosi (1988) has discussed two major consequences. First, these new technological and organizational innovations increase the efficiency of small-scale production (Shepherd, 1982). Second, they are likely to reduce the importance of plant-related scale economies, which were one of the main sources of both productivity growth and of the production rigidity exemplified in "classical" Fordist automation.

In trying to analyze the role of small firms and competition, be it in the United States or Czechoslovakia, we agree that the observed intra-industry distributions of firms by size are affected by sector-specific technologies and opportunities of scale as well as by the trade off between scale and production flexibility (White, 1982). Indeed, there may be a certain number of technology-specific size distributions, by plant and firm, which represent, following Dosi (1988), "evolutionary equilibria." That is, a variety of firms and plants coexists at roughly similar performance levels (Mills and Schumann, 1985) by exploiting more economies of scale with less flexibility, more economies of scope with less economies of scale. However, the distribution of firms or plants, coexisting with similar levels of efficiency, applies not only to technological variety but also to the behavioral diversity of firms within identical environmental incentives (Acs and Audretsch, 1989a). The firms use different strategies related to innovation, pricing, R&D, and investment (Freeman, 1982). Further, the coexistence of firms is not only a result of this process but also of the very form of competition among firms (Geroski and Pomeroy, 1987). Thus, what we find in market economies, as opposed to in the Czechoslovak economy, is that as a result of the processes mentioned above, the market economy has been able to develop a size distribution of firms (i.e. the coexistence of firms with different sizes and behavioral patterns) which has greatly contributed to technological change and the proliferation of consumer tastes. The critical implications for economic transformation in Czechoslovakia of this relationship between technology, start-ups, and the development of a harmonic distribution of firm size is discussed in Section 5 below.

We shall try to reflect some of these hypotheses as we analyze the dynamics surrounding firm structure and declining competitiveness in

Czechoslovakia, which appears to have sunk into the mire of mass production while many developed market economies have tried to reignite themselves with an increase in the role of small firms and the adoption of greater "flexible specialization."

3. Decline and firm size in manufacturing

3.1 Decline of productivity and competitiveness

Even though variability of the economic development level of Czechoslovakia exists among previous analyses (Zamrazilova, 1990), the generally accepted range of Czechoslovak GDP is between 53 percent and 83 percent of Austrian GDP for 1985. These figures demonstrate Czechoslovakia's overall lead in economic level (GDP), by nearly 50 percent of that of Poland and 20 percent of that of Hungary. However, the "mature" Czechoslovak economy over the 1980s has approached the lowest average figures of total factor productivity (TFP) growth rates among the European CMEA countries. Following the production function theory (Brown, 1971), TFP growth captures the macroeffects of economies of scale production. A drop in TFP growth, when not compensated by product and process innovations (as has been the case of Czechoslovakia), represents a decrease in the benefits derived from economies of scale production. The drop in TFP growth, which can be seen in Figure 8.1, thus led to the gradual deceleration of average annual rates of growth of the net material product (Mejstrik, 1990).

The decline in the competitiveness and performance of Czechoslovak manufacturing can be seen more clearly through the fall in export capabilities. According to Mejstrik (1990), in the period 1965–1986 in various branches of manufacturing, prices per unit of weight of Czechoslovak exports into the EC market developed quite differently from those of competing countries (see Figure 8.1). Essentially, these ratios can be characterized by a general negative relationship between Czechoslovak prices and those of their competitors. The most notable and prolonged decrease in these ratios of average prices per unit of weight has occurred in the engineering industry. The average export prices per unit of weight of products exported by Czechoslovakia to the European Community have dropped from 52 percent (1965) to 47–48 percent (1986) of the prices attained by other countries' exports in the European Community. The worst situation has been in high-tech industries (i.e. electronics), while the low-tech industries (i.e. metallurgy) have fared relatively better: the corresponding figure for metallurgy was 73 percent in 1986. These trends

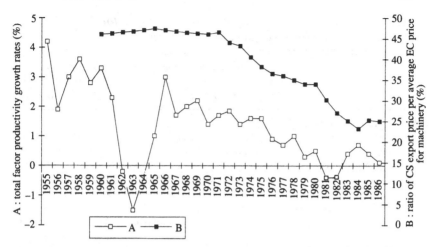

Figure 8.1 Decline of Czechoslovak factor productivity, 1955–1986 (A) and decline of Czechoslovak export manufacturing competitiveness, 1965–1986 (B). *Source:* Mejstrik and Cermak (1990).

were accompanied by a decrease of Czechoslovak export shares of trade in the EC machinery market – 0.35 percent (1965) to 0.14 percent (1983), a 60 percent fall in market share. We must thus try to discern which factors can be attributed to the decline of Czechoslovak international performance and competitiveness. Rather than learning from firms in advanced capitalist countries, many of whom developed a more flexible, scaled-down production structure (as discussed in Section 2.3 above), Czechoslovakia continued to follow large economies of scale production in export manufacturing.

3.2 *Manufacturing employment at the firm level*[2]

We see from Table 8.4 that for the smallest 5 percent of firms in terms of employment in the Czechoslovak export manufacturing sector[3] (which comprises 67 percent of the total number of manufacturing firms) in 1988, the average size is still 900 employees per firm and the corresponding quantile is 1,232. The emphasis and preference for large-scale firms can be further seen in the jump from the 8th to the 10th decile in average firm size – from 8,504 to 36,712 employees per firm, respectively. These figures are exceptionally high when compared to contemporary Western developed nations. For example, in Japan in 1983, firms with over 1,000

Table 8.4. *Czechoslovak state export manufacturing sector, 1988, firm size distribution by employment quantiles and deciles*

	Employment quantile and decile categories				
	0.0–0.05	0.05–0.1	0.1–0.2	0.2–0.3	0.3–0.4
Employees per firm (high end)	1,232	1,649	2,329	2,912	3,690
No. of firms	114	72	104	79	63
Av. no. of employees	900	1,443	1,994	2,606	3,288
Av. total sales (Kcs)	628,310	588,823	774,871	907,124	1,386,224

	0.4–0.5	0.5–0.6	0.6–0.7	0.7–0.8	0.8–0.9
Employees per firm (high end)[a]	4,572	5,666	7,413	11,168	23,454
No. of firms	51	41	32	25	14
Av. no. of employees	4,114	5,160	6,479	8,504	16,690
Av. total sales (Kcs)	136,014	1,423,219	1,762,791	4,082,009	7,009,155

	Employment quantile categories	
	0.9–0.95	0.95–1.0
Employees per firm (high end)[a]	41,001	41,159
No. of firms	4	1
Av. no. of employees	35,600	41,159
Av. total sales (Kcs)	13,594,068	11,324,670

Note: [a] Denotes the high end of the given employment quantile or decile category.
Source: Czechoslovakia Statistical Bureau (1988).

employees comprised only 13.2 percent of total employment in the manufacturing sector (Sato, 1989). In West Germany in 1986, firms with over 1,000 employees were 49.9 percent of total manufacturing employment (Schwalbach, 1989). By contrast, in 1988 Czechoslovak firms with over 1,000 employees had a more than 95 percent share of employment in their export manufacturing sector and a 91.2 percent share of employment in the whole manufacturing sector (Zemplinerova, 1989a). Moreover, Table 8.5 indicates that, between 1956 and 1988, the share of total manufacturing employment for firms with less than 500 employees fell

Table 8.5. *Enterprise-size distribution of Czechoslovak manufacturing firms between 1956 and 1988; share of total manufacturing employment*

| | Employment size categories | | | | | |
| | In absolute terms (000 workers) | | | In relative terms (%) | | |
Year	<500	500–2500	>2500	<500	500–2500	>2500
1956	193.2	826.2	466.6	13.0	55.6	31.4
1960	154.7	745.4	857.9	8.8	42.4	48.8
1970	37.0	729.0	995.0	2.1	41.4	56.5
1980	26.0	751.0	1052.0	1.4	41.1	57.5
1988	26.0	787.0	1024.0	1.4	42.8	55.8

Source: Statistical Yearly, FCU, SNTL, Prague (various years).

from 13 percent to 1.4 percent, while firms with greater than 2,500 employees represented over 55 percent of the total share.

A further indicator of the priority given to large firms is revealed in shares of total manufacturing sales. As Table 8.4 shows, the five firms comprising the 10th decile account for a staggering 71.5 percent of total sales in this sector, while the 290 firms in the combined 1st and 2nd deciles account for only 4.4 percent of total sales. The data suggests a confirmation of widely-held belief in Czechoslovakia that the economic authorities considered smaller-scale production virtually meaningless, while the largest firms were given full market priority.

The above evidence reveals a very interesting situation in the Czechoslovak export manufacturing sector. While there has been a gradual decline in export competitiveness in the overall economy in Czechoslovakia, the economic authorities have emphasized the need to maintain and support large economies of scale production in the export manufacturing sector. However, as Mejstrik and Cermak (1990) confirm, this emphasis on large-scale mass production has not aided performance of these firms, even when they have strong negotiation power. In fact, their results suggest a negative correlation between the large sizes of Czechoslovak firms in export manufacturing and performance.

We must then consider why the leaders in Czechoslovakia did not respond to the decline of the economy. As is discussed in Section 4, the high concentration of industry gave birth to a perverse coalition structure, which tried to maintain its hold on its economic and political monopoly and subsequently presented itself as a daunting hindrance to economic reform of the country.

4. The coalition structure in Czechoslovakia

As can be seen, Czechoslovak manufacturing is thus experiencing serious problems in international competitiveness. Both the aggregate and disseminated data reveal that the Czechoslovak manufacturing sector has not been able to recover from its decline while the economic authorities have tried to maintain adherence to the increasing economies of scale paradigm. It seems that the existing institutional framework can be considered as a serious influence on firm behavior and, moreover, has not created any response to this steady fall nor any hope for a future turnaround. What is feared is a hysteresis jump downward in export manufacturing (i.e. decreasing productivity and relative quality, and consequently a loss of markets). Radical measures must therefore be taken to restructure industry and reflect world standards.

Economic reformers face a market dominated by large state monopolies (Zemplinerova, 1989b), which were created and maintained by administrative action rather than by economic determination, and almost completely lacking a private sector, even when compared to Hungary or Poland. One could say that Czechoslovakia is home to a double monopoly, that is, a monopoly established simply due to the high degree of market concentration yet combined with a monopolization along the political power structure:

The enterprise in a non-parametrical environment is a coalition of internal and external participants. The internal participants include the "control group" – the power center of the enterprise, the worker aristocracy, and the administrative apparatus. The main goal of this group is not to improve efficiency and innovation, but rather to establish close links with all members of the external hierarchal superiors, i.e., planning commission, industry ministries, and regional Party bosses, as well as with key suppliers and customers. These links help to insure the fulfillment of personal interests of the "control group" – their material and political welfare (Mlcoch, 1990, p. 15).

The coalition structure derives its own system of barter exchange, an informal distribution network of resources, where formal monetary cost plays a secondary role. The trump card in an exchange is the ability to deliver a deficit product, also known as "natural revenues," such as industrial materials in short supply, the inside line on certain consumer goods, or a "natural" bonus system of coveted vacations.

Furthermore, it is necessary to emphasize that the traditional assumption of strict top-down planning is largely a fallacy. The collusion of formal and informal control groups creates an illusion of "plan struggle," so often depicted by Western analysts of centrally planned economies. In reality, the collusive monopoly decides on a distribution of resources and benefits primarily for the internal rewards of the "mafia." (This conception was originally discussed by Mlcoch, unofficially published between 1980 and 1983.) The larger the firm, the greater its political and economic power, inducing the economic authorities to continue their preference for large-scale production. It would be contradictory to their interests to allow development of smaller firms, possibly destabilizing the monopoly of resources and sales revenues.

This coalition structure is deeply rooted in its informal nature, where the behavioral problems cannot be easily changed by the simple, formal transfer of the economy to a market-based position. The country faces, in turn, a very hostile environment for the introduction of a market structure. Barriers to entry include not only those common in developed market economies[4] but also a complete lack of guaranteed supply as well as of market and resource information, most of which is monopolized by the state firms. As already exemplified over the past decade in Yugoslavia, Hungary, and Poland, partial reforms of cuts in state subsidies and liberalization of prices of certain product groups can help decrease the hostility of the environment, yet lead to a system of mutual lending and subsidization within the coalition. For example, in Hungary interfirm debt rose approximately 300 percent between 1987 and 1989 in the state industrial sector,[5] representing a further softening of the firm's budget constraint (Kornai, 1986).

5. The challenges of the reform process

The principal points of departure for reform are the full or partial privatization of state firms as well as the development of a new private sector of small and medium-sized firms. The former process would be prefaced by the break-up of the monopolies and/or the internal decentralization of management decision making, with the hope of easing the rigid and highly centralized nature of the internal organization of state firms.

However, even the formal break-up of these enterprises does not dissolve the coalition structure. In fact, in such a small, closed economy as Czechoslovakia, the individual plants of former state firms would become monopolists in their own right. Czechoslovakia is thus faced with a monumental task of creating basic competition – alternative suppliers and, in turn, alternative selection of the prices and qualities of goods.

Besides opening up the market to foreign competition – a necessary measure which is at a primitive stage of implementation and will prove initially quite costly – we can open and facilitate the expansion of a domestic private sector.

Since legalization of private shops was enacted in January 1989, there has been some expansion in the number of private entrepreneurs, yet only single individuals and their relatives are allowed to operate the business. In anticipation of the full legalization of the private sector, an Association of Private Entrepreneurs was created in February 1990. This is the only existing organization which keeps data on prospective small businesses in Czechoslovakia. However, as of 1991, no national registration office existed, so registration into the Association took place only at local town halls. The data offered, though crude, is the best available at this time.

By the end of 1990, the Association boasted a membership of approximately 220,000 prospective entrepreneurs whose activities include:

%
25.0 – restaurant and food services.
20.0 – transportation and shipping.
30.0 – construction and repair services.
20.7 – diversified activities (i.e. crafts, etc.).
2.3 – willing to start manufacturing firm.[6]

As we can see, there appear to be few healthy prospects for the dynamic formation of a private manufacturing sector. Even those who are willing to venture into manufacturing are primarily interested in exploiting existing shortages rather than in competing with new and innovative products. Prospective entrepreneurs in Czechoslovakia also do not see the opening of markets as an incentive to implement progressive technological equipment or innovative methods of production, but rather as a continuation of past production practices in a shortage economy. Moreover, two principal barriers to investment in new technology still exist. First, the acquisition of new equipment is not tax deductible and the current drafts of a new tax law offers depreciation of equipment only over a 10-year schedule. Second, there is a definite lack of available capital for investment. Not only are credit policies still in the hands of state bureaucrats, but personal saving in Czechoslovakia is virtually non-existent for the ordinary people. In fact, the most recent statistics reveal that, although Czechoslovakia has a savings base of approximately Kcs 267 billion, over one-third is owned by only 5 percent of the population (i.e. past *nomenklatura*, black marketeers), and one-quarter of the inhabitants are without savings altogether. As a result of this environment, what we have is a small group of private owners stimulated to consume capital (savings) for unproductive purposes, rather than to accumulate productive assets.

The new government has recently begun to take steps toward facilitating the development of the private sector. A new law on private enterprises was passed by Parliament in April 1990. The main benefit of this law is that it removes all legal limitations on the number of employees hired and the extent of property acquired by a private firm. However, an implicit barrier was imposed as well: if a firm has more than 25 employees and a yearly income of over 500,000 Kcs, then it must register as a large firm and, in turn, subject itself to the same regulations as a state firm. More specifically, the firm is subject to a double rate of taxation, extensive price controls, and internal administrative procedures dictated by the state.

Furthermore, little attention has been paid to several existing entry barriers, the most severe of which we will now discuss. We have mentioned already the serious lack of available start up capital for private entrepreneurs. Firms will be, for the foreseeable future, subject to relatively high tax burdens and to a general drought of private savings. Although the central bank was formally separated from controlling the commercial banking sector, these "commercial" banks are still fully owned by the state, and there has been little discussion in the ministries for the imminent need to initiate the birth of a private banking sector. In fact, in concurrence with the so-called tight monetary policy of the Finance Ministry, regulations on credit actually increased in the first half of 1991. Moreover, we find that in practice banks prefer formally and informally to loan to large state-owned establishments, making it very difficult for small firms to acquire capital. The state demands as well that private firms must guarantee a relatively high minimum wage and be subject to a steep progressive tax on wage increases. The result is a rigid wage structure, further raising the firms' cost floor.

Foreign trade continues to be heavily regulated. A private firm is permitted to conduct direct foreign trade only after proving that the firm itself improves the product value by at least 30 percent. 30 percent of all hard currency earnings must also be relinquished to the state bank in exchange for domestic soft currency. Consequently, a private firm is further restricted from acquiring resources and equipment from the West. Few will be permitted to carry out any foreign trade activities, and since hard currency is basically available through exports, most private firms will not even have the opportunity to acquire the necessary hard currency to invest in any sort of quality technology or materials. (An internal foreign exchange auction has been established with an unsurprisingly, thin supply of hard currency.) Innovation, competitiveness, and market entry are thus further hampered.

As discussed in Section 2 above, a key factor in the birth and development and the success of small, flexible firms is the opportunity to acquire state-of-the-art technology (Acs and Audretsch, 1989a; Acs, Audretsch and Carlsson, 1991). Without the greater availability of this technology and its related resources, the dynamic growth of small firms, and subsequently a more balanced size distribution of firms, as well as of the entire manufacturing sector will be greatly hampered. Even if reprivatization of the state sector can be implemented successfully, the market will remain highly concentrated, as noted above. Further, this process will take a considerable number of years. The effect of such a oligopolistic, perhaps monopolistic, market is a general lack of competition – sluggish productivity and innovation coupled with inflationary pressures.

However, if, at the same time, enough emphasis can be given to the development of small firms, we can foresee the rapid growth in the number and variety of new firms in the Czechoslovak market. As new firms concentrate their efforts on the production of consumer and manufactured goods as well as expanding output before the state sector can be more effectively organized, the traditional dominance of Sector I over Sector II will be weakened – and with it one of the main structural causes of inflation in centrally planned economies. The proliferation of thousands of new small entrants can help demonopolize the industrial structure and strengthen tendencies toward price competition. Also, since small firms are associated with high rates of job generation (Acs and Audretsch, 1987), they have the ability to soak up much of the unemployment from the bankrupt state factories.

Furthermore, the fairly rapid development of the small-firm sector can greatly aid the proposed plans for the reprivatization of state firms and, in turn, the trading of shares. First, the capital accumulated in these numerous start ups will speed up the selling of the state sector, while also producing a middle class, other than former *nomenklatura*. Second, the economic culture of Czechoslovakia needs to undergo a serious overhaul. The population needs to be educated as quickly as possible regarding the basic practices and principles of economics, business, and investment, if they are to be effective buyers and sellers of privatized state assets. Small business can definitely help facilitate this understanding of economic transactions.

On the political and social side, the public needs to be reassured that their positive future will be tied to their direct and local participation in the development of markets. Economic reformers need to offer a concrete vision of how individuals and groups can themselves take advantage of prospective market opportunities (i.e. through their own creation of a network of interdependent, competitive small and medium-sized firms).

Moreover, a large body of independent, active economic agents can better assure the maintenance and growth of democratic markets.

By providing economic opportunities to those currently without privileges through their involvement in local, smaller firms, it will demonstrate to the people that marketization is not just for the privatized *nomenklatura*, who will try to transfer acquired political capital into economic power. The formation of interdependent small firms as well as local savings and loan banks can greatly reduce the risk that marketization will end up serving a narrow elite concerned solely with export production and exploiting shortages. That is, it will reduce the risk of the existing old boy network (as discussed in Section 4) which already owns a substantial majority of the savings in Czechoslovakia, manipulating their inside line on credit and power to form an oligarchy, becoming not entrepreneurs but the worst sort of capitalists, saving the best industries for themselves and the worst for the state.

Reformers in Czechoslovakia are gradually realizing the need for an industrial policy which actively fosters the development of private small firms in the manufacturing sector.[7] At the minimum, Czechoslovakia needs a distribution of firm sizes which will efficiently foster technological change and the proliferation of consumer tastes. Small firms can rapidly contribute to the development of a harmonic size distribution of firms. Structural barriers, such as those described above, must be removed in the fullest sense if individuals are to have viable access to the economic opportunities of the market. This means more than the legalization of private business, the implementation of anti-trust policy, and the reduction of bureaucratic red tape.

The government, particularly at the regional level, and in cooperation with local social and commerce organizations, such as Civic Forum, Public Against Violence, the trade unions, regional Chambers of Commerce, and the Association of Private Entrepreneurs, needs to establish a business climate which is more hospitable to entrepreneurship – decreasing the costs of creating a new business. That is, given the enormous structural barriers which will continue to exist, if not grow, during the economic transformation of the country, a policy of democratic marketization demands the formation of local institutions which will improve the flow of resource and market information, the skill level of workers, and the provision of credit for new firms.[8] Although the central government can help formulate the general framework of such a policy, the key to its success is the actual implementation and enhancement by a combination of local private individuals and social institutions. Unfortunately, a detailed extrapolation of this policy initiative goes beyond the scope of this chapter.

6. Conclusion

We have tried to give an explanation and an analysis of Czechoslovak manufacturing firms within the context of the economic strategy based on the returns to scale paradigm. This paradigm has been followed to its political and economic extreme in Czechoslovakia, yet did not appear positively to influence the performance and competitiveness of firms, contradicting the assumptions of industrial policy makers and managers.

We have found that in spite of a relatively high economic level inherited from past generations, the mature Czechoslovak economy suffered serious drops in total factor productivity growth rates as well as in the ratio of the Czechoslovak export sale price per average price of foreign competitors in the EC market, especially in the manufacturing sector. Furthermore, the Czechoslovak export manufacturing sector is dominated by firms with well over 1,000 employees, with small firms virtually absent.

The qualitative and quantitative evidence actually suggest an interesting reason for the downfall of communist economies in Eastern Europe. Just as Marx declared of capitalist economies, we can say that communist centrally planned economies, as in the Czechoslovak case, "sowed the seeds of their own destruction." As the regime married itself to ever-increasing scales of production, coalitions of enterprise directors, regional Party officials, and deputies of relevant ministries increasingly acquired economic and political power. These coalitions could virtually blackmail the state into financially and politically supporting their economic structure, while maintaining their economic monopoly and, in turn, a "soft" environment for performance. Internal pressure for structural change could thus be diffused over an extended period of time.

The Czechoslovak manufacturing sector faces a hysteresis jump downward in international competitiveness. The transformation process is presented with the challenge of a persisting coalition structure that is deeply rooted in its informal nature, where the behavioral problems cannot be easily changed by the simple, formal transfer of the economy to a market-based one. From the preliminary data of the newly establishing small-business sector and from the analysis of adopted legislation, one can observe that a very hostile environment continues to exist for the development of dynamic capital and firm formation, which is critical to the survival and success of democratic marketization. Future research should be directed toward the creation of a microinstitutional framework which minimizes the negative behavioral effects of the distorted economic structure.

Notes

1 Czechoslovak statistics record only the number of laborers in firms, excluding calculation of the number of white collar employees.
2 According to Brown and Phillips (1989), the employment measure is a standard criterion to gauge firm size.
3 Export manufacturing firms are defined in Czechoslovakia as those which pursue export activities, yet also contribute (often principally) to domestic production.
4 Standard entry barriers in leading developing countries are typically high capital requirements, scale economies, advertising, and R&D (see Geroski and Schwalbach, 1991). By contrast, entry barriers are vastly more complicated and widespread in Czechoslovakia.
5 This was revealed through investigations of the state industrial sector in Hungary by Gerald A. McDermott in 1989, as a Thomas J. Watson Foundation Fellow.
6 What is not included in the above data are those small, productive units currently within a state firm, which want to break off and form their own private company. No clear picture regarding this group will be available until the further formation of new commerce and ownership laws.
7 For concrete policy recommendations in developed market economies, see Storey and Johnson (1987).
8 Tony Levitas (1989 and 1990) began arguing for similar initiatives for Poland in 1990.

References

Acs, Zoltan and David Audretsch (1987) "Innovation, Market Structure, and Firm Size," *Review of Economics and Statistics*, **69**, 567–576.
(1988) "Innovation in Large and Small Firms: An Empirical Analysis," *American Economic Review*, **78**, 678–690.
(1989a) "Small Firms and Technology," *Beleidsstudies technologie/economie*, Ministry of Economic Affairs, The Netherlands.
(1989b) "Entrepreneurial Strategy and the Presence of Small Firms," *Small Business Economics*, **1**, 193–213.
Acs, Zoltan, David Audretsch, and Bo Carlsson (1991), "Flexible Technology and Firm Size," *Small Business Economics,* **3(4)**, 307–320.
Audretsch, David (1989) *The Market and the State*, New York: New York University Press.
Blair, J. (1948), "Technology and Size," *American Economic Review*, **38(2)**, 121–52.
Brock, William and David Evans (1989) "Small Business Economics," *Small Business Economics* **1**, 7–20.
Brown, H. S. and B. Phillips (1989) "Comparisons Between Small Business and Data Base (USEEM) and Bureau of Labor Statistics (BLS) Employment Data 1978–1986," *Small Business Economics*, **1**, 273–284.

Brown, Murray (1971) *Technological Change and the Production*, New York: New York University Press.

Carlsson, Bo (1989) "The Evolution of Manufacturing Technology and Its Impact on Industrial Structure: An international Study," *Small Business Economics*, **1**, 21–37.

Chandler, Alfred (1977) *The Visible Hand: The Managerial Revolution in American Business*, Cambridge, MA: Harvard University Press.

Dosi, G. (1988) "Sources, Procedures of Microeconomic Effects of Innovation," *Journal of Economic Literature*, **26**, 1120–1171.

Evans, David and L. Leighton (1989) "The Determinants of Changes in U.S. Self-Employment, 1968–1987," *Small Business Economics*, **1**(2), 111–120.

FitzRoy Felix (1989) "Firm Size, Efficiency, and Employment: A Review Article," *Small Business Economics*, **1**(1), 75–80.

Freeman, C. (1982) *The Economics of Industrial Innovation*, London: Francis Pinter.

Galbraith, John (1967) *The New Industrial State*, Boston: Houghton Mifflin.

Geroski, Paul and R. Pomeroy (1987) "Innovation and the Evolution of Market Structure," London Business School, *Working Paper Series*, **36** (November).

Geroski, Paul and Joachim Schwalbach (eds.) (1991) *Entry and Market Contestability: An International Comparison*, Oxford: Basil Blackwell.

Kolko, Gabrial (1963) *The Triumph of Conservatism*, New York: Macmillan.

Kornai, Janos (1986) *Contradictions and Dilemmas*, Cambridge, MA: MIT Press.

Leibenstein, Harvey (1976) *Beyond Economic Man*, Cambridge, MA: Harvard University Press.

Lenin, Vladimir (1916) *Imperialism as the Latest Phase of Capitalism*.

Levitas, Tony (1989) "Strategic Choices and Democratic Marketization (Solidarnosc i Ryneor)," *Res Publica* (May).

   (1990) "Solidarity Banns: Infrastructure From the Bottom Up," *Communist Economics*, **2**(1).

Mejstrik, Michal (1990) "Czechoslovak Transition to a Market Economy," NBER Lecture, Cambridge, MA (June).

Mejstrik, Michal and M. Cermak (1990) "Analysis of Size and Performance of State Industrial Enterprises," Research Report, Institute of Economics, Prague.

Mills, D. E. and L. Schumann (1985) "Industry Structure With Fluctuating Demand," *American Economic Review*, **75**, 758–767.

Mlcoch, Lubomir (1990) "The Behavior of Czechoslovak Enterprises," *Research Paper*, **348**, Institute of Economics, Prague.

Nelson, R. and S. Winter (1977) *An Evolutionary Theory of Economic Change*, Cambridge, MA: Belknap Press.

Piore Michael and Charles Sabel (1983) "Italian Small Business Development: Lessons for US Industrial Policy," in John Zysman and Laura Tyson (eds.), *American Industry in International Competition*, Ithaca: Cornell University.

   (1984) *The Second Industrial Divide*, New York: Basic Books.

Pryor, Z. P. and F. L. Pryor (1975) "Foreign Trade and Interwar Czechoslovak Economic Development 1918–1938," *Vierteljahrschrift für Sozial und Wirtschaftgeschichte*, **62**.

Reich, Robert (1983) *The Next American Frontier*, New York: Times Books.

Sato, Yoshio (1989) "Small Business in Japan: A Historical Perspective," *Small Business Economics*, **1**(2), 121–128.

Scherer, F. M. (1980) *Industrial Market Structure and Economic Performance*, Chicago: Rand McNally.

Schumpeter, Joseph (1950) *Capitalism, Socialism, and Democracy*, New York: Harper & Row.

Schwalbach, Joachim (1989) "Small Business in German Manufacturing," *Small Business Economics*, **1**(2), 129–136.

Shepherd, W. (1982) "Causes of Increased Competition in the U.S. Economy, 1939–1980," *Review of Economics and Statistics*, **64**(4), 613–626.

Storey, David and S. Johnson (1987) *Job Generation and Labor Market Change*, London: Macmillan.

Teichova, Alice (1988) *The Czechoslovak Economy 1918–1980*, London: Routledge.

Triska, Dusan (1990) "Bargaining and Search in Imperfect Markets: A Centrally Planned Economy," in Richard Quandt and Dusan Triska (eds.), *Optimal Decisions in Markets and Planned Economies*, Boulder: Westview Press.

Wheelwright, S. C. (1985) "Restoring Competitiveness in US Manufacturing," *California Management Review*, **27**, 27–34.

White, L. J. (1982) "The Determinants of the Relative Importance of Business," *Review of Economics and Statistics*, **64**, 42–49.

Zamrazilova, Eva (1990) "International Comparisons of Economic Development Levels Between East and West European Countries," *Jahrbuch des Ost-Europa Wirtsschaft* (November).

Zemplinerova, Alena (1989a) "Monopoly in a Centrally Planned Economy," *Research Paper*, **333**, Institute of Economics, Prague.

(1989b) "Monopolization of the Czechoslovak Economy," paper presented at the EARIE Conference, Budapest.

9 The evolution of small business in East Germany

Hans-Gerd Bannasch

1. The process of German unification: economic conditions for small business

The evolution and the perspectives of small business in East Germany is of course directly connected to the German unification process. On July 1, 1990, the currency unification of Germany started, and I am convinced that the market forces will contribute to a fast change towards a better structured economy in the eastern part of Germany. At the heart of the transformation process is the development of a vital base of entrepreneurial activity.[1] According to Román (1989) and Puchev (1990), the existence of such entrepreneurial activity has been markedly absent throughout the Eastern European countries since the Second World War. According to Román (1989, p. 396), "Small business as an entrepreneurial sector is still small, lacks dynamism, and is far from being innovative enough to have a significant impact on structural adjustment."

Now we have a completely new situation for firms in the former German Democratic Republic, and one hears again and again – it is a historical moment (which happened very often in the first six months of 1990) in this high-speed development process. There are good reasons for hope, but also concerns about the risk of unemployment and the necessity to close many enterprises due to inefficiency. So top managers, young entrepreneurs and scientists are living between high expectations about economic growth and success and concern about the risks of the transitional period from an outdated centralized system towards a social market economy.

2. The combine system

To describe the conditions for the development of small business in East Germany it is necessary to explain the rapidly changing enterprise structure of the past. Throughout the 1980s, the international competitiveness of East German goods decreased steadily and the international worth of the currency dropped by 15 percent. This was largely attributable to the creation and growth of the system of combines during the previous three decades. A combine, the equivalent of a giant conglomerate in the West, typically consists of hundreds of individual plants. In essence, East German economic planners believed that large, centrally controlled plants would generate economies of scale far beyond anything in the West. In East Germany, bigger was better, easier to control, and the key to economic growth. One giant firm, the combine, was responsible for virtually all plants within each major industry. Smaller manufacturing plants and firms were gradually closed or merged, and their workers were shifted to or placed under the control of new combines. While the government dramatically changed the ownership, management, and control of firms, it did very little over four decades to upgrade and modernize the plants.

It should be emphasized that the relationship between each individual establishment, or plant in the manufacturing sector, and its parent combine is somewhat different than that between an establishment and the parent firm in the West. The East German combines generally had rigid control of the individual establishments, whereby most of the important decisions were centralized and made at the combine and not at the establishment level.[2]

What the combines gained in size – a workforce that generally equalled the equivalent of twenty to forty establishments in the West – they lost in flexibility and entrepreneurial innovation.[3] As of 1989 there were 224 combines in existence, of which 180 were in the manufacturing sector. County authorities controlled 95 of the combines, and 126 were controlled by government officials in East Berlin (Audretsch, 1990). The East German policy of centralization provides a striking contrast to the entrepreneurial revolution built around the explosion of new small firms in Western economies, particularly in the United States. The absence of such entrepreneurial activity deprived East Germany of the West's greatest source of dynamism and innovation.

Table 9.1 indicates the evolution of the extent of industrial combines since 1970 in East Germany. There are two important trends apparent in this table. First, the number of industrial combines has substantially increased over the last two decades. Second, the share of economic activity – measured alternatively by industrial output, employment, output of consumer goods, and exports – accounted for by these combines rose drastically between 1970 and 1987.

As a result of the system of combines, the share of manufacturing establishments, or plants, in East Germany with at least 500 employees

Table 9.1. *Industrial combines in East Germany*[a]

Year	Number of combines	Industrial production	Employment	Consumer goods	Exports
1970	35	33	33	6	38
1980	130 (93)	98 (92)	99 (94)	100 (97)	99 (85)
1985	129 (95)	98 (95)	100 (95)	100 (97)	100 (96)
1986	127	98	100	100	100
1987	126 (93)	98 (95)	100 (95)	100 (97)	100 (97)

Note: [a] The combines controlled by District Economic Councils are listed in parentheses. Otherwise, all combines were controlled by an industrial ministry.
Source: Statistisches Jahrbuch der DDR (1988).

was almost ten times as great as that reported by Michael Fritsch for West Germany in Chapter 3 of this volume. In the German Democratic Republic 40 percent of the plants have over 500 employees. Similarly, while in the Federal Republic of Germany about 88 percent of the plants have fewer than 100 employees, only 18 percent do in East Germany (Acs and Audretsch, 1990). In terms of unemployment, this disparity in establishment size is even greater. About four-fifths of employment is in plants with at least 500 employees. Most strikingly, only 1.1 percent of manufacturing employees are in plants with fewer than 100 employees.

One of the major goals of a combine in the old system was to be able to function autonomously to react to evolving economic conditions. To facilitate this goal, combines typically undertook research and development (R&D) activities spanning the entire industry. In addition, combines often included the capacity for plants producing crucial inputs as well as for plants producing final goods. A combine also had the capacity to engage in marketing and sales at a national level and, in certain cases, in international markets.

Not surprisingly, with the increase in the share of economic activity accounted for by the industrial combines came a sharp concentration of economic power. This economic concentration was largely the product of a policy designed to exploit administrative economies and therefore continuously to reduce the number of independent industrial plants.

Table 9.2 shows that there were only 13 percent as many industrial enterprises in existence in East Germany in 1987 as there had been in 1950. This dramatic reduction in the number of enterprises over the last four decades is a striking contrast to the explosion in new firms in most Western countries. Just as the number of enterprises throughout the

Table 9.2. *Index of number of enterprises and employment in East German manufacturing, 1950–1987 (1950 = 100)*

Year	Number of enterprises	Employment
1950	100	100
1960	68	135
1970	49	138
1980	19	150
1987	13	153

Source: Statistisches Jahrbuch der DDR (1988).

Table 9.3. *Number of establishments in East German manufacturing by size class, 1971–1987*

Number of workers and employees	1971	1978	1987
less than 25	3864	716	131
25–50	2559	1084	186
51–100	1812	1130	343
101–200	1147	946	519
201–500	845	1074	861
501–1000	405	517	558
1001–2500	406	480	540
2501–5000	133	178	215
5001–10,000	62	69	75
10,001–20,000	15	16	21
20,000 +	5	3	–
Total	11,253	6,213	3,449

Source: Statistisches Jahrbuch der DDR (1988).

Western economies had been rapidly expanding, there had been an overwhelming increase in economic concentration in East Germany. Similarly, while the average plant size reduced substantially during the last twenty years in the United States it increased considerably in East Germany.

Table 9.3 shows that the total number of establishments in East German manufacturing had fallen from over 11,000 in 1971 to 3,449 by 1987. Most striking was the reduction in the number of plants with fewer than 25 workers, from 3,864 to 131.

One of the historical artefacts of the combines is that, over time, some plants were included in combines for administrative reasons, and not because they provided an economic contribution. The inclusion of such inefficient plants has placed a burden on overall economic growth.

Starting from this enterprise development there is now the task and the chance to create new enterprises on an economic basis in accordance with the approach of countries with advanced economic performance in the West. Transformation of establishments into enterprises could narrow the gap between the two German states, especially in the manufacturing sector, where productivity levels reached only 50 percent in comparison to the western part of Germany. Three reasons can be cited for that low level:

- One-third is accounted for by outdated organization which includes a lot of bureaucracy of the "command-economy."
- One-third is accounted for by the old technologies (high efforts necessary in the repair sector).
- One-third is related to motivation, lack of incentives for higher performance including real entrepreneurship.

In accordance with our research work, I agree with assessments which are drawing the following conclusions about future chances for the existing combines:

- 5–8 are internationally competitive.
- 50–70 are competitive, but it is necessary to stabilize them.
- 50 or more need to be redeveloped, but it is worthwhile.
- 20 are not able to be stabilized.

That means that one-third of the single firms have a good chance in the market economy, 50 percent are capable of being restructured and 20 percent have no chance. The appropriate way will be reprivatization of the large units via the divestiture of plants, the creation of new enterprises and the formation of joint ventures with firms from the West with the help of finance promotion from the government there. Not surprisingly, there is little private investor interest in the approximately 8,000 establishments now under government trusteeship through the *Treuhandanstalt*, which is the state trust agency responsible for privatization and reorganization of state-owned combines. The German government sold only DM 1 billion of assets in 1991 out of a total plant valuation of roughly DM 600 billion. Burger King, Siemens, Lufthansa, Daimler–Benz, General Motors, and Volkswagen have all entered into pioneering joint ventures with spinoffs from the former combines.

For the 12,000 small firms that were nationalized in 1972 (large plants and firms were nationalized shortly after East Germany was created in 1949), the *Treuhandanstalt* approved 582 joint ventures with Western partners, predominantly West German firms, in 1990.

3. Historic development of small business

Especially prior to 1972, there was a relatively strong sector of small business in East Germany. As Table 9.4 shows, it consisted of private handicrafts, handicraft cooperatives, semi-state enterprises and private enterprises.

From the 1950s up to the erection of the Wall in 1961, there was a sector of small business in the East but at a declining level. After that time, private entrepreneurs also tried to establish and develop their small plants on a very small scale in certain restricted areas. This period was nearly finished in 1972: in 1972, 6,700 semi-state enterprises, 2,900 private enterprises, and 1,900 cooperatives were taken over by the government and became state owned. After that time period, economic development was characterized by the centralized "command-economy" with all its problems and negative results especially for the small business sector.

Interestingly, the former private enterprises and semi-state plants can now play an important role in the new state. Every former owner has the right to get their enterprise back in connection with the privatization process. There are already some encouraging examples, but it is too early to assess the possible results of these developments. Nearly 50 percent of former owners have signaled their interest in getting their plant back, but so far only 4 percent are already acting as a new entrepreneur.

Despite the crippling effects of massive uncertainty, the reprivatization of combines and individual plants is beginning and the establishment of small, new firms shows signs of flourishing. By the end of 1990, there were 59,435 registered new start ups, 60 percent in the service sector and tourism. These start ups typically involve several employees, require modest financing, and provide personal services, such as shoe or auto repairs, that are in enormous demand.

On the other hand, we are at the beginning of a very interesting period of the creation of small and medium-sized enterprises via the reprivatization process of big economic units and the foundation of new enterprises in the future. The ambitious target has been set by Elmar Pieroth, economic advisor of the government from the West to create 500,000 new enterprises in East Germany in the near future. That means

Table 9.4. *Share of small business in the number of firms, employment and Gross National Product*

Year	Private handicrafts	Cooper- atives	Private enterprises	Semi-state enterprises	Total	Total share of employment	Total share of GNP
1950	91.5	–	6.7	–	98.2	42.0	31
1956	91.0	0.1	6.1	0.1	97.3	29.7	20
1961	87.7	1.5	3.9	3.5	96.6	27.4	17

Source: Statistisches Jahrbuch der DDR (1988).

that millions of jobs (there is a figure of 4 million jobs) could be created in all sectors of the economy in order to reach the productivity level of the FRG within 5–8 years.

4. Forecast and expectations for the future

In the present situation it is nearly impossible to provide scientifically-based hypotheses and conclusions for the small-business sector in East Germany because of the current economic uncertainties. Indeed, one cannot find a comparable process in the economic history of any other country. At the same time it is, of course, an exciting development for the scientists and advisors of managers to influence this process.

From my own point of view, it is essential to promote especially three preconditions to facilitate a vital entrepreneurial sector:

(1) The creation of an economic environment that is conducive to entre-preneurial activity.
(2) The alleviation of political and administrative barriers which impede the creation of new firms.
(3) The creation of an institutional network that will provide the infra-structure for promoting, financing, and facilitating new business.

In this process it is very important to see the necessary connection to the western part of Germany, and to EC 1992. There are 7,000 firms in East Germany already involved in intra-German trade, and this process should be much more internationalized. The figure of about 2,000 joint ventures is an indicator for entrepreneurial activities.

I think the next few months will see a fast-growing sector of small business, and I am very optimistic that we can expect in the coming years something that in the past has often been called an "economic miracle": I do have the hope that the new freedom and openness will lead to a successful period of economic development. I am convinced that especially this part of the economy will play one of the most important roles in the transformation process in East Germany.

Notes

1 See Steinitz (1989).
2 "Norbert Walter zur deutschen Konjunktur," *Wirtschaftswoche* (June 22, 1990) p. 29.
3 That is, as Diwan (1989) and Carlsson (1989) point out, one of the liabilities of larger-enterprise inflexibility and sluggishness in reacting to change. In fact, both Carlsson (1989) and Diwan (1989) attribute the recent emergence of small firms in Western economies to the inherent flexibility associated with smaller firm size.

References

Acs, Zoltan J. and David B. Audretsch (1990) "Kleine Unternehmen, Schaffung von Arbeitsplätzen und Technologie in den USA und der Bundesrepublik Deutschland," in Johannes Berger, Volker Domeyer and Maria Funder (eds.), *Kleinbetriebe im wirtschaftlichen Wandel*, Frankfurt: Campus Verlag, 35–60.

Audretsch, David B (1990) "Investment Opportunities in a Unified Germany," *Global Economic Policy,* **2(2)**, 14–24.

Carlsson, Bo (1989) "Flexibility in the Theory of the Firm," *International Journal of Industrial Organization,* **7(2)**, 179–204.

Diwan, Romesh (1989) "Small Business and the Economics of Flexible Manufacturing," *Small Business Economics*, **1(2)**, 101–110.

Puchev, Plamen (1990) "A Note on Government Policy and the New 'Entrepreneurship' in Bulgaria," *Small Business Economics*, **2(1)**, 73–76.

Román, Zoltán (1989) "The Size of the Small-Firm Sector in Hungary," *Small Business Economics*, **1(4)**, 303–308.

Steinitz, K. (1989) "Innovationsprobleme und Strukturwandel in der DDR," *Politik und Zeitgeschichte* (March).

10 The implications of the Polish economic reform for small business: evidence from Gdansk

Simon Johnson and *Gary Loveman*

1. Introduction

In January 1990, the Solidarity government in Poland introduced the "Balcerowicz Plan," which was designed quickly to transform the centrally planned Polish economy into a market economy. The Plan included monetary policy reforms to slow the existing hyperinflation (which was running at roughly 4000 percent per year) and make the zloty a freely convertible currency, and it also called for an end to the protection and subsidization of state-owned enterprises. While the details of privatization of state-owned assets remained to be resolved, state-owned enterprises would lose their monopoly positions and their large subsidies, and would be left to compete effectively or perish. The disruptive nature of this style of rapid economic reform was well known to its architects, and the results nine months into the Plan reflected both high costs and impressive progress: monthly inflation slowed from 100 percent to about 4 percent, the zloty was stable against the dollar, real interest rates had gone from a large negative magnitude to roughly zero, and both real output and real wages had fallen (according to official statistics) by about 25 percent.

While stabilization of Poland's macroeconomic circumstances is a crucial precondition for economic reform, institutional reform and privatization are fundamental to Poland's prospects for economic growth and an improved standard of living. Unfortunately, the legacy of 40 years of communist rule is an institutional structure particularly vulnerable to the type of reform program now in place. In particular, Polish policy under the communists was explicitly directed at severely controlling both private production and, closely related, small-scale production. The proportions vary over time and the statistics are themselves problematic, but the

190

data suggest that from 1960 to the mid-1980s less than 5 percent of Polish non-agricultural employment was in private enterprise.[1] The *Statistical Yearbook* for 1989 gives total non-agricultural private sector employment as 954,304 in 1985 and 1,287,693 in 1988 (with a total labor force in 1988 of 17.83 million). Meanwhile, Polish state enterprises became larger, so that even state employees typically worked in very large organizations. Lipton and Sachs (1990) report that in 1986 the average Polish state enterprise had 1,132 employees with an average plant size of 378. For the purposes of comparison, industrial plants in Austria, Belgium, France, Italy, Japan, and Sweden, had an average plant size of 80. Indeed, only about 1,000 Polish state enterprises employed fewer than 100 people, and only 10 percent of industrial employment was in establishments of fewer than 100 employees. The above group of Western countries had 35 percent of industrial employment in establishments with 10 to 100 employees.[2]

The absence of a significant small-business sector in Poland raises severe problems for the Balcerowicz Plan. As the large state-owned firms begin to contract and, eventually, go bankrupt, and as privatization and reorganization of these firms take place, the economy must rely on smaller businesses to provide employment and output to sustain the economy, at least during the transition to a market economy. But it is precisely these small businesses that have not existed to any significant degree in Poland for decades. An absolutely central issue for economic reform in Poland therefore is whether a small-business sector will emerge quickly enough and effectively enough to stimulate the economy during the contraction of the state sector. From a policy perspective, the reform program must be expanded to include measures that will facilitate entrepreneurship and small-business development. However, given the novelty of these phenomena in Poland, very little is known about the current state of the small-business sector, if such a sector can expand, or what specific problems are presented by the economic reform for small-business development.

The current Polish circumstances offer, paradoxically, both tremendous opportunities and great difficulties. Recent research (Sengenberger, Loveman and Piore, 1990; Friedman, 1988) has documented the crucial role of a small business in the economic performance of market economies such as Japan, Italy and the Federal Republic of Germany, and has identified important differences in institutional structures across countries that significantly influence the nature and performance of the small-business sector. In addition, evidence from many Western industrialized countries suggests that, after decades of decline, the employment shares of small enterprises and establishments have increased since the late 1970s. The relative youth of a significant private small-business sector in Poland means that Poles are still creating the necessary institutional structure. The weak economic system inherited from the communists places few inhibitions on institutional innovation, unlike, say, the United States, where long-established regulations and practices make institutional change much more difficult. Amidst the very full agenda facing Polish policy makers, room must be made for a debate on the future role and structure of the small-business sector.

This chapter reports on the beginning of an ongoing effort to understand the development of small business in Poland during the transformation from central planning to a market economy. The results and arguments presented below are drawn from a study of small businesses in the area around and including Gdansk. The sample of roughly thirty firms, about twenty of which are private, is by no means a random sample. Rather, it includes the most successful and highly visible entrepreneurs in the area, as well as some relatively successful state firms. In addition, small-business growth has been more extensive in Gdansk than in other areas, for reasons that are discussed below. The sample selection bias is obviously considerable if the goal is to draw inferences about the general population of small businesses in Poland. Our goal is more modest. We seek to answer the question: how can Polish policy makers and business persons begin to build institutions that will support a growing small-business sector capable of generating more employment and competing with large firms (including foreigners) in both product and labor markets?

Section 2 profiles the current private small-business sector in Gdansk. Several factors are identified which contributed to the development of small business. First, there were some liberalizing influences even under the old planned system which allowed the continued existence of "craft" production, especially in handicrafts and retailing. Second, there was a breakdown in the planned system after 1980, resulting in the weakening of central control over state enterprises as well as further liberalization for the private sector and the destabilization of the macroeconomy. There emerged new small private firms, the most important of which used private economic activity to support their work in the political opposition (underground Solidarity). Third, there was the economic reform in 1990, involving still further liberalization and stabilization of the macroeconomy. These measures have allowed some experienced entrepreneurs to produce radically new goods. Despite significant differences across firms, there is also a great deal of similarity between them. In particular, all of them have successfully tailored organizational structures and human resource strategies to fit their product market strategies.

Section 3 examines the current situation in small state enterprises (the situation in large-scale state firms involves a different set of issues, and is not discussed here). There is considerable heterogeneity across state firms. First, there are monopolies which have not been seriously affected by the collapse of the old system. Second, there are firms which have been forced by the breakdown of the old system to compete with the private sector. Third, there are firms responding in a desperate way to a worsening in their situation during 1990 and looking for their own salvation through a radically new product. The important similarity between all of these state firms is that they all have problems with their product market and human resource strategies, because these were assigned rather than designed by themselves.

Finally, Section 4 concludes with an assessment of the current prospects for the Polish small-business sector, and makes some tentative policy prescriptions. While the outlook is quite bright, there are several clear dangers. Some of these dangers, such as that posed by a backward banking system, can be eliminated by appropriate policy interventions. Our policy prescriptions deal first with immediate and obvious impediments to small-business development, and then turn briefly to policies aimed at building an institutional structure to support small business in the years to come.

2.   A profile of private firms

Despite differences in product strategy, all the private firms share important features. These features are especially apparent after interviewing both private and state firms. In particular, they all have a product strategy which emphasizes quality, along with a matching human resource strategy that provides incentives for maintaining quality. In most cases this involves a pay-for-performance compensation scheme. The careful matching of product with human resource strategy has been essential to the survival of private firms.

For many years the most important constraint facing private business was the availability of inputs. Successful entrepreneurs found ways to organize scarce labor and capital as there were no input markets of the sort found in the West. In Poland it was primarily a firm's human resource strategy which determined its output strategy, in contrast to the usual pattern in the West. If an entrepreneur could organize production, the output could usually be sold. It is only in 1990 that market conditions became more important than the rules and restrictions governing business.

2.1 *Available inputs*

Almost all of the entrepreneurs interviewed had at least five years' experience in private business. Many had not worked for themselves for all that time: about half had changed companies, either to adopt a new product line or to work with different people.

Only two businessmen had firms before 1980. The rest started in private business between 1983 and 1986, because opportunities in the state sector were so poor. They differ, however, in whether they were denied jobs in the state sector (e.g. in universities) for political reasons or whether they merely regarded the pay and work in state firms as unsatisfactory.

Many of the most successful firms had important links to academia and most employees had worked in the same "network" of people *before* joining the firm, although the network varied from student enterprises to underground Solidarity. Most firms still hear about potential employees through their own and existing workers' networks. These private firms have been remarkably successful in attracting the type of labor force which they want. All have low turnover rates. Those that employ skilled labor have "skimmed off" the best workers from the state sector, because they can afford to pay much higher wages. However, many firms said they were constrained by a lack of skilled labor. None had an organized training program, although most offered some on-the-job training.

All the firms are capital constrained. Most of them have very little in the form of fixed assets – with the exception of those firms which managed, often with extreme difficulty, to buy premises or land previously (usually for cash). Many of the firms raised capital through some form of industrial services – painting or repair work. Often they borrowed from their families. There is little evidence of informal credit markets – other than some trade credit and taking equity stakes in new start ups.

None of these firms feels that its operations are very risky, primarily because they know their products and markets very well and because they have very little debt. When asked about their prospects, their reaction is usually to point to something they do better than anyone else and to something new they intend to do in the near future which will be better still. This apparently nonchalant attitude to risk is not found in small firms in the West and the underlying reasons stem largely from the fact that the businesses were started with very little capital, and rarely with the proceeds from mortgaged assets. Hence, the downside risk is limited, and even business failure causes no substantial loss of reputation for the entrepreneur.

2.2 *Organization of work*

Most firms have "autocratic" management – the same one person consistently makes decisions and takes responsibility. The nature of the firm depends on this person's personality and experience.

Even in the private firms which are ostensibly cooperatives, there is one person who clearly makes the final decision. However, in these firms there is always consultation and a great deal of trust between the top manager and some close associates. In striking contrast with state firms, there was hardly an administrative hierarchy in the private businesses, and most expanding firms felt uneasy about how to create and manage a hierarchy. Some individual owners thought this was not an issue only because they could not think of sharing managerial control, and while these firms may grow considerably they will remain one-person operations.

Almost all of the private firms had some kind of pay-for-performance scheme. Such schemes are easier to arrange when the firm's product is a series of distinct projects. All firms which did project work paid employees according to performance on each project (this is not generally true of state firms). For example, a team which is paid to overhaul a turbine will receive a lump-sum payment for this job, subject to achieving satisfactory quality. Several firms have also established pay-for-performance schemes in manufacturing and in product development.

Some private firms are organized as cooperatives, but only because before 1988 this was the easiest way to form a private company with limited liability. These firms are usually composed of a group of highly skilled workers or professionals. Managers in these firms want to form several separate companies to run their different activities, but they are constrained by property forms. They are now waiting for legal changes, which they hope will allow them to divide the original cooperative's property and form a joint stock company. This transformation is intended to resolve the question of who owns the firm and how earnings should be divided between owners and employees. The resolution of this issue will affect how the cooperatives involve themselves in spinoff companies – for example, whether they retain an equity stake and some kind of managerial involvement.

2.3 *Product market strategy*

All the firms have relatively high-quality products. Most of them attribute their survival to success in positioning themselves in the high-quality end of the market. They also consider this to be a principal reason for their continued prosperity in 1990, despite the "demand barrier" created by the Balcerowicz Plan.

The successful private manufacturers usually see their competitors as one or two inefficient state firms. The service sector is more competitive, with more private firms, but most of the firms we interviewed believe they have defeated private competitors by retaining the business of loyal state enterprises through consistently providing high quality. Our sample lacks low-quality producers, probably because these firms do not survive for long. High quality is difficult to organize – particularly in Poland – so it is no accident that our sample is comprised primarily of well-organized firms.

Almost all these private firms try to innovate. In the firms composed of highly skilled workers, the leader organizes work, but often the innovation comes from below – their strength is in motivated, highly skilled labor. Otherwise, the entrepreneurs are themselves the innovators in their firms (so the innovations come "from above").

3. State firms

3.1 Current circumstances

State-owned enterprises can be segmented according to their product strategy. However, this strategy is usually not a conscious decision, but rather an endowment. The three types of firm differ in the market position with which they were endowed by the collapse of the old central planning system.

Many state firms have no effective competition, and feel content to continue with their existing products, although these may be of poor quality and have dubious prospects. Other firms already face substantial domestic or foreign competition, and as a result have already defined a clearer product strategy than have the monopolists. Finally, there are firms which have completely lost their previous market and are now desperately seeking new products.

There were also some differences in the way these state firms managed their human resources. Their human resource strategies were also endowments, the result of labor relations since at least 1980. In most of the firms, product and human resource strategies did not seem to fit together well. All state firms were much more hierarchical than private firms with the same number of employees, and there was a much clearer division between employees and managers. While the firms facing significant competition had pay-for-performance schemes similar to those in the private sector, the monopolies paid a fixed monthly wage (usually with a meaningless bonus).

All the state firms felt their prospects were unclear (and hence are not inclined to expand) until privatization issues are resolved. As sections 3.1.1–3.1.3 describe, managers of state firms differed considerably in their attitudes to privatization.

3.1.1. The monopolists

State firms with some monopoly power have yet to adapt to the new environment. Although managers in these firms can recite the rhetoric of economic change, they have no strategies to deal with the incipient entry by domestic private firms into their sector, and have little idea about the effects of foreign competition. These firms do have useful human and physical assets, but the prospects and value of the firm depend on whether management can develop a product strategy and reorganize their human resources so as to look more like successful private firms.

A state firm in shipping services was reasonably successful in the past because it had permission to conduct foreign trade. But any firm can now trade, so this once precious permission is now valueless. The state firm has no clear strategy to deal with the new situation, other than to hope that some foreign partner will turn up. What happens to this firm will depend in part on the form and speed of entry by other firms into its sector.

Almost all the banks interviewed were also monopolies. Reform of the banking system has left significant monopolies, especially in loans to the food-processing sector, as well as establishing an effective cartel of so-called "commercial banks." These banks are doing little to improve their products, particularly money transfer service and the organization of credit, although to some extent they are held back by the extreme caution of the National Bank of Poland (NBP). The banking sector may become a real brake on Polish economic development because the existing services are so poor and because the NBP controls both entry and the level of services in the cartel. There is a startling discrepancy between the delays in improving bank services and the rapid changes in state firms which face more market competition.

3.1.2. The competitors

The two "competitive" state firms which we interviewed were in construction services. One competes with private firms to provide repairs to public buildings, and the other manages the export of construction services from a consortium of local firms.

Both state firms organize their work into projects (which seems natural for construction), give project leaders considerable discretion and total control over quality, and pay workers according to the performance of a particular project. Both feel that their previous success and future prospects rest upon providing relatively high-quality services.

The repair service firm has problems with its workers. Management recognizes that it has too many administrators and unskilled workers, especially now that acquiring materials has become so much easier. There is also a tense relationship between management and the firm's Solidarity union and workers' council. On the other hand, the firm has an established and successful training program for workers – in association with the local technical college. Even this firm, one of the most successful state firms in the region, will probably have to reduce its unskilled labor force by a third. However, it is currently seeking to increase its number of skilled workers.

The export firm employs most of its workers part-time, for particular projects. It pays workers substantially more than they earn in their usual jobs and appears to have no labor problems. This is one state firm which was set up to pursue a well-defined product strategy and its success has always been based on management's ability to organize its human resources to fit this strategy. The firm also has an extensive network of foreign contacts and has new projects under way in West Germany, Czechoslovakia and the Soviet Union.

3.1.3.   The gamblers

We interviewed one firm which is taking a huge gamble. Its traditional business – exporting to the Soviet Union – has stopped. The firm is actually just a branch of a conglomerate state firm, with headquarters in Warsaw, but the central office has no good ideas about how to respond to the crisis. In the Gdansk branch, a strong central figure has already organized the highly skilled engineers to produce prototypes of two new electronic products – one for the West and one for the domestic market. Pay will probably be strictly according to performance. However, the prospects of this firm are uncertain for two reasons. First, its management has no experience with selling on any market. Second, in contrast with private Polish firms – which all built up their capital themselves – this firm is waiting to see if it can get assets "free" when (and if) the conglomerate is broken up. Interestingly, the leaders in this firm did not view the risks of this strategy as being excessive. The management and workers do not feel they have much to lose, and there is little chance that failure will result in the loss of personal property.

3.2 Privatization

Managers in all these state firms want to be privatized, but each type has different views on what will result from privatization. Each firm also has its own particular property form with its own issues. Until these property issues are resolved and it becomes clear who owns the firms, none of them will significantly reorganize their labor force (and fire people) and none will undertake substantial investment.

Three of the state firms are owned by other state firms and one firm is owned by the local council. In none of them does the central government have a clear ownership claim – it was an established practice to "hide" good assets in small firms as far from central ministries as possible.

Before 1990, each of these firms can be characterized as having maximized the value of real wages paid – subject to keeping higher authorities content. Obviously, all of them now want the best possible deal for employees, but they differ about how privatization can achieve this.

The monopolies are fairly content with the status quo. In any privatization they want as much of the assets as possible to pass without charge to the employees. They feel that employee ownership was the *de facto* situation previously and that it should continue. The banks are aware that this may be politically impossible, and as a result are in no hurry to be privatized. Thus firms which receive economic rents in the product market are waiting for handouts in the asset market.

The competitors are extremely dissatisfied with the status quo. They believe their businesses can do well, and seek just to resolve the property issue – so there are clear rules about ownership and the division between wages and profits. For them "privatization" means stabilizing and codifying income shares and the initial ownership of assets.[3] One firm is "owned" by the local council, and would not object to the council becoming a shareholder. The other firm is "owned" by member firms, and the staff of this firm (which is quite small) wants to assure their own share in profits.

If these competitor firms think the price set by the current owners on any of their fixed assets, such as buildings, is too high, then they are willing to set up the firm in another location. They are interested in attracting an infusion of capital through issuing shares, and diluting their ownership rights.

The gambler is also dissatisfied with the status quo, but for a different reason. This firm thinks that the central office has lost its usefulness and the assets of the conglomerate should be divided up. The new products were developed only in Gdansk, and they do not see why Warsaw should share in any of the profits. There is, however, about $20–30,000 in machinery (valued at replacement cost) at this branch, and it would be extremely difficult for the firm to raise this amount of capital by itself.

We expect the firms in this sector to contract in the short term. Their sales will stagnate and their employment will fall, as workers leave for higher paying jobs elsewhere. There is a danger that the skimming off of skilled workers by the private sector will create state sector "zombies" – firms that are incapable of producing properly, but which continue to control potentially valuable capital assets. The real wages for unskilled labor left in such firms will probably fall.

The property issue obscures the long-term potential of every firm. It is very hard to tell who is a good manager. Most of them are "good" *nomenklatura* – who were promoted for their ability rather than their political connections – and some of them are from Solidarity, connected to the same networks as the leading private firms.

In all cases the net effect of privatization will probably be a reduction in the employment of unskilled manual workers and in older white collar workers in the "administration" of the firm. Privatization will probably increase the demand for skilled labor.

4. Conclusions and policy implications

Our sample is small and is biased towards successful firms. Nevertheless, it is possible to make some broad inferences for at least the small-business sector in Gdansk. Currency stability and relatively low inflation, both products of the economic reform, have helped firms to calculate what is profitable, and to import goods. It is now much easier to buy materials and most of the firms interviewed had experienced only a small fall in demand. However, most of the businessmen expressed disappointment that the government has not (as they saw it) improved tax regulations and eliminated biases against the private sector.

Most of these firms are positive about their future. The obstacles they cite are primarily internal to the firm. In the old regime, management competed largely on the basis of exploiting loopholes in regulations and finding ways to procure scarce inputs. As the economy is reformed, managers must begin to compete on the basis of the variables that influence success in Western economies (e.g. product strategy, innovation, and marketing). The growth of each firm will be determined largely by how well it transforms its management. Much more than before, although not completely, private sector managers feel in control of their own destinies.

4.1 Immediate policy prescriptions

While the individual firms face many specific strategic and managerial hurdles, there are several important government measures which would help the private sector. These measures fall roughly into three groups: regulation and taxation, banking and privatization.

Regulations of all kinds should be simplified, kept stable and made more uniform between different legal forms. In particular, entrepreneurs suggest the following:

(a) There should be no tax or other advantages for joint ventures, and no minimum capital requirement for joint ventures (at present it is $50,000).

(b) The excess wage tax should be lifted from all private firms. (This is a form of tax-based incomes policy designed to penalize firms if they give "excessive" wage increases per worker, but under some conditions it can effectively limit the expansion in employment.)

(c) The taxation system should be restructured; in particular, there should be investment tax credits and an end to the double (and in some cases triple) taxation of dividends. Of over 1,000 joint stock companies in the Gdansk region, less than twenty paid a dividend in 1989.

At best these restrictions waste resources, as firms devote considerable energies to avoiding them. At worst these restrictions prevent growth in the private sector by, for example, preventing small-scale joint ventures. The perception of private businessmen is that regulations and taxes are at least as unstable as under the old regime. Furthermore, the regulations are still implemented by aggressive regional tax offices. These must be the most frequently inspected small businesses in the world.

Many businessmen were disappointed by the recent tax holiday for new companies. This measure is unpopular because it "discriminates" (a word used by several businessmen) against existing business and will probably lead many firms to close and reopen under new names, with fictitious owners.

Businesses cited banking as their most pressing problem with Polish infrastructure. Firms need to transfer money rapidly, to any part of Poland and abroad. Many small firms incur considerable wasted time in the transfer of money, and for most it is a serious impediment to transacting foreign business. The NBP appears to have taken no steps to improve this service. The problems are not technological, but organizational. Every bank has a telex machine and couriers are used locally. Nevertheless, it can take two weeks to transfer money 10 miles. Part of the problem is that banks use the delay in making payments to finance their own operations (in some branches of the Bank for Food Economy, this provides one-third of their funds). Some entrepreneurs suggest that an independent money transfer office should be established, with the explicit goal of transferring money to anywhere in Poland within the working day. Small business remains extremely skeptical about the organizational ability of Polish banks.

Most small firms also need capital. Start up firms need relatively small amounts, $2–3,000 for fairly long periods and may not be able to make immediate payments. Private business people do not think that the established state-owned banks are willing and able to provide these loans. It is true that the administrative costs per unit of credit are higher for smaller firms, but banks are reluctant to lend, primarily because they see this as a risky activity in which they have no experience. More importantly, there is no competitive pressure, and a weak profit motive, for an individual bank to lend to the private sector.

The entry of new banks is essential to make the market for loans to small firms more competitive. Of course, adequate regulation is required, especially after the Grabelny affair (in which an unlicensed "banker" absconded with several million dollars of deposits). But it would be a mistake to allow regulatory caution to preserve the banking cartel. The most dynamic private business networks, such as those in Gdansk, are beginning to establish local banks, to share their financial resources and promote new activities. But technical assistance and sources of capital are definitely needed to encourage bank start ups in other towns.

4.2 *Small firms and privatization*

The debate about Polish privatization has so far centered on the need to balance a wide distribution of ownership (because this is fair) and a concentration of control, to make managers more sensitive to profits (because this is efficient). One currently discussed plan is to allocate firms' shares to a number of mutual funds, and then distribute mutual-fund shares at no cost to the population. The mutual-fund shares would eventually be tradeable, and fund managers would be given incentives effectively to control the restructuring of the firms.

However, our interviews suggest that this policy will not have a large or immediate impact on small state firms. Most of these firms are not "owned" directly by the central government. The central government lacks the legal authority or managerial capacity to deal with many small-firm privatizations. Most of our interviewees think that many small firms will be privatized without major problems, through first having their assets "unbundled" by the existing owners and then rebundled by the firms' management. The unbundling or separation of a firm into its component assets will be the essential first step for most firms.

The most valuable physical asset involved in small firms is the building they occupy. Usually this asset is owned by another entity – often the local council. Frequently the existing tenant will be offered a long-term lease at a market level of rent (already paid by most private firms, but not usually by state firms).

The other valuable asset is the human capital in the firm: skilled labor and managerial experience. In principle, these human resources could move directly to private companies. But in practice it is unlikely that such a move would be rapid and without substantial unemployment while people searched for jobs. In most cases the employees will be allowed to buy the company (minus the building and any machines) at a low price, with reasonable financing terms.

Employees (usually just the management) will then choose whether to buy or lease the machines and buildings. If the employees want an infusion of capital, they will offer a partnership with the building's owner, usually the local council. The privatized company will therefore choose the level and form of its capital stock and its own debt–equity ratio.

However, this "spontaneous" or "from below" privatization (both terms are used in Poland) could meet with three types of difficulties. First, the firm and the existing owners may not agree on how to unbundle the existing assets. This seems likely to be a problem in conglomerate state firms, where branches want to break away but the head office does not want to lose control. The second potential problem is that management and workers will not agree on how to allocate ownership within the firm and on how to rebundle the firms' assets. This conflict is more likely to occur where there is a strong workers' council or Solidarity presence. Finally, there may be conflict between different groups of workers, for example between existing employees ("insiders") and potential employees ("outsiders"), skilled and unskilled, old and young, or full-time and part-time. This kind of conflict has yet to emerge, so it is too early to predict its form.

4.3 *Building institutions to support small business*

There is no doubt that small business is growing rapidly in the Gdansk region, both in terms of the number of businesses and employment in existing businesses. What is less clear is the nature of the small-business sector that will result from this growth. Unlike most countries, Poland is in the process – consciously or unconsciously – of building a set of institutions, more or less from scratch, that may endure for many years. The inadequacy of the inherited communist institutions is not even debated: the debate centers on what to put in their place. The remainder of this chapter addresses two broad issues that we think are central to the establishment of an institutional structure conducive to the sustained growth of small businesses in Poland: constraints on the strategic choices available to small businesses, and the promulgation of collaboration amongst small businesses.

Sengenberger, Loveman and Piore (1990) and Loveman and Sengenberger (1991) compare the legislative and institutional constraints on small businesses in the largest industrialized Western economies, and find tremendous cross-country variance in the nature both of strategies pursued by small firms, and of interfirm relations. In the United States, for example, relatively few constraints are placed on small businesses, and indeed, they are exempted from many obligations placed on larger firms. The minimum wage is low as a proportion of the mean wage, there are no industry-wide negotiated minima, unionization is quite low, and small firms offer much less non-wage compensation (e.g. pensions, health insurance) than do large firms. Consequently, small firms often choose to compete on the basis of low labor costs and poor working conditions, resulting in low-cost, standardized products (the "low road"), rather than competing on the basis of more highly skilled, higher paid labor and higher-quality, more specialized products (the "high road").

Furthermore, while small businesses are a powerful political force, there is very little by way of small-firm association to pool R&D, hiring and training, materials' acquisition, import–export, etc. Moreover, there are rarely any collaborative arrangements between small employers and educational institutions to provide skilled labor and facilitate their mobility when business conditions require fewer employees. Small firms are at a resource disadvantage when competing with large firms unless they can pool some of the critical resources to reduce cost. The inability of small firms in the United States to form such associations has often left them unable to compete with large firms world-wide, relegating them to either a supplier position or a presence in markets avoided by larger firms.

In Germany, on the other hand, small employers are bound by a variety of constraints that preclude a strategy of competition on the basis of low labor costs alone. Industry-wide bargaining agreements set high minimum wages applicable to all employers, and small firms offer non-wage benefits much closer to those of large firms than is the case in the United States. Despite these constraints, German small firms account for a larger share of employment than in the United States in, say, manufacturing industries, and compete very effectively in many international markets.

A significant reason for the competitiveness of small German employers is the long-standing vocational training system that supplies well trained craftspeople to small firms at a fairly low cost. The combination of an adequate supply of skilled labor and the inability to pay very low wages to unskilled labor gives small firms a clear incentive to pursue a product market strategy based on high-quality, customized goods (the "high road"). The collaboration of small firms in a variety of other ways helps to provide the other necessary resources for competition with larger firms, both domestically and internationally.

Poland now faces a very delicate situation in which the need for employment and output growth must be balanced with any desire for small businesses to follow the "high road" strategy. Perhaps the most likely current outcome is that Polish policy makers will do little to shape the course of small-business development. Our evidence from Gdansk suggests that the foundation for local small-firm collaboration is firmly in place in the form of the networks that connect entrepreneurs. The most important requirements for the growth of small business appear to be previous experience in the private sector and external networks which spread this experience within the local economy. We expect private business to do well in Gdansk, because it has the best imaginable (given recent Polish history) combination of these features. But in other towns without these features, we are not so confident about the prospects for small enterprises. In all cases where the economic network was based on shared political goals, the emergence of democratic party politics in Poland will require changes in the network structure.

At the moment, small businesses are attracting skilled labor away from the moribund state sector firms by paying much higher wages. Nonetheless, many growing small businesses complain that it is very difficult to obtain skilled labor, while at the same time there is a growing number of unemployed unskilled workers. Unfortunately, most small firms lack the resources to provide major worker training themselves. In Gdansk, but not in all parts of Poland, there are community initiatives to retrain workers, but the effects of these efforts will not be seen for some time. At some point, the restructured large firms will again compete effectively for these workers, and the absence of an institutional mechanism to supply skilled labor to small firms may become a serious problem.

The networks of entrepreneurs may also not be capable of assuring an adequate supply of non-labor resources. The expansion of private business in the first half of 1990 was in activities which could be financed by the firms' own modest resources. If this expansion is to continue, small firms must find ways both to pool resources and to obtain outside funding. There has been a debate between potential aid donors about whether funds should be provided either to the state sector or to the private sector. Most small businessmen do not understand this dichotomy, because they see the activities of *local* government as critically important to private sector development. It is local governments which are underwriting the new small banks, and which are trying to retrain unskilled labor. Providing large amounts of foreign aid to big state firms will not help the private sector much, but targeting expertise and financial resources to local governments could help the private sector a lot. In this respect, close collaboration between small businesses and local governments will be critical.

The need for collaborative relationships is most evident when considering the transformation that most Polish small firms must make to compete effectively with either imports or revitalized large domestic firms. Many small firms survived in niches created by the incompetence of the state sector. These niches may disappear over the next years due to foreign competition or as the result of improved large-firm efficiency (perhaps through the privatization of state firms). The prosperity of craft firms (which have one well-known product) will depend on whether they can create interfirm relations in the form known in the West as "industrial districts" or "craft communities." More innovative private businessmen appear to have much better prospects and may grow to be large firms. However, even they need further development in the institutional structure which supports business by making it easier to acquire materials, premises, skilled labor and the results of R&D.

For the near term, Polish labor costs will remain far below those of Western countries. Nonetheless, policy makers, including those in unions, must consider how wages will vary across employee-size groups. While low wages and contingent compensation may be a good idea in small firms during the first few years of the economic reform as a means for employment generation and output growth, the failure to consider meaningful constraints on small-firm strategies will lead Polish small business down a road more like that of the United States than that of Germany. The choice between these broad alternatives is not obvious, but it is a choice leading to distinct outcomes.

Notes

This chapter is based on interviews conducted in January, March, July and September 1990, with over 30 firms (private, cooperative and state), bankers, city councillors, the Economic Foundation of Solidarity, the Gdansk Entrepreneurs' Club and officials of the Ministry of Finance. In order to conceal their identities, the details of firms' activities have been kept vague.

Generous funding was provided to Gary Loveman by the Division of Research, Graduate School of Business Administration, Harvard University, and to Simon Johnson by the Pew Charitable Trusts.

For all their help the authors thank researchers at the Center for Marketization and Property Reform in Gdansk, especially Maciej Grabowski, Anthony Levitas, and Janusz Lewandowski.

1 Aslund (1985).
2 These data are taken from Table 2 in Lipton and Sachs (1990). The original sources are the *Statistical Yearbook of Industry*, Warsaw: Central Statistical Office, and Ehrlich (1985).
3 The most valuable physical assets are buildings.

References

Aslund, Anders (1985) *Private Enterprise in Eastern Europe*, New York: St. Martin's Press.

Ehrlich, Eva (1985) "The Size Structure of Manufacturing Establishments and Enterprises: An International Comparison," *Journal of Comparative Economics*, **9**, 267–295.

Friedman, David (1988) *The Misunderstood Miracle: Industrial Development and Political Change in Japan*, Ithaca, NY: Cornell University Press.

Lipton, David and Jeffrey Sachs (1990) "Creating a Market Economy in Eastern Europe: The Case of Poland," *Brookings Papers on Economic Activity*, 75–147.

Loveman, Gary and Werner Sengenberger (1991) "The Re-emergence of Small-Scale Production: An International Comparison," *Small Business Economics*, **3(1)**, 1–38.

Sengenberger, Werner, Gary Loveman and Michael Piore (eds.) (1990) *The Re-Emergence of Small Enterprises – Industrial Restructuring in Industrialised Countries*, Geneva: International Labor Organization

Statistical Yearbook of Industry, Warsaw: Central Statistical Office.

11 The development experience and government policies: lessons for Eastern Europe?

Hans-Peter Brunner

1. Introduction and preview

Improving the performance of the manufacturing sector implies improving the myriad of firms and economic agents within it. The base of manufacturing in both developing as well as developed economies is the small and medium-scale enterprise (SME) sector. While the large firms play a vital role in developing the frontiers of processes and technology and constitute a major share of employment and value added, the SMEs account for the majority of firms, and a significantly large share of employment and value added.[1] They are also an important part of the system of technology production and assimilation. In many instances SMEs are productively linked to the large-firm sector.[2]

The East is faced today with the very issues which the South faced thirty years ago, and still faces. These are: how to diversify the firm-size structure of an economy; how to open up channels of technology transfer for small enterprises; how to close the productivity gap looming between an underdeveloped economy and the Western industrialized economies while simultaneously closing the productivity and technology chasm that has opened up between a largely informal small-industry sector and an overbearing government supported large-scale sector.[3] The experience of the South in the last thirty years contains useful lessons which now for the first time can be brought to the attention of policy makers in those Eastern European countries which are ready to follow the South in their own SME development efforts.

I will start with two all too common hypotheses which are generally assumed to be valid and have led in the past to generally untenable SME development schemes in economically lesser-developed countries (LDCs). I will show why they are untenable on theoretical and empirical grounds. Then I will outline a simple neoclassical analytical framework which will help us later to focus on the important policy goals. The simple neoclassical framework of analysis however is incapable of explaining dynamic transformations of firms, as the Indian case study below will show. In sum, in the South I observe four movements which I think ought to be of central concern for successful SME development: a movement (1) from low-skill to high-skill industry products; (2) from low-productivity to high-technology products; (3) from capital poor to capital intensive industrial sectors; and (4) from an undiversified industry structure to an industry structure where large, competitive innovators coexist with small-firm challengers. Next, in response to the Indian experience, I will sketch elements of a more sophisticated dynamic, disequilibrium approach to SME development. Some general policy conclusions for Eastern Europe will then become readily apparent.

2. Two common but misleading hypotheses regarding the role of small firms in developing economies

Governments in the South have generally relied on two types of policy measures for the development of SME firms: (a) they have sponsored special, subsidized financial programs for them; and (b) they have given special preferences for investments and markets to SMEs (industrial policy such as licensing exemptions, entry restriction for large firms, government purchase requirements). Both policy approaches are justified by governments largely by the alleged employment creation potential of SMEs and their size-related handicaps. I will show now that these justifications are not sufficient to legitimize these policy measures, and are actually inappropriate.

Hypothesis 1

Relatively labor intensive production by small firms makes them an ideal vehicle for employment creation, if one only removes the financial constraint on small firms.

Even neoclassical economic theory does not support a facile connection between capital support to SMEs and employment generation. Bruton (1976) established in theory that the rate of *employment growth is a function of* (a) the elasticity of substitution between capital and labor; (b) the difference between labor productivity change and the increase in wages; and finally (c) the rate of capital formation and productivity.[4]

The employment creation effect of a rise in labor productivity is magnified in precisely those cases where the elasticity of substitution between capital and labor exceeds unity. Empirical evidence shows the greater

Table 11.1. *Elasticities of substitution in developing countries*

ISIC No.	Industrial category	Elasticity of substitution	Standard error	R^2
311	Food	1.14	0.39	0.96
313	Beverages	0.81	0.32	0.97
314	Tobacco	1.17	0.47	0.96
321	Textiles	0.59	0.41	0.98
322	Clothing	0.58	0.26	0.99
323	Leather	1.06	0.25	0.97
331	Wood	1.18	0.31	0.98
332	Furniture	1.78	0.33	0.98
341	Paper	0.65	0.29	0.98
342	Printing	0.83	0.25	0.98
355	Rubber	1.11	0.17	0.98
35	Chemicals	0.91	0.15	0.77
36	Non-metallic minerals	0.57	0.45	0.97
371	Iron and steel	0.97	0.54	0.82
381	Metal products	0.02	0.12	0.73
382	Non-electric machinery	0.57	0.20	0.99
383	Electric machinery	1.21	0.28	0.99

Note: Data are for individual LDCs converted to US dollars by exchange rates. Data for value added, employment, and wage rates are taken from United Nations, 1969 and 1970. Exchange rates are from *International Financial Statistics*. The same set of countries could not be used in each regression.

magnitude of the elasticity of substitution between capital and labor in those industries that are traditionally dominated by small-size firms: food and tobacco industries, wood and furniture production, leather goods, rubber wares, and transport equipment such as bicycles, the only exception to the rule being electrical machinery (see Table 11.1). So there is good reason to see SME development as a vehicle for employment creation in comparison to large firms.

As Bruton has shown theoretically, if employment grows more rapidly than value added at constant wage rates, labor's share of value added will rise. A high growth in labor's share of value added again *magnifies* any *employment effect arising from increased labor productivity*. The capital constraint is thus not the only constraint on employment growth. At least two other parameters constrain employment creation: substitution elasticities and labor productivity advances. Policy makers need to pay attention particularly to the latter parameter.

In a dynamic sense it is growth in total factor productivity (TFP) that increases the competitiveness of modern industries and firms which leads to *sustainable job growth*. It is not very useful to create and fund jobs in industries and firms which may have employment potential in the short run due to high elasticities of substitution, when in the long run they become uncompetitive and are not able to adjust technologically and thus have shrinking total output and value added. Financial support specific to SMEs does not automatically make them a vehicle for employment creation.

Hypothesis 2

Small firms and medium-size firms have different attributes than do larger ones with respect to sectoral affiliation, wage rates, capital cost, entry and exit rates, export orientation, level of productivity and competitiveness. Hence there is reason for the government substantially to differentiate industrial policy with respect to firm size.

Small and medium-size firms in developing countries are clustered in sectors which exhibit high elasticities of substitution (see Table 11.1), which are high in labor content, which require a fairly unskilled labor force and where wage levels are lower. Table 11.2 identifies those industries: food products and beverages, textiles and footwear, wood products and furniture, paper products, pottery and china. That is also the experience for SMEs in Indonesia, Pakistan, Sri Lanka, Ecuador and Mexico.

The direction of structural change or industrial deepening is reflected in changes in the structure of manufacturing output. The industrial development process leads to an increase in the share of value added relative to all manufacturing in those sectors that are either skill intensive or capital intensive, or both. When compared to the world average in 1975, LDCs display lower shares of value added in high-skill or capital intensive manufacturing sectors, and higher shares in those sectors which are neither. The former sectors include in particular electrical and non-electrical machinery, chemical industries, paper products and publishing. The latter include food and beverage firms, and textile production.

Figure 11.1 gives the structure of manufacturing value added of LDCs and compares it to the world average, broken down by 2 digit ISIC code (industrial sectors). In comparison to the rest of the world LDCs tend to have an excessively large food, textile, and basic chemical sector, and a far too small machinery sector. Figures 11.2–11.5 display the ratio of the shares of value added in the various sectors of four sample countries to the world average share of the sectors in total manufacturing value added.[5] In general the ratio is above 1 in those industries which are labor

Table 11.2. *Characteristics of manufacturing branches*

ISIC No.	Industrial sector	Factor intensity[a]	Skill requirement[b]
311–312	Food products	L	L
313	Beverages	L	L
314	Tobacco	K	L
321	Textiles	L	L
322–324	Wearing apparel and footwear	L	L
331	Wood products	L	L
332	Furniture	L	L
341	Paper products	L	L
342	Printing and publishing	K	H
351	Industrial chemicals	K	H
352	Other chemicals	K	H
355	Rubber products	L	L
356	Plastic products	K	L
36	*Non-metal products*	–	L
371	Pottery, china	L	L
362	Glass and products	K	L
369	Other non-metal	L	L
37	*Basic metals*	–	–
381	Metal products	K	H
382	Machinery, non-electric	L	H
383	Electrical machinery	L	H

Notes:
[a] L denotes labor intensive and K capital intensive industries. The dividing line between the two is the average capital intensity for the manufacturing sector as a whole.
[b] L denotes low, and H high, skill requirements. The level of skill requirement is measured from the proportion of skilled labor in the workforce, and the mean is used for separating L and H industries.
Sources: United States, Department of Commerce (1978, Table 929); Lary (1968); Hufbauer (1970); UNIDO (1981).

and low-skill intensive, and where SMEs are concentrated, and it is below 1 in those sectors which are more capital intensive as well as skill intensive. A comparison of the ratios for two sample countries, Pakistan and Indonesia, reveals an insignificant trend towards an increase in the ratio in the more capital and skill intensive sectors between 1977 and 1985. Unfortunately no clear trend can be detected away from labor intensive, low-skill industries. Table 11.3, however, reveals a clear trend of small firms to become more capital intensive as well as more skill

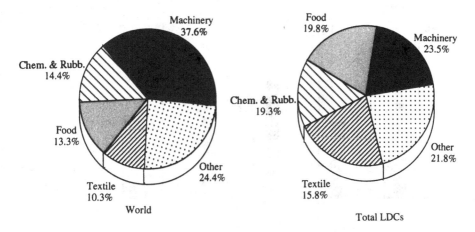

Figure 11.1 Structure of manufacturing value added, the world and LDCs, 1975.
Note: food includes – beverages and tobacco; textiles: apparel and footwear; chemical: rubber and coal.

intensive (reflected in higher labor productivity) when countries reach a higher level of development. This most likely reflects both an increasing capital and skill intensity when SMEs develop within a sector, but it also implies a shift of SMEs towards those sectors that are less traditional, more capital and skill intensive, in the process of economic development.

In terms of characteristics such as capital intensity or skill intensity SMEs change over time, and in the course of the economic development process. Such characteristics thus cannot serve as fixed points or anchors for policy differentiation, simply because they are not fixed: their values themselves are changing and fluctuating over time, and according to development stages. Rather SMEs have to be perceived by policy makers as components of the entire industrial system, which itself is undergoing a process of dynamic transformation. SME-specific policies should be decided on only in the context of enhancing the SMEs' role as agents of change in tandem with a related, if unsimilar, role for large firms.

3. The analytical framework

For simplicity, I find it appropriate to start my exposition of the analytical framework of study with the familiar neoclassical production function. I am of course fully aware of the very limited utility of such a model in explaining evolutionary dynamic processes of observed change.

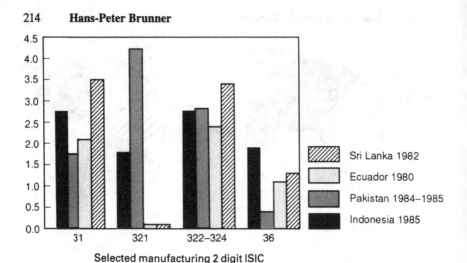

Figure 11.2   Ratio of manufacturing value added to world average, labour
intensive and low-skill sectors.
Note: compared with world average in 1975. 31 food, beverages and tobacco;
321 textile; 322–24 apparel, leather and footwear; 36 Non-metal mineral.

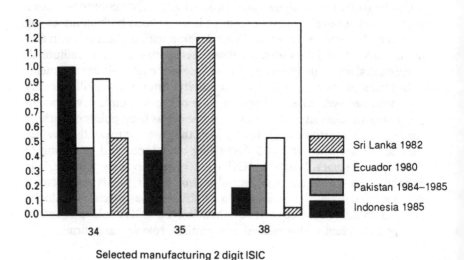

Figure 11.3   Ratio of manufacturing value added to world average, capital
intensive and high-skill sectors
Note: compared with world average in 1975. 34 paper, printing and publishing;
35 chemical, coal and rubber products; 38 machinery.

Neoclassical economics simply lacks vital institutional ingredients. Nonetheless it is a good point at which to start.

In the familiar language of neoclassical microeconomics, the transition from a manufacturing sector producing primarily low-skill intensive and low value added products to one which has a larger component of

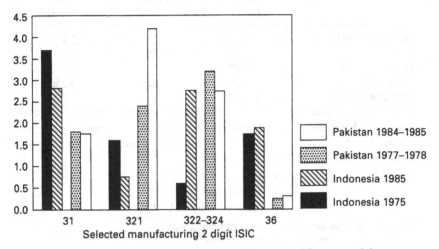

Figure 11.4   Ratio of manufacturing value added to world average, labor intensive and low-skill sectors.

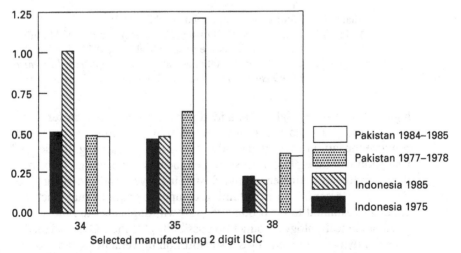

Figure 11.5   Ratio of manufacturing value added to world average, capital intensive and high-skill sectors

Table 11.3. *Comparative capital intensity, capital productivity and labor productivity of SMEs*

	Capital intensity (K/L) (US$)	Capital productivity (Y/K) (ratio)	Labor productivity (Y/L) (US$)
Pakistan (1976)	1,762	1.2	2,185
Philippines (1975)	3,746	0.78	2,933
Thailand (1976)	5,480	0.48	2,652
Malaysia (1973)	3,197	1.01	3,246
Singapore (1978)	13,413	0.73	9,790

Note: The figures were computed in local currency and converted into US dollar equivalents at official exchange rates of the respective data year. The respective index is computed as below:

Capital intensity: (K/L)
Capital productivity: (Y/K)
Labor productivity: (Y/L)

Where: K stands for value amount of fixed assets
   Y stands for amount of value added
   L stands for number of employees

Sources: Pakistan: Census of Manufacturing 1975/1976.
   Philippines: National Census of Statistics Office, unpublished version of 1975 Census results.
   Thailand: Tambunlertchai, Lochawenchit (1980).
   Malaysia: Department of Statistics (Malaysia), Census of Manufacturing Industries, Peninsular Malaysia, 1973.
   Singapore: Department of Statistics (Singapore), *Report on the Census of Industrial Production* (1978) unpublished version.

high-skill intensive, high value added products, requires transfer of resources to, and sustained growth momentum in, those sectors which produce the latter category of products. In a dynamic setting, the desired transition will take place with sustained increases in average labor productivity for an entire economy. Sustaining levels and growth in productivity is essential to maintaining competitiveness in manufactured exports. Sustained labor productivity growth duplicates the move outward of the technology (production possibility) frontier. Overlaid on this outward dynamic movement is a substitution movement on the production possibility frontier. Increasing specialization in high-skill high value added SME sectors demands a concomitant increase in capital stock.

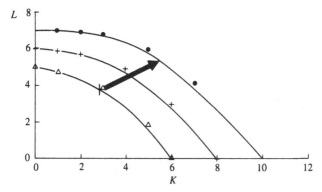

Figure 11.6   The production possibility frontier, capital–labor substitution and productivity.

Both of these movements, the outward productivity increase and the capital–labor substitution effect, are depicted in Figure 11.6.

A straightforward extension of the production function approach to incorporate simple institutional change is easily made. Basically institutional improvements make the economic exchange process more efficient. The costs of transacting (transaction costs) are key to the performance of an economy, its firms and banks. Traditional and primitive agricultural economies are characterized by high transaction costs. Therefore exchange is limited, personalized and localized. For example, the lack of an institutionalized banking system leads small producers to rely on personal or family income, or local money lenders, for financing of investment.

High transaction costs in economically lesser-developed countries lower the efficiency of SMEs considerably and prevent them from realizing their employment generation potential. Heavy reliance by sub-borrowers on localized, personalized sources of investment capital and other key inputs such as raw materials and machinery persist. Market access is limited by inordinate transaction costs. All this is indicative of the extent of the burden that SMEs still face in terms of excessive transaction costs, despite past efforts in institutional and technical development. A comprehensive recent survey of the SME sector undertaken in Ecuador in 1985 shows that 50 percent of start up firms relied primarily on the proprietor's own resources for investment capital. Over 80 percent of 3,934 establishments in the survey were of recent origin. Those firms using imported goods had to rely primarily on intermediaries for their supplies. Most sold their goods directly to customers in local markets. Very few exported any products. Perceived barriers to exports

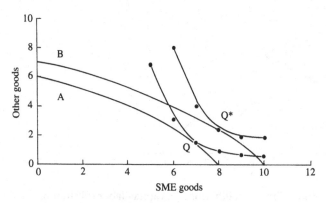

Figure 11.7   Institutional impact on production possibilities.

included lack of credit, the need for information and market or product studies.

In Indonesia, the 1986 census of small manufacturing enterprises revealed that more than half of the 94,500 firms questioned relied primarily on private funds for their investment. The survey also showed that small and medium-size firms relied largely on agents and wholesalers for marketing their products outside the local market. Only 8.7 percent of the firms marketed their products on a nation-wide basis; a very small minority of about 1 percent attempted to undertake marketing of products in export areas. SMEs in Indonesia sold one-third of their production directly to the customer, 72 percent of it was passed on to wholesalers. About 10 percent of the firms answered that they were subcontracting to another, presumably larger, firm.

To help us understand the essence of this short discussion on institutions, let us visualize the issue with yet another diagram (Figure 11.7). Under "inefficient" institutional arrangements for SMEs an economy produces goods at point Q. Some goods are produced by large firms and the service sector and some by small and medium-size enterprises. An improvement of institutional arrangements for SMEs enables the country to move its production point to Q^*, which lies on a higher production possibility frontier (Bromley, 1989, pp. 109–47).

In other words, with a fixed amount of units (labor and capital) the small or traditional industry sector is able to produce more goods. Growth in TFP has occurred. This will also result in a relatively smaller increase in productive efficiency in other sectors of an economy due to spillover effects. The relative larger increase of productive efficiency in the traditional or SME sector will result in increasing economic returns to that sector. This will change relative factor prices as well. It will increase the price of labor relative to capital when the supply of labor turns out to be inelastic or, which is more likely, in SME sectors where labor supply is deemed to be very elastic, increasing economic returns will translate into employment generation.

Small and medium-size firms in developing countries are generally conscious of the need for institutional improvements in order to generate TFP growth. As part of the 1986 small and medium-scale-firm census of Indonesia the question was posed to over 94,500 businesses as to the main difficulties they faced in their operation. The results show that nearly half of the firms surveyed were concerned with access to units such as raw materials and machinery, managerial and training assistance, or marketing; less than 40 percent were deeply concerned with capital supply. Marketing problems figured prominently, with one-third of the respondents facing serious difficulties in that respect.[6] The general impression remains that SMEs value technical and institutional assistance at least as much as ease of access to capital. The sketchy evidence supports the conclusion that effective technical and institutional assistance would go a long way towards increasing overall productivity (TFP) in the SME sector.

4. The relative role of SMEs over time – the case of the Indian computer industry[7]

As the evidence from industrialized countries suggests, in some industrial sectors small and medium-size firms are a more significant conduit for technical change than are large ones (Acs and Audretsch, 1987, 1988, 1989). There is no reason to believe that SMEs are potentially any less significant as a seed bed for innovation and technological entrepreneurship in newly industrializing countries, as the case of the Indian computer industry will show. Increases in innovative capacity and technological leadership of firms in turn affect industry structure in a dynamic sense (note the suggested direction of causality here!). The concern in the industrial organization literature with the development of a broader understanding of the nature and economic consequences of technological change dates back to Schumpeter (1942), and has been aptly summarized in Ch. 18 of the *Handbook of Industrial Organization* (Cohen and Levin, 1989).

What was the contribution of small-scale and medium-scale firms to India's narrowing of the technology gap? To find some answer to this question I analyzed the literature which identifies essential innovations in

Table 11.4. *Essential innovations and firm size*

		Innovations categorized by firm size		
Year	Total (nos)	Small firms (nos)	Medium firms (nos)	Large firms (nos)
–1976	3	0	0	3
1976–1977	0	0	0	0
1977–1978	2	1	0	1
1978–1979	5	2	0	3
1979–1980	1	1	0	0
1980–1981	1	0	1	0
1981–1982	3	1	2	0
1982–1983	7	3	1	3
1983–1984	5	1	3	1
1984–1985	4	0	1	3
1985–1986	5	0	1	4
1986–1987	6	0	0	6
Sum	42	9	9	24
Percent	100.0	21.4	21.4	57.1

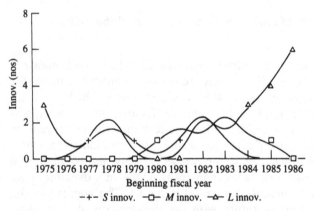

Figure 11.8   Firm size and innovation, number of innovations.

the international (mainly US) micro- and minicomputer industries. This resulted in a list of key innovation events. The list then served as an objective guideline for the selection of essential technology changes in India's industry to be included in a list of essential changes associated with the names of particular Indian companies.

Table 11.5. *Firm-size categories*

	Total firm-size categories				
	Firm (nos)	Small firm (nos)	Medium firm (nos)	Large firm (nos)	Unknown (nos)
1975–1976	1	0	0	1	0
1976–1977	2	0	0	2	0
1977–1978	5	2	0	3	0
1978–1979	8	2	2	4	0
1979–1980	11	3	2	4	2
1980–1981	18	3	6	5	4
1981–1982	25	5	7	6	7
1982–1983	30	3	9	9	9
1983–1984	32	5	14	10	3
1984–1985	34	4	16	11	3
1985–1986	34	4	12	18	0

Notes:
Small ≤ 50 employees.
Medium ≤ 200 employees.
Large > 200 employees.
Sources: Company interviews, brochures and annual reports; GOI, Bureau of Public Enterprises, *Public Enterprises Survey* (annual issue); "The Dataquest Top Ten," *Dataquest* (March 1984) pp. 32–65; "The Dataquest Top Ten," *Dataquest* (March 1985) pp. 45–67; "The Dataquest Top Ten," *Dataquest* (August 1986) pp. 11–49.

The results of this exercise are shown in Table 11.4. An initial period of innovative activity between 1977 and 1979 by small- and large-scale industry was followed by a lull in innovative efforts during the years 1980–1981. In 1981–1982 small and medium-size firms temporarily became a driving force in innovation. This was also the time when a new wave of small companies entered the Indian computer industry. Some of these entrants then kept growing in terms of employment and market share, and by 1985 had achieved large-scale status (see Table 11.5). It is thus justified to conclude from our data that these were the same firms that then rekindled innovative activities as large-scale firms in the mid-1980s (see Figure 11.8 for a visual display of these patterns).

Table 11.5 classifies the 34 observed companies in the Indian computer industry (excluding IBM) according to their size category for each fiscal year between 1975–1976 and 1985–1986. With computer firms thus classified between 1975 and 1986, Table 11.5 clearly shows a continuous movement of firms from small- to medium- to large-scale in terms of employment size. Small firms, and to some extent medium-size firms, are thus transitory creatures, seeking to mature and reach large-scale status. The reason for this drive to become large in terms of employment can be found in the nature of computer industry technology.[8]

5. Beyond a summary: innovative views of the role for SMEs in developing economies, and the quest for new theory

While it is perfectly reasonable to start the process of economic development with heavy support for industrial sectors, and within those sectors of firms which utilize abundant unskilled labor relatively intensively, it is not justifiable on theoretical and empirical grounds to support small firms simply as a means to an end, namely employment creation. I discussed this point earlier. Nor should SMEs be singled out only because they exhibit different characteristics to their larger brethren. Rather, SMEs have to be seen and treated as part of, and integrated with, the domestic manufacturing system, a system which itself is then linked to similar systems in other nations. At times large and small firms may complement each other, at other times and in certain sectors they may substitute for each other. SMEs need to be supported in fulfilling their role as suppliers, providers of jobs, innovators, and in their general role of agents of economic change.

Transforming a manufacturing sector with a large share of low-skill intensive, relatively low value added products to one which produces a large proportion of products using higher skills generating higher value added, is a major development challenge. The existing structure of manufacturing has to be understood and policies to transform it put into operation. These policies should address the needs of the sub-sectors and the producer firms, the institutions and support infrastructure, and the mechanisms of resource flows to manufacturing. The policies have to be timed and sequenced to sustain the efforts of firms, while at the same time they have to address the pressing issue of unemployment. The employment issue, however, should not distract policy makers from the central concern with four principal movements observed in previous sections: (1) from low-skill to high-skill products; (2) from low-productivity to high-technology products; (3) from capital poor to capital intensive industries; and (4) from an undiversified industry structure to an industry structure where large, competitive innovators coexist with small-firm challengers.

At certain times and in certain industries SMEs are only transitory creatures. I have used the case of the Indian computer industry to illustrate the at times transitory nature of SMEs. They are small as long as they are new and inexperienced, but still unburdened by past investments in ideas, knowledge and machinery. They are flexible in responding to new demands. When they are successful some small firms will grow and become large. As large firms they behave differently than when they were small. They may pursue technological innovations that are R&D intensive and not very tangible, while when they were small they relied on commercialization of ideas and knowledge that were readily available and codified. Small firms are at least as innovative as large ones, but they are innovative in different ways. They are thus worthy of government support at least as much as, but not more than, large firms. The example of the Indian computer industry also underlines the point that it is inappropriate to box in SMEs, as SMEs, through various policy restrictions (reservation, favors). "Small" is not an interesting and valid policy variable *per se.*

If for policy reasons we want better to understand why firms come in different sizes, what makes firms of different size behave differently, the role SMEs play in the evolution of industrial sectors, and the dynamic relationship that exists between SMEs and large firms and macroeconomic variables such as value added and employment, we necessarily have to venture beyond the neoclassical framework of analysis.

An industrial sector can be perceived as an open system undergoing transformation. The outcome of transformation is the elevation of the system onto a higher level of economic activity: a system that is higher in terms of quantity *and* quality of output, that is higher in terms of quantity *and* quality of factor inputs, that is higher in terms of internal density and integration, and that is likely to be increasingly responsive to exogenous potentially destabilizing influences and disturbances (Radzicki, 1990, p. 58). An increase in complexity, organization and variety in the industrial sector comes about because of the need for more sophisticated skills to support the making of competitive advantage in a rapidly changing environment determined by new technologies. To move the industrial system from a lower to higher level of activity, it has to become more and more integrated, and information flows about technology and markets have to increase both in quantity and in speed.

6.   The role for government: lessons for Eastern Europe?

In the end, a different analytical framework carries with it a different policy approach. I will outline such an approach before I draw some broad conclusions for Eastern Europe.

From the experience and from the analytical approaches outlined it becomes clear that the government's role in the South is one of helping firms of any size to upgrade their capabilities, and to improve their linkage, both within the domestic economy, as well as with foreign businesses. In some industries this means integrating smaller supplier firms with larger producer and exporter firms. In other industries it means opening channels of technology and market information between importers, producers, and exporters of all sizes. It means decreasing barriers to entry and exit for firms, both large and small, so that they can avail themselves of new economic opportunities which they learn of through improved channels of information and knowledge acquisition.

Four lessons come to mind for Eastern Europe: two as to what not to do, and two that indicate in broad terms what to do.

First, governments should not institute expensive financial schemes for SMEs in the name of employment creation. As we have seen the connection is not as simple and not certain: the employment effect may rather result from an overall effort of industrial and educational policies to increase the labor productivity in industry as a whole. *Second*, Eastern European governments should not fall into the trap in which most governments in the South were caught, of putting SMEs in quarantine. Rather, and here I move to the *third* lesson, governments should recognize the sector-specific role of SMEs in terms of suppliers, innovators, employers, and of agents that introduce diversity and quality into the product range of a country. In many sectors, but not in all, SMEs have to be viewed as transitory, as future winners which can develop into large corporations that can exploit economies of scale, if existent, in domestic and foreign markets. My *fourth* lesson is that governments should make it easy for SMEs to enter the market and pursue emerging economic opportunities, and to gain access to necessary information and factor inputs (including adequate human resources). Government has an important role in integrating the domestic industrial economy, that is, connecting firms and industrial sectors through efficient information and knowledge links and creating efficient ways of moving products along the value added chain. Furthermore, government can help to integrate domestic sectors and firms with the world economy.

So my general advice is: (1) Build on your present strength in specific industrial sectors, no matter how irrelevant any particular strength may seem right now. (2) Identify windows of opportunity in export markets which are as close as possible to present strengths. It is important to realize, however, that government organizations, no matter how well intentioned, have difficulty in conducting the required analysis by themselves. What is needed is rather a concerted effort by the private sector and government. (3) A concerted effort is essential to encourage active innovation in selected sectors by providing the incentives for structural change and diversification. Most important here is the creation of free room for competition. Competition can be brought about – not only by breaking up existing oligopolistic and monopolistic economic structures, but also through injection of new technological (institutional) opportunities. Such policy allows small, efficient entrants to expand the market for new substitute products, or for products at a higher level of quality than those offered by entrenched competitors. (4) All this will not take place, however, without a parallel development of human resource skills, a scientific base, informational channels, and basic technological as well as institutional infrastructure in support of targeted industrial sectors.

Notes

The findings, interpretations, and conclusions expressed in this chapter are entirely those of the author and should not be attributed in any manner to any organization. I thank David Audretsch for his excellent comments on my paper.

1 See the contributions in this volume by Fritsch (Chapter 3), Hughes (Chapter 2), Invernizzi and Revelli (Chapter 7), and Thurik (Chapter 5), on details for the Western European experience with SMEs.

2 A study by the United States Congress describes linkages between Japanese firms in detail (United States Congress, OTA, 1990, pp.129–148).

3 This refers to the discussion of issues by East European authors in this volume (in Chapter 9). In addition Régnier (1993) presents South Korea's experience with respect to dealing with the issues of diversifying firm-size structure and closing the productivity and technology gaps.

4 The following equation (Bruton, 1976, p.73) establishes the rate of growth of the demand for labor rL, or the employment effect, as a function of the rate of growth of capital input rK, the rate of productivity growth of capital rPK, the rate of productivity growth of labor rPL, the wage increase rW, the labor share of VA, LS, and the elasticity of substitution between labor and capital, s:

$$rL = rK + rPK - rPL + (s \cdot LS)(rPL - rW).$$

Assuming a sufficient rate of growth of capital inputs and productivity, and given the elasticity of substitution, employment increases depend essentially on an increase in the labor share of value added *and* a rate of labor productivity growth which is larger than the wage effect.

5 The figures are based on Annex 2.1 and 2.2 in Leechor *et al.* (1983) as well as on country industrial Census information.

6 Many firms gave multiple answers as to input problems.

7 For more details see Brunner (1991).

8 It is beyond the scope of this chapter to explain the regime character of microelectronics technology and to distinguish industrial sectors by technology regime dynamics. For details see Brunner (1990) and Winter (1984).

References

Acs, Zoltan J. and David B. Audretsch (1987) "Innovation, Market Structure, and Firm Size," *Review of Economics and Statistics*, **69(4)**, 567–574.

—— (1988) "Innovation in Large and Small Firms: An Empirical Analysis," *American Economic Review*, **78(4)**, 678–690.

—— (1989) "Small-firm Entry in US Manufacturing," *Economica*, **56(22)**, 255–265.

Bromley, D. W. (1989) *Economic Interests and Institutions: The Conceptual Foundations of Public Policy*, Oxford: Basil Blackwell.

Brunner, Hans-Peter (1991) "A Triple T(reat) for Industrial Policy of NIEs: Technological Capacity, Technological Regime, and Total Market Size," Wissenschaftszentrum Berlin (Social Science Center), *Discussion Paper, FS IV 91–19*.

—— (1991), "Small Scale Industry and Technology in India: The case of the computer industry," *Small Business Economics* **3(2)**, 121–129.

Bruton, Henry J. (1976) "Employment, Productivity and Income Distribution," in Alec Cairncross and Mohinder Puri (eds.), *Employment, Income Distribution, and Development Strategy*, New York: Holmes & Meier.

Cohen, Wesley M. and Richard C. Levin (1989) "Empirical Studies of Innovation and Market Structure," in Richard Schmalensee and Robert D. Willig (eds.), *Handbook of Industrial Organization*, vol. II, Amsterdam: North-Holland, 1059–1107.

Ecuador (1985) *Small Industry Census*, Quito: Government Printing Office.

Hufbauer, G. C. (1970) "The Impact of National Characteristics and Technology on the Commodity Composition of Trade in Manufactured Goods," in R. Vernon (ed.), *The Technology Factor in International Trade*, New York: NBER.

Indonesia (1986) Jakarta: Biro Pusat Statistik, *Small-scale Manufacturing Statistics*.

Lary, H. B. (1968) *Imports of Manufacturers from Less Developed Countries*, New York: NBER.

Leechor, Chad, Harinder S. Kohli and Sujin Hur (1983) *Structural Changes in World Industry: A Quantitative Analysis of Recent Developments*, World Bank Technical Paper, Washington DC: World Bank.

Radzicki, Michael J. (1990) "Institutional Dynamics, Deterministic Chaos, and Self-organizing Systems," *Journal of Economic Issues*, **24(1)**, 57–102.

Régnier, Phillipe (1993) "The Dynamics of Small and Medium-Sized Enterprises in Korea and Other Asian NIEs," *Small Business Economics*, 5.

Scherer, Frederic M. (1984) *Innovation and Growth*, Cambridge, MA: MIT Press.

Schumpeter, Joseph A. (1942) *Capitalism, Socialism and Democracy*, New York: Harper.

UNIDO (1981) *World Industry in 1980*, New York: United Nations.

United Nations (1969 and 1970) *The Growth of World Industry*, 1967 and 1968 edns, New York: United Nations.

United States, Department of Commerce (1978) *Statistical Abstract of the U.S.*, Washington, DC, Table 929.

United States Congress, OTA (1990) *Making Things Better: Competing in Manufacturing*, Washington, DC: US Government Printing Office.

Winter, Sidney G. (1984) "Schumpeterian Competition in Alternative Technological Regimes," *Journal of Economic Behavior and Organization*, **5**, 287–320.

12 Conclusion

Zoltan J. Acs and *David B. Audretsch*

What has been learned from the preceding chapters comparing the role of small firms across a broad spectrum of nations? Table 12.1 provides a detailed summary from the country studies contained in this book and compares both the small-firm share of manufacturing employment, as well as the shift in the share of manufacturing employment accounted for by small firms over time across all of the countries studied. Small firms account for the least amount of Western manufacturing employment in the Anglo–Saxon countries. Just over one-third of manufacturing employment in the United States is in small firms, while small enterprises account for about 40 percent of manufacturing employment in the United Kingdom. By contrast, small firms account for a relatively high share of economic activity in Portugal, where nearly three-quarters of all manufacturing workers are employed by small firms. While Portugal is considerably less developed than either the United Kingdom or the United States, the small-firm presence is also relatively large in the Federal Republic of Germany, where small firms account for well over one-half of manufacturing employment. There is thus little evidence suggesting that a singular firm-size distribution is common across Western countries with a similar level of economic development. Rather, it appears that the role of small firms varies considerably across countries, even when the stage of economic development and type of economic system is fairly similar.

Another striking result emerging from Chapters 1–7 is that a distinct and consistent shift away from large firms and towards small enterprises has occurred within the manufacturing sector of every developed Western country. While the magnitude of this shift varies considerably among nations, the direction does not. This shift in the firm-size distribution ranged from an increase of 1.9 percentage points in the small-firm employment share in the United States between 1976 and 1986 to an increase of 10.9 percentage points between 1981 and 1987 in the North of Italy, and to an increase of 9.8 percentage points between 1976 and 1986 in the United Kingdom.

Table 12.1. *Summary from country studies of small-firm share of manufacturing employment and shift over time[a]*

Country	Year	Small-firm employment share (%)	Year	Small-firm employment share (%)	Change
United Kingdom	1986	39.9	1979	30.1	+ 9.8
Federal Republic of Germany	1987	57.9	1970	54.8	+ 3.1
United States	1987	35.2	1976	33.4	+ 1.9
Netherlands[b]	1986	39.9	1978	36.1	+ 3.8
Portugal	1986	71.8	1982	68.3	+ 3.5
Italy[c]					
North	1987	55.2	1981	44.3	+ 10.9
South	1987	68.4	1981	61.4	+ 7.0
Czechoslovakia	1988	1.4	1954	13.0	− 11.6
East Germany	1986	1.1	–	–	–
Poland[b]	1985	10.00	1937	33.0	− 23.0

Notes:
[a] A "small firm" is defined as an enterprise with fewer than 500 employees, unless designated otherwise.
[b] A "small firm" is defined as an enterprise with fewer than 100 employees.
[c] A "small firm" is measured as an enterprise with fewer than 200 employees.

There are two striking consistencies emerging from the country studies of Eastern Europe. First, the role of small firms throughout the Eastern European countries is remarkably small, especially when compared to that in the Western nations. That is, while small firms account for only one-tenth of manufacturing employment in Poland, the small-firm employment shares are just over 1 percent in Czechoslovakia and East Germany. Second, while the developed Western countries all experienced a shift in economic activity in manufacturing away from large firms and towards small enterprises, the trend was exactly the opposite in Eastern Europe. The shift away from small firms and towards large enterprises in the Eastern European nations reflects the conscious policy under centralized planning to centralize and concentrate economic assets.

Comparing the experience between the Western and Eastern nations makes it clear that while it is virtually impossible to identify anything approaching an optimal firm-size distribution, the newly established democracies in Eastern Europe have inherited an industrial structure that is strikingly lopsided. One of the challenges confronting nations throughout Eastern Europe is to generate or regenerate the entrepreneurial sector in order to achieve a more balanced industrial structure.

The findings from the preceding chapters shed at least some light on the existence of any direct relationship between the size of the domestic market and the firm-size distribution. That is, a larger domestic market may tend to be associated with a tendency towards larger firms and establishments, since scale economies can be more greatly exploited with a larger geographic extent of the market. In fact, the largest domestic market, the United States, has the smallest presence of small firms, while Portugal, which has one of the smallest domestic markets (of the Western nations) has the largest presence of small firms. However, this relationship is confounded by the differences in the level of economic development between Portugal and the United States. In addition, the Federal Republic of Germany, which is the second largest country listed in Table 12.1, has the second largest small-firm share of manufacturing employment. No simple or obvious relationship between firm size and the extent of the domestic market thus emerges from the findings in this book.

As already stated in the introductory Chapter 1, it is not the goal of this book to provide systematic empirical tests of hypotheses explaining either reasons why the role of small firms varies across countries, or why the observed shifts in the firm-size distribution have taken place. However, a number of tentative explanations are offered throughout the volume and deserve emphasis, because these suggest a set of hypotheses which need to be more systematically tested in subsequent research.

One explanation, at least for Great Britain, was provided by Alan Hughes in Chapter 2. Hughes suggests that the growth in small-firm employment shares is attributable to productivity increases in large firms, which have resulted in the displacement of workers in the largest corporations. That is, large firms have been substituting capital for labor. An alternative explanation was provided by Acs and Audretsch in Chapter 4, where the shift towards smaller enterprises in the United States is linked to the adaptation of flexible technologies. A similar case for the importance of flexibility in both production and management was made in Chapter 7 by B. Invernizzi and Riccardo Revelli. Based on the Italian experience Invernizzi and Revelli argue that the increase in the relative importance of firm flexibility accounts for at least some of the increase in the role of small firms, which tend to have an advantage with flexible production techniques. This is partially the result of a highly turbulent industrial structure, where there is a high propensity for firms to enter, grow, decline, and subsequently exit from the industry within a remarkably short period of time.

Michael Fritsch, in Chapter 3, attributes the overall shift in the Federal Republic of Germany away from large enterprises and towards small firms to the compositional transformation of economic activity out of manufacturing and into services. However, in Chapter 4, Acs and Audretsch note that the shift towards small firms in the United States has actually been more pronounced in the manufacturing sector than in services or finance. In fact, one explanation for the comparatively small shift in the US manufacturing size distribution of firms shown in Table 12.1 is the very low growth rate of manufacturing. Since virtually all of the new jobs in the American manufacturing sector were generated by small firms between 1976 and 1986, while the large corporations actually decreased employment, a higher growth rate in manufacturing would have resulted in an even more pronounced shift in the firm-size distribution.

The extent to which technology and/or managerial techniques have directly resulted in a reduction of scale economies was addressed by Roy Thurik in Chapter 5. Based on a simple cost model, Thurik finds that scale economies have decreased in 52 out of 68 Dutch manufacturing industries. His results support the claim by Shepherd (1982), and Nguyen and Reznek (1991 and 1992) that scale economies have decreased over time, thereby reducing inherent scale disadvantages confronting small enterprises.[1]

The preceding chapters have carefully attempted to document the role of small firms across a broad spectrum of countries, and to identify the manner in which the role of small firms has evolved in recent years. In addition, at least some tentative explanations for the observed shifts were provided. It is left to future research to carry out the painstaking systematic empirical analyses required to transform a tentative explanation into a scientifically tested hypothesis.

Of the five important issues characterizing the contemporary debate about the efficacy of large and small firms identified in the introductory Chapter 1, one remains beyond the scope of this book – the welfare implications. That is, the empirical evidence presented in the preceding chapters makes it clear that the role of small firms in Western economies is increasing in importance. But is that desirable? Is the relatively substantial shift away from large firms in the United Kingdom towards small enterprises evidence of the emergence of a dynamic, vital, innovative entrepreneurial sector, or rather the reflection of the inability of the large incumbent corporations to prevail in the increased presence of international competition? While a handful of studies, most notably the 1990 study by Brown, Hamilton and Medoff, have addressed the welfare implications of large vs small firms, thoughtful and imaginative research is clearly needed to pave the way in a relatively new field. However, as we emphasized throughout the introductory Chapter 1, the facts have to be set straight before arguments about their interpretation can be made with any confidence. To find the right facts and get them straight has been the primary task of the preceding chapters.

Notes

1 Nguyen and Reznek (1991) use the Longitudinal Research Data Base of the United States Bureau of the Census to estimate translog production functions for large and small manufacturing establishments in 1977 and 1982. They find that, while significant differences exist in the production technology between small and large establishments, based on the scale parameter estimates, the small establishments tend to be equally efficient as their larger counterparts. They conclude that "large size is not a necessary condition for efficient production." In their 1992 study, Nguyen and Reznek use the same data base to show that small establishments are more flexible than large plants in substituting capital for labor.

References

Brown, Charles, James Hamilton and James Medoff (1990) *Employers Large and Small*, Cambridge, MA: Harvard University Press.

Nguyen, Sang V. and Arnold P. Reznek (1991) "Returns to Scale in Small and Large U.S. Manufacturing Establishments," *Small Business Economics*, 3(3), 197–214.

(1992) "Factor Substitution in Large and Small U.S. Manufacturing Establishments: 1977 and 1982," *Small Business Economics*, 4.

Shepherd, William G. (1982) "Causes of Increased Competition in the U.S. Economy, 1939–1980," *Review of Economics and Statistics*, 64(4), 613–626.

Index

233